W9-BSM-058

Editorial Manager
Karen J. Goldfluss, M.S. Ed.

Editor in Chief
Sharon Coan, M.S. Ed.

Cover Artist
Chris Macabitas
Jeff Sutherland

Art Coordinator
Denice Adorno

Creative Director
Elayne Roberts

Imaging
Ralph Olmedo, Jr.

Product Manager
Phil Garcia

Publishers
Rachelle Cracchiolo, M.S. Ed.
Mary Dupuy Smith, M.S. Ed.

Practice and Learn

Fifth Grade

Compiled and Written by
Char-lee L. Hill

Teacher Created Materials, Inc.
6421 Industry Way
Westminster, CA. 92683
www.teachercreated.com
©1999 Teacher Created Materials, Inc.
Made in U.S.A.

Table of Contents

Table of Contents (cont.)

Table of Contents (cont.)

Introduction

To Teachers and Parents

The wealth of knowledge a person gains throughout his or her lifetime is impossible to measure, and it will certainly vary from person to person. However, regardless of the scope of knowledge, the foundation for all learning remains a constant. All that we know and think throughout our lifetimes is based upon fundamentals, and these fundamentals are the basic skills upon which all learning develops.

Within this book are hundreds of pages designed to teach and reinforce the skills that are mandatory for a successful completion of fifth-grade curricular standards. To use this resource effectively, simply refer to the contents list to find the practice sheets that correspond to the desired skills.

Skills are reinforced in the following areas:

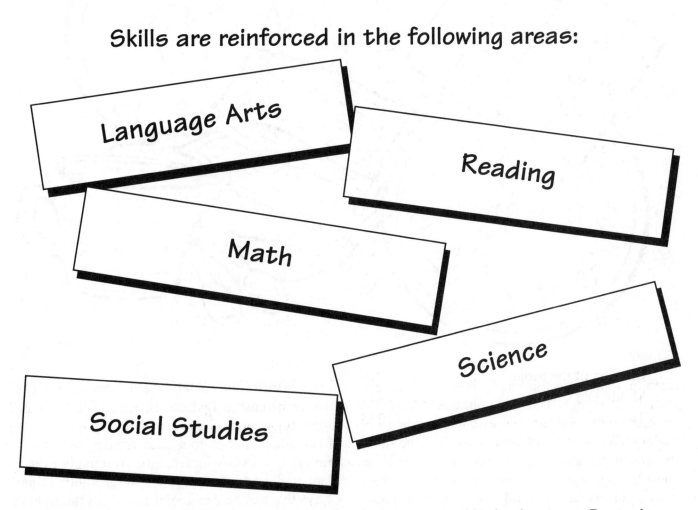

Language Arts

Reading

Math

Science

Social Studies

The practice sheets within this book are ideal for both use at home and in the classroom. Research shows us that skill mastery comes with exposure and drill. To be internalized, concepts must be reviewed until they become second nature. Parents may certainly foster the classroom experience through exposing their children to the necessary skills whenever possible, and teachers will find that these pages perfectly complement their classroom needs.

Introduction (cont.)

In addition to this resource, there are many hands-on materials that will prove vital when reinforcing basic skills. These include math flash cards, measuring spoons, cups, weights, Celsius and Fahrenheit thermometers, a clock or a stop watch, a variety of math manipulatives, a globe, maps, charts, and graphs. Kinesthetic learners will also benefit from items they can manipulate and use for figuring and writing, and every child will enjoy hands-on science experiences of all kinds.

Keep in mind that skills can be reinforced in nearly every situation, and such reinforcement need not be forced. As parents, consider your use of basic skills throughout your daily business, and include your children in the process. For example, while grocery shopping, let your child manage the coupons, finding the correct products and totaling the savings. Also, allow your child to measure detergent for the washing machine or help prepare a meal by measuring the necessary ingredients. You might even consider as a family the time you spend viewing television and calculate how much of the allotted time goes to advertisements. Likewise, there are countless ways that teachers can reinforce skills throughout a school day. For example, assign each child a number and when taking roll, call out math problems with those numbers as the answers. The children will answer "present" when they calculate the problems and realize that their numbers are the answers. You might also play the game of bingo with parts of speech, matching problems, or vocabulary words.

Since basic skills are utilized every day in untold ways, make the practice of them part of your children's or students' routines. Such work done now will benefit them in countless ways throughout their lives.

What is a Research Report?

A research report presents information that the writer has learned through a detective-like search for the facts. Facts are found in books, magazines, newspapers, encyclopedias, atlases, computer programs, and even in personal interviews. You will become an expert on your topic by the time you are done.

How do you choose a subject?

Find something that interests you and something that you would like to learn more about. You might want to spend time in the library to see how much information is available on your topic. If you are having a problem deciding on a topic, keep reading.

Ideas for Subjects

Read the possible topics below. Circle all those that interest you.

- dogs
- trains
- baseball
- football
- basketball
- space exploration
- pets
- movie stars

- inline skates
- ocean
- fish
- presidents
- government
- a country
- a wild animal
- a state

- Grand Canyon
- historical event
- cars
- a famous person
- world wars
- Frisbee

Choose four favorite topics from above and write them on the lines below. After each, write a more specific topic that might make your report more manageable.

Favorite Topic	**More Specific Topic**
Example: Planets	Mars

1. _____   _____

2. _____   _____

3. _____   _____

4. _____   _____

Researching on the Internet

As Robert Louis Stevenson says, "The world is full of a number of things . . . ." And they can all be found on the Internet!"

The Internet is a network of computers that are all connected so they can "talk" to each other. For example, ten-year-old Matthew needs to write a research report about life on the Mississippi River during the times of Tom Sawyer because his class just read the book *The Adventures of Tom Sawyer.* Since Matt is at school using the computer lab, he decides to look up his topic on the Internet. He manages to connect with a university library in another state and finds more information than he can use.

Sounds great! However, before you go "online," keep in mind some important safety rules.

Be Safe and Not Sorry Online

1. Never give any personal information about yourself or your family, such as your full name, where you live, or your telephone number.

2. You will meet many friendly people online, but remember—they are strangers.

3. If you find yourself having an online conversation that makes you uncomfortable, report that person to your online service.

4. Never give away your password.

5. Never agree to meet anyone you've chatted with online unless your parents agree to the meeting and go with you to a public place.

6. Don't send someone you've met online your picture or anything else without first checking with your parents.

Whether you have access to the Internet at your local public library, your school, or at home, you will want to have some practice in researching a topic if you are new to Internet research. Even if you have experience, practice will enable you to research a topic faster. You will be able to find more information within the time limitations necessary when going online.

Using Encyclopedia Volumes

An encyclopedia is a set of books or a CD-Rom with an encyclopedia on it, which contains information on just about everything in the world. The books contain information that is arranged in alphabetical order, beginning with the A's in the first volume and ending with the Z's in the last volume. Your library will have an encyclopedia; it may have several. Many CD-Rom encyclopedias will allow you to click on a table of contents or an index to help you search for a topic, or you can type an idea into a box to find related topics. Most will have a list of books to read at the end of the article. Your school library will probably have them also. An encyclopedia is a good place to find information for your research paper.

Write each of the subjects below on the spine of the encyclopedia volume in which they would be found.

- photography
- dinosaurs
- Hawaii
- chocolate

- rattlesnakes
- lightning
- wildflowers
- computers

- The Beatles
- volcanoes
- space shuttle
- gorillas

Facts and Opinions

When you write a research paper, you must be very careful to stick to the facts. A research paper is written to give people information that is true or that can be proven true.

Is this a fact?

"France is the best place in the world to live."

Whether you agree or not, it is just someone's opinion. It is not a fact.

In the blanks before each sentence below, write **F** for fact or **O** for opinion.

Many plants have thorns. (fact)

Thorny plants are not good in gardens. (opinion)

_____ 1. The moon orbits the earth.

_____ 2. The moon is inspirational to all who see it.

_____ 3. A banana tastes disgusting.

_____ 4. A banana is a fruit.

_____ 5. Abraham Lincoln was killed.

_____ 6. Abraham Lincoln was the best president.

_____ 7. Canada has the most beautiful lakes in the world.

_____ 8. Canada has many lakes.

_____ 9. Red and yellow mixed together make orange.

_____ 10. Orange is the prettiest color.

Now write one fact and one opinion about your school.

1. Fact: _____

2. Opinion: _____

10

Wild Animal Research

Directions for Writing

1. Choose six wild animals from the pictures on pages 14–16 and create your own book about them. Each page will represent one of the animals.

2. List the animals on which you wish to report.

_____   _____

_____   _____

_____   _____

3. Do some research to find interesting facts about the animals you have chosen. Use page 12 to record your findings.

4. Write a paragraph about each animal on six different wild animals. Use the form on page 13.

5. When you make your actual book, be sure to use your best writing skills—grammar, punctuation, and spelling—so your readers will understand and enjoy what you have written.

6. Cut out the pictures from pages 14–16 of the animals you chose. Glue each on the appropriate wild animal book form (page 13). As an alternative, you may wish to illustrate the animal yourself. Fill in the background of your picture with the animal's habitat.

7. Make a front and back cover for your book. Complete your book by stapling the covers and pages together.

8. Share your animal books with someone.

Wild Animal Research (cont.)

Animal_____

Description (size, color, etc.) _____

Habitat (where it lives) _____

Its food _____

Its enemies _____

Caring for its young _____

Other interesting facts _____

Animal_____

Description (size, color, etc.) _____

Habitat (where it lives) _____

Its food _____

Its enemies _____

Caring for its young _____

Other interesting facts _____

Animal_____

Description (size, color, etc.) _____

Habitat (where it lives) _____

Its food _____

Its enemies _____

Caring for its young _____

Other interesting facts _____

Wild Animal Research (cont.)

_____

(animal)

Wild Animal Research (cont.)

You may choose from these pictures to illustrate your book.

Kangaroo

Rhinoceros

Gorilla

Tiger

Wild Animal Research (cont.)

You may choose from these pictures to illustrate your book.

Polar Bear

Koala

Sloth

Penguin

Wild Animal Research (cont.)

You may choose from these pictures to illustrate your book.

Panda

Wolf

Elephant

Alligator

Nouns

Nouns are words that name a person, place, thing, or idea.

- **Persons** include both names of people and categories.
    Mr. Blue   children   policemen   teacher   girl   boy

- **Places** can name both specific and general places.
    New York   school   park   department stores   homes

- **Things** refer to objects.
    door   shoes   newspaper   table   globe

- **Ideas** tell about feelings or thoughts.
    love   pain   philosophy   care   liberty   freedom   belief   rules

A. Underline the nouns in the following sentences. The number at the end of the sentence tells how many nouns to look for.

1. Summer is a wonderful time of the year. (3)

2. The weather is hot and many children enjoy swimming. 34)

3. Most schools are closed and people have time to go on vacations. (4)

4. The days are longer and we have more hours of sunlight. (3)

5. It is wonderful to go to the pool, beach, or lake. (3)

6. My teacher, Mr. Dawson, visited the Metropolitan Museum of Art in New York City in July. (5)

7. He said that great care and concern are shown by visitors. (3)

8. My friends, Tim and Carol, went to the Statue of Liberty and to Ellis Island. (5)

9. The scent of beautiful flowers drifts across Central Park as we eat our lunch outside. (4)

10. We like to cook hamburgers on the grill and picnic in the backyard. (3)

B. Use the back of this paper to write each of the following words under the correct heading of **person**, **place**, **thing**, or **idea**.

• France	• shoelaces	• city	• loyalty	• love	• building
• happiness	• bicycles	• Ms. Litz	• glasses	• table	• fairness
• clouds	• science	• sounds	• Dr. Forest	• pain	• Texas

Verbs

Verbs are words that express action or being.

An *action verb* describes physical action, that which can be seen.

> *Example:* Tom collected stamps and coins.

Sometimes the verb expresses mental action, that which cannot be seen.

> *Example:* Candice knew all the answers on the test.

A *linking verb* joins or links the subject of a sentence with a word or words in the predicate. It tells that something *is* or *was*.

> *Example:* The pot on the stove was hot!

Common Linking Verbs include the following:

am	*be*	*feel*	*has been*	*is*	*been*	*sound*
have been	*are*	*being*	*taste*	*was*	*will be*	*look*
had been	*were*	*become*	*appear*	*seem*		

Directions: In each of the sentences below, underline the verb. Label each verb *action* or *linking*.

_____ 1. Lightning flashed across the sky.

_____ 2. The quarterback raced down the field.

_____ 3. The winner crossed the finish line.

_____ 4. The crackling fire looked beautiful!

_____ 5. The roasting marshmallows smelled delicious!

_____ 6. The hunters captured a turkey and a deer.

_____ 7. Hailstones are little ice balls.

_____ 8. Fog covered the airport, preventing the planes from landing.

_____ 9. Trucks skidded on the snow-covered highways.

_____ 10. Dew formed on the grass in the early morning.

_____ 11. The magician pulled a bouquet of flowers from the scarf.

_____ 12. Mike appears frail after his operation.

_____ 13. Kitty seems to be the fastest runner in the sixth grade.

_____ 14. The young boys became excellent ranch hands.

Tall Tale Pattern Story

Use the form below to create a tall tale. Fill in the blanks with the correct words. Then illustrate the tall tale and share it with someone.

Many years ago _____ was born in
                                        (hero)

_____ . _____was so big
        (place)   (hero)

that he/she slept in a _____ . Each morning.
                                (noun)

_____ ate _____ ,
        (hero)   (noun)

_____ , and _____ for breakfast. As
        (noun)   (noun)

_____ grew older, he/she decided to learn to
        (hero)

_____ . He/She became so good at
            (verb)

_____ that he/she could _____
        (verb)   (adverb)

beat anything or anybody. One day _____ found a/an
                                                    (hero)

_____ and rescued it from
            (animal)

_____ . _____ named his/her new
        (noun)   (hero)

friend _____ . People were amazed when they saw
            (name)

_____ traveling with a/an _____
        (hero)   (animal)

Then the two rescued _____ from a
                                (famous person)

_____ . Since then, _____
        (danger)   (hero)

and _____ have become favorites of people everywhere.
        (animal name)

Adjectives and Adverbs

Adjectives describe nouns and pronouns.

Adverbs modify verbs, adjectives, and other adverbs.

A. Cross out the word on the right that **cannot** be used to describe the word on the left.

1. sing   joyfully, beautiful, well, loudly
2. train   fast, yellow, electric, slowly
3. Ms. Woods   thinly, jumpy, comical, kindly
4. freedom   more powerful, limited, very, desired

B. Circle the adjectives.

1. pretty glass
2. big dog
3. green door
4. happy boy
5. thin cookie
6. round ball
7. wet towel
8. excellent work
9. broken pencil
10. smelly shoe

C. Circle the adverbs.

1. running slowly
2. turning quickly
3. quickly hit
4. falling down
5. joyfully leaping
6. writing sloppily
7. watching closely
8. sipping loudly
9. driving badly
10. throwing wildly

D. Think of three nouns and write them below. Write an adjective to go with each noun on the line next to it.

Noun	Adjective
1. _____	_____
2. _____	_____
3. _____	_____

E. Think of three verbs and write them below. Think of an adverb. Write the adverb on the line next to each verb.

Verb	Adverb
1. _____	_____
2. _____	_____
3. _____	_____

Glad Libs

With a partner, fill in each blank with the appropriate part of speech. When all the blanks have been filled in, read the story aloud. Try writing your own story on the back of the paper.

Fairy Tales Can Come True

Once upon a _____, there was a(n) _____
(noun)   (adjective)

little girl named _____. She _____ reading
(proper noun)   (verb)

_____ fairy tales. One morning she _____ ran to her
(adjective)   (adverb)

bookshelf where, much to her surprise, she saw a (an) _____ fairy god-
(adjective)

_____. "_____!" she said, "You startled me!"
(noun)   (exclamation)

"Nonsense!" said the fairy, "I'm here to grant you _____ wishes; but first,
(number)

you must guess my name, fit into the golden _____, and
(noun)

_____ dangle your long _____ hair out of the window.
(adverb)   (adjective)

"Easy," replied the girl. "Your name is _____, this item fits like a glove,
(proper noun)

and I will _____ dangle my hair out the window."
(adverb)

She was granted her wishes. The first things she did were _____,
(verb)

_____, and _____. Then everyone lived happily ever
(verb)   (verb)

after!

Make Your Own Word Search

Choose 10 or more words to build the puzzle. The words must all be nouns, verbs, adverbs, or adjectives. Write your words in the word box. Fill the words in the grid below. Put other letters in the empty boxes until they are all full. Give the word search to another person to solve.

Word Box

_____   _____   _____

_____   _____   _____

_____   _____   _____

Where's My List?

A comma is used between words in a series. Three or more things together make a series.

> *Example:*   *We will be talking today about muffins, kittens, and lollipops.*

Add the missing commas to the sentences below.

1. All birds have feathers wings and beaks.

2. My sister is sleepy grumpy and clueless.

3. I would have done my homework, but I was abducted by aliens was left in Siberia and had to wait for the Marines to rescue me.

4. I ordered a pizza with cheese pickles and sliced cherries.

5. Please go to the store and get flypaper chopsticks and kumquats.

6. I went to the door with rollers in my hair a mud mask on my face and wearing my bathrobe.

7. My dog has brown spots a short tail and fuzzy feet.

8. My little brother can't go anywhere without his blanket his stuffed duck and his rabbit's foot key chain.

9. When I go to college, I am taking a stereo a microwave and a treadmill.

10. For her birthday, Mindy wants some edible flowers sparkly socks and a pony.

✧   ✧   ✧

A comma is also used between two or more describing words (adjectives).

> *Example:*   *A friendly, playful dog makes a good pet.*

Add the missing commas to the sentences below.

1. My rabbit has long floppy ears.

2. A large heavy sparrow could weigh 200 pounds.

3. My teacher has a green pointy nose.

4. My dad used to have curly frizzy hair.

5. A friendly playful giraffe ate all my spaghetti.

When and Where?

A comma is used when writing a date. The comma separates the date and the year. It is also used to separate the day and the date.

A. Insert commas where needed in the sentences below.
1. My parents bought their first home on January 13 1976.
2. My mom was born on March 31 1948.
3. We went to Disneyland on Tuesday August 18 and it was really crowded!
4. My brother's birthday is November 17 1973.
5. On Saturday April 19, we are flying to my grandma's house.
6. I get my tonsils out on Monday September 16 and then I can eat lots of ice cream.
7. Our puppies were born on February 14 1997.
8. It rained cats and dogs on January 18 1995.

B. Write these dates using commas correctly.
1. today's date and year_____
2. today's day and date _____
3. your birthday _____
4. your favorite day of the year (besides your birthday)_____
5. the birthdate of a member of your family (and tell who)

Use a comma between the city and state (country or province) in an address.

C. Add commas to the following sentences.
1. Yesterday, I met a girl from Canberra Australia.
2. A hurricane went on shore at Acapulco Mexico.
3. I've never been to Seattle Washington.
4. It can get very cold in Buffalo New York.
5. Yesterday, I received e-mail from Bordeaux France.
6. Many movie stars live in La Canada-Flintridge California.
7. Alexandria Virginia, is an interesting historic town.
8. You can take a great train ride in Durango Colorado.
9. Have you been on the roller coasters in St. Louis Missouri?
10. The mountains are really high in Vail Colorado.

D. Answer the following with the name of a city and state or a city and province.
1. Where were you born? _____
2. Where was your mother born? _____
3. Where do you live today? _____
4. Name where one of your grandparents lives. _____
5. Where is the last place you visited? _____

Days, Months, and Holidays

There are some names of holidays on this page. They are not capitalized correctly. Capitalize the holidays by changing a lowercase letter to a capital letter where it is needed. As you write each capital letter, color the same letter in the heart.

1. What letter did the colored hearts make? _____

2. Write the names of two holidays that begin with this letter.

_____

_____

3. Color the rest of the heart.

What's in a Name?

Did you know that your name is a proper noun? It is, and **you should always capitalize your first and last names and middle name if you have one**. And what about your pet snake? If you call your snake "George," "Rex," or "Samantha Slither," you should capitalize that, too. And if your stuffed animal is named "Old MacDonald" that name should be capitalized, with the M of Mac (or Mc) capitalized and the D of Donald also capitalized. Your little brother has the nickname, "Punkin"? That would also be capitalized.

Rewrite the following names so that they are properly capitalized.

1. amanda panda _____

2. jeffrey r. hardy_____

3. carlos custard appleseed _____

4. gilbert mcgillicutty_____

5. leslie q. presley_____

Do you have any pets at home? If you do, write the names of your pets (or any other pets you know) here.

_____

_____

_____

_____

Here are some pets without names. Think of a name for each pet. The names can be fancy or simple, long or short, but they should all be capitalized. The first one has been done as an example.

Malcolm Angus McCollie McDuff   _____   _____   _____

                                                    _____   _____   _____

Extension: Make a *Names Notebook*. In a small notebook, write all the creative names you can think of in alphabetical order. Be sure to capitalize! Keep your notebook handy. The next time you write a story, you will have lots of interesting names from which to choose.

End Marks

Every sentence must end with a punctuation mark. As you have been learning, **a sentence may end with a period, a question mark, or an exclamation point**.

- A **period** comes at the end of a sentence that tells something.

  Examples: I have a purple bicycle. Turn left at the corner.

- A **question mark** comes at the end of a sentence that asks a question.

  Examples: What color is your bicycle? Is that your house?

- An **exclamation point** comes at the end of a sentence that contains a strong feeling.

  Examples: Watch out for that car! What a wonderful surprise!

The following sentences need end marks. Think about which end punctuation each sentence needs. Then write the correct punctuation mark at the end of each sentence.

1. I love my purple bicycle ☐

2. I saved enough money to buy it last year ☐

3. Would you like to try it ☐

4. My brother has a blue bicycle ☐

5. One time he crashed into me, and I fell off my bike ☐

6. Have you ever fallen off your bike ☐

7. Did you skin your knee ☐

8. I was so mad at my brother ☐

9. He told me he was sorry ☐

10. I'm so glad that my bike did not break ☐

11. Watch out for the glass in the road ☐

12. Don't ride your bike in the street ☐

13. Can you park a bike right here ☐

14. I have to go inside now ☐

15. Will I see you tomorrow ☐

Capitalization Review

It is time to see how much you have learned about capitalization. Circle all the letters below that should be capitals. (*Hint:* There are 63 of them.)

1. the first day of school is exciting.

2. freddy wilson's frog peepers hopped into mrs. woolsey's purse.

3. as i walked outside, i smelled smoke.

4. In the play, robin hood was played by lieutenant bronksy.

5. the fourth thursday in november is thanksgiving.

6. i like halloween best when it is on a saturday.

7. aunt susan went to yellowstone national park.

8. connie lives on maple street in bismark, north dakota.

9. brazil, argentina, and peru are in south america.

10. the mediterranean sea and the atlantic ocean touch spain.

11. the letter was signed, "love always, esther."

12. davis medical center opened in january last year.

13. one of the religions practiced by many african people is islam.

14. italians and germans belong to the caucasian race.

15. last tuesday ruben walked his dog spotty down tulip street to central park.

Building Sentences

Writing sentences can be fun. The following sentences are all about someone special–you! Add words to complete each of the sentences. When you are finished, cut out the box, glue it to a piece of decorative paper, and add a photograph of yourself.

1. My favorite sport is _____ because _____
_____ .

2. My favorite song is _____ because _____
_____ .

3. My favorite animal is _____ because _____
_____ .

4. My favorite class at school is _____ because _____
_____ .

5. My favorite TV show is _____ because _____
_____ .

6. My favorite place to go is _____ because _____
_____ .

7. My favorite dessert is _____ because _____
_____ .

8. My favorite story is _____ because _____
_____ .

9. My favorite time of the day is _____ because _____
_____ .

10. My favorite movie is _____ because _____
_____ .

TV Review

Complete the following TV program review. Then use the space on page 31 to write about the program and your reactions to it based on the information on this page.

Name of Program _____

1. Summary of episode _____

2. Explain how the show depicts the mother. _____

    _____

3. Explain how the show depicts the father. _____

    _____

4. Name and describe a child who is a main character in the episode. _____

    _____

    a. What problem or dilemma does he or she face in this episode? _____

        _____

    b. How is it resolved? _____

5. Name and describe a second child character. _____

    _____

    a. How is he or she related to the other character you described?_____

        _____

    b. What role did this character play in the main character's problem? _____

        _____

6. Do you think the program portrays a realistic family? Explain your answer._____

    _____

7. How is your family like this TV family? _____

    _____

    How is it different? _____

    _____

8. Would you like to be a part of this TV family? Explain why or why not. _____

    _____

TV Review (cont.)

_____
Title

_____

_____

_____

_____

_____

_____

_____

_____

_____

_____

_____

_____

What Happened Next?

When you write about something that happened to you or something that you do, it must be in the right time order. Another name for this is *chronology.* The things you write about in a paragraph should usually be in *chronological* (or time) *order* to make sense.

Here are some lists of events that are out of order. Put them in chronological order by marking them from first (1) to last (5). The first one has been done for you.

A.

___2___ eat breakfast

___1___ get up

___5___ go to school

___4___ go out the door

___3___ brush teeth

B.

_____ bait a hook

_____ clean a fish

_____ eat a fish

_____ catch a fish

_____ cook a fish

C.

_____ mail the letter

_____ put the letter in an envelope

_____ write a letter

_____ wait for an answer

_____ seal the letter

D.

_____ write a book report

_____ click on word processing

_____ turn on the printer

_____ turn on the computer

_____ print the book report

E.

_____ slap your arm

_____ see a mosquito

_____ feel a bite

_____ hear a buzz

_____ scratch a bump

F.

_____ buy popcorn

_____ leave the theater

_____ stand in line

_____ buy a ticket

_____ watch a movie

G.

_____ find an old Halloween mask

_____ clean up your room

_____ sneak up on your brother

_____ put it on

_____ jump out at him

H.

_____ snap on the leash

_____ guide your dog back home

_____ get the leash

_____ whistle for your dog

_____ walk your dog

Choose one of the lists above and, on a separate piece of paper, make it into a paragraph. Be sure to write a good topic sentence.

Extension: Using the lists above, make sets of cards (five cards in a set). On each card write a phrase, such as "sneak up on your brother," and illustrate it. Take the cards to the children in younger grades and have them put the cards in order.

Write Your Own Story

Choose one of the following story ideas. Follow the steps to develop your ideas into a several-paragraph story. Illustrate the story if you wish.

The Beautiful Horse

Step 1: You are a beautiful horse leaning over a fence. You long to walk the trails, but people rarely come to ride. One day, you notice a hole in the fence. What happens next?

Step 2: Describe the action.

Step 3: Continue the action.

Step 4: Create an ending. Perhaps you can make your story end as it began, with you, the beautiful horse, leaning over a fence. If you have a better title in mind, give your story a new title.

The Eagle

Step 1: You are an eagle perched high on a rock crag. Far below, you spot a gray and brown jackrabbit. What is going to happen?

Step 2: Describe the action.

Step 3: Continue the action.

Step 4: Tell how it ends. Make your story end where it began, with you, the eagle, perched on your rocky crag. If you have a better title in mind, give your story a new title.

Write Your Own Story (cont.)

Choose one of the following story ideas. Follow the steps to develop your ideas into a several-paragraph story. Illustrate the story if you wish.

The Little Caterpillar

Step 1: You are a little caterpillar sitting in the middle of a path. Here comes a human holding a jar and a net. Oh, no! Describe the human from where you are, sitting in the middle of the path. Decide what you are going to do. Perhaps you will want to add some dialogue. Rewrite the first two sentences making them into a story beginning.

Step 2: Create some action.

Step 3: Continue the action.

Step 4: Tell how it ends. Make your story end where it began, with you, the little caterpillar, on a path. If you have a better title in mind, give your story a new title.

The Waterbug

Step 1: You are a waterbug floating in a stream that is trickling down a mountainside. You hear the sound of water rushing fast and hitting rocks up ahead. What is going to happen to you now? Rewrite the first two sentences, making it into a story beginning.

Step 2: Create some action.

Step 3: Continue the action.

Step 4: Tell how it ends. Make your story end as it began, with you, the waterbug, floating in a stream. If you have a better title in mind, give your story a new title.

Paragraph Starters

You might want to set a goal for yourself of writing each day. You will see your writing improve if you do this. You will find ideas on what to write about below and on page 36. Look them over and circle the ones about which you would like to write. Use these paragraph starters when you need inspiration while practicing paragraph writing. You might want to use some of these ideas for writing an essay, a report, or a story.

Gorillas make good pets.	If I were my teacher, here are three things I would do.
There are many uses for popcorn.	It's a good idea for all students to invite the principal to dinner.
Collecting bugs is an interesting hobby.	Kids should be allowed to drive when they are 10 years old.
There are many things shaped like a circle.	There are lots of reasons why I am glad to be a member of my family.
I would like to be invisible.	I really like math (science, English, social studies, etc.).
I have three favorite foods.	I should have my own room.
I know my brother/sister is an alien.	I deserve a raise in my allowance.
I would like to join the circus.	Eating is one of my favorite activities.
If I could stop time, there are three things I would do.	We should remember to wash our hands.
I would make a great president.	I would like to visit Mars.
I would like a giraffe for a pet.	It's a good idea to learn a foreign language.
It would be a good idea to build a roller coaster in my backyard.	I love music.
Airplanes are not a good idea.	I would like to remodel my house.

Paragraph Starters (cont.)

A smelly monster lives under my bed.	Snakes make great pets.
People should not be expected to wear matching shoes and socks.	I make the best peanut butter sandwiches.
It would be a good idea if we all lived in tents.	A woman should be president.
Gravity is a good idea.	I don't like earthquakes.
We should be allowed to bring our pets to school every day.	I love to read because . . .
Eating is a very weird thing to do.	I am afraid of the ocean.
We need pocket computers.	There are three good reasons for wearing a hat.
Anyone can draw.	Red is the best color for food.
I would rather starve than . . .	It's hard to wake up in the morning.
I put ketchup on everything.	I love roller coasters.
I don't like fish.	Even when I'm sick, there are some interesting things to do.
Rainy days are the best.	I think we need three arms and three hands instead of just two of each.
I would not like to lose my big toe.	It would be better if the sun stayed up all the time.

Ben Franklin

Preview the words in exercise A before reading the following selection. Then complete the exercises below.

Benjamin Franklin was a great American. He had many outstanding accomplishments in his lifetime. He was a printer, a publisher, a writer, an inventor, a scientist, a diplomat, a statesman, and an inspiration to those he met.

At age 42, Franklin decided to devote himself to the study of science. During this time, he was one of the world's greatest scientists, inventing and experimenting and loving his work. He proved that lightning was electricity and that things could be positively or negatively charged with electricity. Among the many things he made were the world's first battery, lightning rod, bifocal glasses, and an energy-efficient, wood-burning stove. However, he never patented any of his inventions. He preferred, instead, to share what he had learned freely with the world.

A. These words were used in the selection you just read. Match the words from the list on the left with their proper meaning.

_____ 1. diplomat

_____ 2. devote

_____ 3. inspiration

_____ 4. statesman

_____ 5. patent

a. official rights to the inventor

b. wise or experienced leader

c. a person who represents a country

d. give attention

e. sudden or original idea

B. Use the back of this paper to answer the following questions.

1. What are some of the many outstanding accomplishments Ben Franklin achieved in his lifetime? List three of them.

2. What did he decide to do when he was 42 years old?

3. What did he prove about lightning?

4. Did he patent any of his inventions? Why?

5. Which one of his inventions do you feel helped the world the most and why?

Our National Anthem

Preview the words in exercise A before reading the following selection. Then complete the exercises below.

In 1814, Francis Scott Key composed a poem, "The Defense of Fort McHenry," as he watched the bombardment of Ft. McHenry during the War of 1812. Later, Key's words were set to the tune of a popular English drinking song, "The Anacreaon in Heaven." Although the United States had been using the song in ceremonies for many years, it did not become the official national anthem until March 3, 1931, when President Herbert Hoover signed the bill that made "The Star-Spangled Banner" our national anthem.

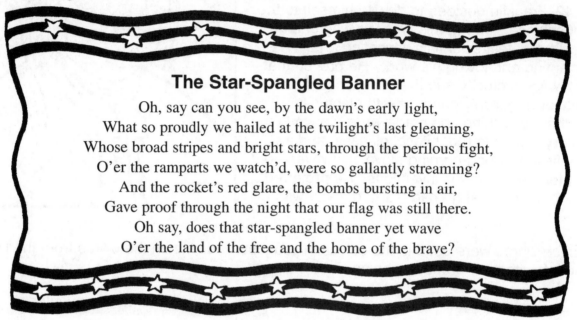

The Star-Spangled Banner

Oh, say can you see, by the dawn's early light,
What so proudly we hailed at the twilight's last gleaming,
Whose broad stripes and bright stars, through the perilous fight,
O'er the ramparts we watch'd, were so gallantly streaming?
And the rocket's red glare, the bombs bursting in air,
Gave proof through the night that our flag was still there.
Oh say, does that star-spangled banner yet wave
O'er the land of the free and the home of the brave?

A. These words were used in the selection you just read. Match the words from the list on the left with their proper meanings.

_____ 1. defense   a. in a position of authority

_____ 2. bombardment   b. song of patriotism or praise

_____ 3. ceremonies   c. protection from attack or harm

_____ 4. official   d. continued attacking

_____ 5. anthem   e. formal acts performed as a ritual

B. Use the back of this paper to answer the following questions.

1. What was the name of the poem that Francis Scott Key wrote?

2. What was happening when he wrote it?

3. When did it become the official national anthem?

4. Who was the president that signed the bill?

5. Do you think that this song is the right one for our national anthem? Explain your answer.

Morse Code

Preview the words in exercise A before reading the following selection. Then complete the exercises below.

Today, we commonly use telephones when we want to transmit a message over a long distance. However, before the use of telephones, other means of communications were used. Messages were often sent on paper. More urgent messages may have been sent by Morse code.

Morse code is a system of dashes and dots. Each combination of dashes and dots represents a different letter in the alphabet. Samuel F. B. Morse developed this language in 1835 to send messages over long distances with a telegraph machine. Morse code is still commonly used in emergencies by people today when telephone services are interrupted or unavailable.

The telegraph is used to send messages over long distances.

A. These words were used in the selection you just read. Match the words from the list on the left with their proper meanings.

_____ 1. transmit

_____ 2. interrupt

_____ 3. unavailable

_____ 4. message

_____ 5. code

a. series of symbols

b. to send from one person to another

c. to stop

d. not able to obtain or get

e. words sent from one person to another

B. Use the back of this paper to answer the following questions.

1. What symbols are used in Morse code?

2. Who developed this code?

3. Is a telephone used to send messages with Morse code?

4. Who most commonly uses Morse code today?

5. Describe when you might need to use Morse code and what you could use to send the message?

Totem Poles

Preview the words in exercise A before reading the following selection. Then complete the exercises below.

As you travel through Vancouver and Victoria, British Columbia, you can see many totem poles. Stanley Park in Vancouver and Thunderbird Park in Victoria, British Columbia, each has a wonderful collection of totem poles.

Totem poles have been used by many Native Americans as a way to record history. Tribes, clans, and families used them as a symbol. A totem pole is a carving of animals, birds, fish, plants, or other natural objects that represent a Native American tribe.

A family would place its totem pole in front of its home. At the top of the pole was the family totem or symbol. When a totem pole was erected, there was a festival called a potlatch.

A. These words were used in the selection you just read. Match the words from the list on the left with their proper meanings.

_____ 1. clan　　　　　　　　　　a. something that stands for something else

_____ 2. carving　　　　　　　　b. group of people (usually related)

_____ 3. potlatch　　　　　　　c. a shape made by cutting with a sharp object

_____ 4. collection　　　　　　d. group of objects

_____ 5. symbol　　　　　　　　e. festival

B. Use the back of this paper to answer the following questions.

1. Where can you find a wonderful collection of totem poles?

2. What is the purpose of totem poles?

3. What is carved on a totem pole?

4. What was put at the top of the totem pole?

5. Describe what your family's totem pole would look like. You can draw it on another piece of paper.

Frisbee™

Preview the words in exercise A before reading the following selection. Then complete the exercises below.

The Frisbee™ story began in the late 1800s with the Frisbee Pie Company in Bridgeport, Connecticut. Their pies, which came in a ten-inch-wide round tin with a raised edge and wide brim, were popular with students at nearby Yale University. At some point, pie-tin catch had become a fad among the young collegians. The fad continued into the 1950s but was changed forever with the introduction of a plastic flying dish called Flyin' Saucer invented by Walter Frederick Morrison. First marketed as the Pluto Platter, the toy's name was officially changed to Frisbee when Wham-O's president saw Yale students throwing and catching Frisbee pie plates. However, not until the 1960s did sales of the Frisbee take off. Today it remains a popular toy and sport.

A. These words were used in the selection you just read. Match the words from the list on the left with their paper meanings.

_____ 1. fad   a. thin round object

_____ 2. collegians   b. to make something that has not been made before

_____ 3. marketed   c. something that is popular for a short time

_____ 4. disk   d. college students

_____ 5. invent   e. sold or offered for sale

B. Use the back of this paper to answer the following questions.

1. When did the Frisbee Pie Company begin?

2. What did the college students do with pie tins?

3. What name was the Flyin' Saucer marketed as before it was changed to Frisbee?

4. When did the sales of the Frisbee take off?

5. What would you have called this toy and why?

WD-40

Preview the words in exercise A before reading the following selection. Then complete the exercises below.

During the early 1950s, the aerospace industry began looking for a product to eliminate moisture from electrical circuitry and to prevent corrosion on airplanes. A satisfactory product was invented by Norman Larsen, who was the president and head chemist at the Rocket Chemical Company. His water displacement formula was developed on his fortieth try, thus the name WD-40. When it was discovered that WD-40 worked well to quiet squeaky doors and unstick stuck locks, a number of employees began sneaking the product home. In 1958, the product was made available to the public.

The WD-40 Company makes more than one million gallons of the lubricant each year. When astronaut John Glenn circled the earth in Friendship VII in 1964, the spacecraft was covered with WD-40 from top to bottom.

A. These words were used in the selection you just read. Match the words from the list on the left with their proper meanings.

_____ 1. corrosion   a. vehicle designed to travel into space

_____ 2. displacement   b. slippery substance used to lubricate parts

_____ 3. lubricant   c. person trained to travel into space

_____ 4. astronaut   d. act of wearing away (i.e., rusting)

_____ 5. spacecraft   e. to take the place of

B. Use the back of this paper to answer the following questions.

1. During the early 1950s, what was the aerospace industry looking for?

2. Who invented the formula later called WD-40?

3. How did it get its name?

4. What spacecraft was covered from top to bottom with this product?

5. What would you have called it and why?

Beatlemania

Preview the words in exercise A before reading the following selection. Then complete the exercises below.

Just how did four boys from Liverpool make it so big? Their story began in 1957 when John Lennon invited 15-year-old Paul McCartney to join his group, "The Quarrymen." Guitarist George Harrison and drummer Pete Best had joined the group by August 1961. In 1962, Best was replaced by Ringo Starr. After record store owner Brian Epstein became their manager, they signed with a recording company. It was not long before the Beatles became England's biggest-ever idols. Their live performances were accompanied by hordes of screaming fans. After their February, 1964, appearance on *The Ed Sullivan Show,* "The Fab Four," as they were sometimes called, became transatlantic chart-toppers. While their first album had combined pop-soul songs with some of Lennon's and McCartney's original compositions, later albums reflected the whole group's efforts.

A. These words were used in the selection you just read. Match the words from the list on the left with their proper meanings.

_____ 1. transatlantic   a. person in charge of someone's business

_____ 2. combined   b. joined together

_____ 3. compositions   c. crossing the Atlantic Ocean

_____ 4. hordes   d. works of art, literature, or music

_____ 5. manager   e. large crowds of people

B. Use the back of this paper to answer the following questions.

  1. Who first started the group?

  2. What was the name of the first group?

  3. Who replaced Pete Best?

  4. What show made them famous in America?

  5. Why do you think that this group was so popular all over the world?

Butchart Gardens

Preview the words in exercise A before reading the following selection. Then complete the exercises below.

One of the most beautiful flower gardens in the world is located in Victoria, British Columbia. This garden spreads out over many acres and features a Japanese garden, a rose garden, and a sunken garden.

In most of Canada, spring-like weather does not arrive until after St. Patrick's Day on March 17. However, before spring arrives in Victoria, Flower Count Week is celebrated. During this week people all over the city go out and actually count how many flowers and buds they see. Children are given an hour off from school to help count. There are special centers to which the numbers are called, and a graph of the number of flowers counted is posted at Eaton Centre, a large shopping mall downtown.

A. Match the words from the list on the left with their proper meanings.

_____ 1. acre   a. placed information for others to see

_____ 2. celebrate   b. garden below the ground level

_____ 3. locate   c. area of ground equal to 4,840 square yards

_____ 4. posted   d. to observe a special occasion

_____ 5. sunken garden   e. to find

B. Use the back of this paper to answer the following questions.

1. Where is Butchart Gardens located?

2. What are three of the types of gardens that you can find there?

3. What do people do during Flower Count Week?

4. What special privilege do children get?

5. If you could plant a garden, would it be a flower or vegetable garden? Explain your answer.

Spider-Man

Preview the words in exercise A before reading the following selection. Then complete the exercises below.

Spider-Man's real identity is Peter Parker, the freelance photographer. Peter was not born with any special powers or talents. However, when he was a teenager, he was accidentally bitten by a spider that had been exposed to huge amounts of radiation. As a result, Peter became strong and agile like a spider and was able to cling to any surface, including walls and ceilings.

He made a red and blue uniform for himself and created a mechanism for shooting a web. He decided to call himself the "Amazing Spider-Man," making sure to keep his real identity a secret. After Spider-Man's uncle was killed by a burglar, he quit his acting career and was determined to devote his life to fighting crime.

A. These words were used in the selection you just read. Match the words from the list on the left with their proper meanings.

_____ 1. freelance

_____ 2. identity

_____ 3. radiation

_____ 4. agile

_____ 5. mechanism

a. parts that make a machine work

b. able to move quickly

c. works independently

d. who a person is

e. waves or particles emitted by radioactivity.

B. Use the back of this paper to answer the following questions.

1. What is Spider-Man's true identity?

2. How did he get his special powers?

3. What did he wear when he wanted to be Spider-Man?

4. Why did he give up his career to become a full-time Spider-Man?

5. What do you think Peter's life would have been like if he had never been bitten by the spider?

Olympics in the 1920s

Preview the words in exercise A before reading the following selection. Then complete the exercises below.

The Olympic Games are the world's greatest sports contest. A tradition begun in ancient Greece in 776 B.C. and abolished in A.D. 394, the games did not begin again until 1896. Since then, the modern Olympiads have undergone numerous changes. Some sports, like rugby, have come and gone while others, like track and field, have remained constant.

During the 1920s there were two important changes in the Olympics. The now familiar Olympic flag first appeared in 1920. In 1924, the first winter Olympic games were held in Chamonix, France. Originally held in the same year as the traditional games, the schedule changed in the 1990s, with the summer and winter games held two years apart.

A. Match the words from the list on the left with their proper meanings.

_____ 1. tradition　　　　　　a. first; the source

_____ 2. ancient　　　　　　　b. the passing of customs to the next generation

_____ 3. numerous　　　　　　c. form of football

_____ 4. Rugby　　　　　　　　d. many; a lot

_____ 5. original　　　　　　　e. very old

B. Use the back of this paper to answer the following questions.

1. When were the first Olympics?

2. Have they stayed the same all these years?

3. Where were the first Olympic Games held?

4. Are the winter games and summer games held in the same year?

5. What sport would you like to participate in at the Olympics and why?

Barbie™ Doll

Preview the words in exercise A before reading the following selection. Then complete the exercises below.

In 1959, the Barbie™ Doll made her debut. Today, she is the best-selling toy in American history. Her inventor is Ruth Handler, a former secretary and housewife. Ruth noticed that her daughter preferred to play with teenage dolls rather than those designed for her own age group. The problem was that the teenage dolls available at that time were paper cutouts. Ruth designed a more grown-up doll that would wear fashionable clothing and be a little girl's dream of things to come. Barbie™, named after Handler's daughter, made her debut at the 1959 New York Toy Show. A huge success, it sold $500 million worth in its first eight years. Ruth Handler went on to become vice president and then president of Mattel, Inc., the company that manufacturers Barbie™.

A. These words were used in the story you just read. Match the words on the left with their proper meanings.

_____ 1. debut   a. a good result

_____ 2. designed   b. liked better

_____ 3. fashionable   c. in the latest style

_____ 4. preferred   d. made a plan for

_____ 5. success   e. seen in public for the first time

B. Use the back of this paper to answer the following questions.

1. When did Barbie make her debut?

2. Who invented Barbie?

3. Why did she invent Barbie?

4. Who went on to become president of Mattel, Inc., the company that manufacturers Barbie?

5. Do you think Barbie is a doll that should be sold in toy stores? Explain your answer.

Hula Hoop™

Preview the words in exercise A before reading the following selection. Then complete the exercises below.

The Wham-O toy company manufactured the Hula Hoop™ in the 1950s. For six months it enjoyed great success as the Hula Hoop became the fastest-selling toy in history. Just as quickly, however, the craze seemed to die down. Every generation since then has seen a resurgence of the unusual toy. Based on a wooden hoop used by Australian youths, the plastic Hula Hoop was invented by Richard Knerr, a partner in the Wham-O toy manufacturing company.

A. These words were used in the selection you just read. Match the words on the left with their proper meanings.

_____ 1. manufactured   a. popular for a short time

_____ 2. craze   b. a circular frame

_____ 3. resurgence   c. people who grew up and lived at the same time

_____ 4. generation   d. made

_____ 5. hoop   e. having become popular again

B. Use the back of this paper to answer the following questions.

1. How long was the Hula-Hoop the fastest selling toy in history?

2. Did the craze last for a long time?

3. What was the Hula Hoop based on?

4. Who invented the Hula Hoop?

5. Invent a game you could play with the Hula Hoop. Briefly describe how to play.

The Endangered Sea Otter

Preview the words in exercise A before reading the following selection. Then complete the exercises below.

In the mid-1800s, the fur trade was thriving. Hunters up and down the West Coast were trapping and trading furs for goods. Demand for precious furs was high. Unfortunately, the sea otter was one of the animals prized for its pelt. Hunters traveled from Alaska to Southern California to capture them. As a result, the playful sea otters were hunted almost to extinction by the late 1800s. Since then, the government has taken an interest in sea otters and has placed a ban on the hunting of these creatures. Although there are still hunters who illegally poach these animals for their fur, the population of sea otters off the coast of California is increasing.

A. These words were used in the selection you just read. Match the words from the list on the left with their proper meanings.

_____ 1. thriving	a. against the law
_____ 2. endangered	b. no longer exists
_____ 3. illegally	c. group of the same kind of animal
_____ 4. extinct	d. healthy
_____ 5. species	e. to be in danger
_____ 6. pelt	f. animal skin

B. Use the back of this paper to answer the following questions.

1. What kind of trade was thriving in the mid 1800s?

2. Why did the hunters want the sea otters?

3. Why can't people hunt sea otters today?

4. What is happening to the sea otters off the coast of California today?

5. Do you think that we should be able to hunt seal otters today? Explain your reasons.

Spider-Woman

Preview the words in exercise A before reading the following selection. Then complete the exercises below.

No one knows the real identity of Spider-Woman. She kept it a well-guarded secret. She refuses to reveal her identity because she wants to protect the people she cares about from being harmed by her enemies. Unlike Spider-Man, it is unknown whether Spider-Woman was born with special powers or if she acquired them later in life.

Spider-Woman has extraordinary strength, endurance, and agility. Spider-Woman can move her body like a spider, climbing up walls and across ceilings. Spider-Woman's intuition is only average. She is not able to sense danger any better than the ordinary person. However, her psychic ability is exceptional. She can create a web by concentrating intensely and does not need any kind of device. Spider-Woman uses the web to trap criminals. One problem with the web is that it becomes increasingly weaker the further away it is from Spider-Woman. Therefore, a criminal can easily break loose if caught in the outer boundaries of the web. If Spider-Woman loses consciousness, she cannot create or maintain a web.

A. These words were used in the selection you just read. Match the words from the list on the left with their proper meanings.

_____ 1. identity   a. lines or limits where something ends

_____ 2. extraordinary   b. who a person is

_____ 3. psychic   c. able to read another's mind

_____ 4. concentrate   d. with utmost strain

_____ 5. intensely   e. beyond what is ordinary

_____ 6. boundaries   f. focus on common center

B. Use the back of this paper to answer the following questions.

1. Who is the real Spider-Woman?

2. How did she get her special powers?

3. How does she create a web?

4. Can she sense danger like an ordinary person can?

5. How can a criminal break loose from her web?

6. What super power would you add to Spider-Woman?

The Walt Disney Story

Preview the words in exercise A before reading the following selection. Then complete the exercises below.

Walter Elias Disney was born on December 5, 1901, the fourth of five children. Disney's early years were spent on a farm in Missouri, where he developed an interest in drawing.

In 1919, Disney and a friend formed an art company and made some animated cartoons.

Four years later he moved to California, where he and his brother, Roy, began Walt Disney Productions. Disney created a character he called Mortimer the Mouse. His wife, Lillian, suggested a name that was less stuffy, and Mickey was born. In 1928, with Disney providing his voice, Mickey Mouse starred in *Steamboat Willie*. The success of Mickey Mouse was only the beginning. In the thirties, Mickey acquired a number of cartoon pals, including Donald Duck, Pluto, Minnie Mouse, and Goofy. Walt Disney died in 1966, but the studio he founded continues the Disney tradition, bringing new technology to films. Disney's spirit lives on in his memorable characters and theme parks.

A. These words were used in the selection you just read. Match the words from the list on the left with the proper meanings.

_____ 1. stuffy   a. made to seem alive

_____ 2. develop   b. dull

_____ 3. founded   c. use of scientific knowledge

_____ 4. animated   d. to cause to grow; get better

_____ 5. technology   e. brought into being; established

B. Use the back of this paper to answer the following questions.

1. When was Walter Elias Disney born?

2. Where did the name Mickey Mouse come from?

3. Who did Walt go into business with to form Walt Disney Productions?

4. What was the first movie that Mickey Mouse starred in?

5. Describe a character that you would create if you had your own movie company.

The Amazon Rain Forest

Preview the words in exercise A before reading the following selection. Then complete the exercises below.

In 1971, construction began in Brazil for a major trans-Amazon highway to open up and remove areas of the rain forest for settlement and development. Huge areas of the Amazon rain forest were cut down and burned to make way for about one million new settlers. Because the large cities were so overcrowded and most people were unable to find work there, the government offered lucrative incentives to families who moved to the Amazon. Each family would be given a 240-acre piece of land, housing, and a small salary for a few months. Plans were made to build schools, health facilities, and other services. Thousands made the move but had to give up after only a few months because life in the rain forest was so difficult. The project failed, and it led to the destruction of a great deal of the Amazon rain forest. The result of this devastation was that much of the rain forest habitat was lost forever, and the soil eroded and turned into poor agricultural land.

A. These words were used in the selection you just read. Match the words from the list on the left with their proper meanings.

_____ 1. lucrative   a. destruction

_____ 2. facilities   b. that which relates to producing crops or raising livestock

_____ 3. habitat   c. producing wealth, profitable

_____ 4. incentive   d. buildings used for activities

_____ 5. devastation   e. something used to make someone do better

_____ 6. agricultural   f. place where an animal lives

B. Use the back of this paper to answer the following questions.

1. What did construction begin for in 1971?

2. What happened to large areas of the Amazon rain forest?

3. What was each family offered if they moved there?

4. What services would be available to these families?

5. Was this project a success? Explain your answer.

6. Is the rain forest important to the ecology of the rest of the world? Explain your answer.

Robin Hood

Preview the words in exercise A before reading the
following selection. Then complete the exercises below.

Robin Hood is a legendary English hero whose rebellious
nature made him a popular character in stories and
ballads beginning sometime during the 1300s. To this day,
no one knows for sure whether or not he really existed.

The legend begins when Robin Hood is rescued by a
group of outlaws who live in Sherwood Forest. He finds
that he has much more in common with these outlaws
than anyone else so he becomes their leader. Robin
Hood's followers include the beautiful Maid Marian, the
love of his life; Friar Tuck, a good-hearted priest; and Little
John, a seven-foot giant of a man.

Robin Hood's popularity comes from the way he fights
corruption and injustice. He treats corrupt officials, such
as the sheriff of Nottingham, with contempt. However, he treats women and poor people with
respect. He and his band of outlaws steal from the rich and give to the poor. The commoners
praise him as a hero, while authority figures proclaim him an outlaw.

A. These words were used in the selection you just read. Match the words on the left with
   their proper meanings.

   _____ 1. legend   a. a feeling of honor

   _____ 2. rebellious   b. resisting authority

   _____ 3. ballads   c. dishonesty

   _____ 4. commoners   d. ordinary people

   _____ 5. corruption   e. poems or songs that tell a story

   _____ 6. respect   f. story handed down from the past

B. Use the back of this paper to answer the following questions.

   1. Who is Robin Hood?

   2. Who rescues Robin Hood in the forest?

   3. Who are his faithful followers?

   4. How does he treat corrupt officials such as the sheriff of Nottingham?

   5. How does he treat women and poor people?

   6. Do you think Robin Hood was a real person? Explain your answer.

Kristi Yamaguchi

Preview the words in exercise A before reading the following selection. Then complete the exercises below.

Kristi Tsuya Yamaguchi was born in Hayward, California, in 1971. She was born with a clubfoot, but she did not let that stand in the way of her ambitions. She started skating at the age of six and was competing within two years.

When Yamaguchi was 12 years old, she started skating with Rudi Galindo. Together they won the 1985 national junior pairs championships.

In 1990, Yamaguchi and Galindo decided they wanted to concentrate on their singles careers rather than continue with their pairs skating. This gave Yamaguchi more time to devote to her singles training. As a result, her singles skating improved. She started working to make her routines more complicated. This paid off because she was able to become the world champion in figure skating in 1991 and 1992.

Yamaguchi went to Albertville, France, for the 1992 Winter Olympics. She knew that the competition was going to include many excellent skaters. She chose a routine that was technically difficult. She skated with perfection, and the judges rated her routine the highest. Yamaguchi won a gold medal. It had been 16 years since an American woman had won a gold medal in the singles event.

A. These words were used in the selection you just read. Match the words from the list on the left with their proper meanings.

_____ 1. clubfoot   a. deformity of the foot

_____ 2. concentrate   b. strong desire to achieve something

_____ 3. routine   c. a series of regular activities

_____ 4. champion   d. winner of game or contest

_____ 5. ambition   e. to direct ones thoughts on something

B. Use the back of this paper to answer the following questions.

   1. Where and when was Kristi born?

   2. How old was she when she started skating?

   3. What did she decide to do in 1990?

   4. What medal did she win at the 1992 Winter Olympics?

   5. Would you prefer to be a singles skater or a pairs skater? Explain your answer.

The Greatest Airship Ever Built

Preview the words in exercise A before reading the following selection. Then complete the exercises below.

You have probably seen helium-filled blimps gracefully making their way across the sky. These ships are quiet, safe, and fuel efficient, but their cousins, the zeppelins, did not possess all of these qualities. During the 1930s, huge zeppelins more than 40 times the size of modern blimps carried passengers across the oceans.

The largest and most luxurious zeppelin ever built was the Hindenburg. A magnificent airship, it contained observation decks and private sleeping rooms and offered gourmet dining to its rich passengers.

On Monday, May 3, 1937, at 7:30 A.M. the Hindenburg began a routine journey to America. It reached America on May 6. After delays due to bad weather, it finally landed. Suddenly, there was a loud thump, and the tail section explored into flames. The fire spread rapidly throughout the rest of the craft, and within half a minute the blazing air ship was on the ground. With that unfortunate mishap, the age of the zeppelin came to a complete and abrupt halt.

A. These words were used in the selection you just read. Match the words from the list on the left with their proper meanings.

_____ 1. helium   a. a good result without waste

_____ 2. blazing   b. very splendid and comfortable

_____ 3. efficient   c. a very light gas

_____ 4. routine   d. brightly-burning flame

_____ 5. luxurious   e. regular or standard

B. Use the back of this paper to answer the following questions.

1. How much bigger were zeppelins than blimps?

2. What was the largest and most luxurious zeppelin ever built?

3. Where was the Hindenburg going in 1937?

4. What happened to the Hindenburg as it landed?

5. Would you like to ride in a blimp or zeppelin? Explain your answer.

Judy Blume

Preview the words in exercise A before reading the
following selection. Then complete the exercises below.

Beginning with the introduction of her book *Are You
There God? It's Me, Margaret* in 1970, Judy Blume
became a leading children's author.

Judy Sussman Blume was born on February 12, 1938,
in Elizabeth, New Jersey. As a child, Judy Sussman
was an A student and did exactly as she was told, even
though on the inside she wished she could rebel. She
loved to read Nancy Drew mysteries, biographies, and
horse stories but also longed to read about characters
who shared problems that she and other young people
were facing. She attended New York University, and in
1960, the year before she graduated, she married John
W. Blume, an attorney.

Since her first book was published in 1969, Judy Blume has received awards from all over the
United States. In addition to writing several juvenile fiction books, Judy Blume has written
young adult and adult books. Blume also contributed to the project *Free to Be You and Me* for
the Mrs. Foundation in 1974.

In recent years, Judy Blume founded KIDS Find and remains on the council of advisors for the
National Coalition of Censorship.

A. These words were used in the selection you just read. Match the words from the list on
the left with their proper meanings.

_____ 1. rebel	a. resist or fight authority
_____ 2. biographies	b. people who consult or give advice
_____ 3. juvenile	c. completed a course of study
_____ 4. advisors	d. childish
_____ 5. graduated	e. true stories about someone, written by another person

B. Use the back of this paper to answer the following questions.

1. What was the name of the first book that made her famous?

2. What kind of student was she as a child?

3. What kind of books did she like to read as a child?

4. Why did she change her name to Judy Blume?

5. What would be a subject for a book that you would like her to write about?

Annie Oakley

Preview the words in exercise A before reading the following selection. Then complete the exercises below.

Annie Oakley was born in 1860 in Darke County, Ohio. Her name at birth was Phoebe Ann Moses. By the age of eight, she had learned to shoot and helped her family by hunting animals for food. Annie was a professional marksman by the time she was 15. She participated in many shooting contests that took place in Cincinnati. She beat Frank Butler in a shooting match, which sparked a romance between them. Annie and Frank were married in 1876. Soon afterwards, Annie started calling herself Annie Oakley. In 1885, Annie joined Buffalo Bill's Wild West Show. She gave a fascinating performance with the assistance of her husband. She would shoot a dime that was in his hand or a cigarette that was in his mouth. Annie also did a trick during which her husband, who was standing 90 feet (27 m) away from her, threw a playing card into the air and she shot it. Annie's accuracy amazed audiences. She was often called "Little Sure Shot," a nickname that was given to her by Sitting Bull, a Sioux Indian chief.

A. These words were used in the selection you just read. Match the words from the list on the left with their proper meanings.

_____ 1. marksman   a. feelings of love toward someone

_____ 2. assistance   b. person skilled in shooting a gun or rifle

_____ 3. accuracy   c. having the power to charm

_____ 4. fascinating   d. to help

_____ 5. romance   e. freedom from error

B. Use the back of this paper to answer the following questions.

1. How did she help her family when she was eight years old?

2. How did she meet her husband?

3. Describe one of the tricks that she could do.

4. What was her nickname?

5. Why do you think that Annie's performance was so popular?

Statue of Liberty

Preview the words in exercise A before reading the following selection. Then complete the exercises below.

The Statue of Liberty has always been a symbol of welcome and a promise of freedom for immigrants to the United States of America. The statue was given to the United States by the people of France in 1884. They wanted to have it ready by the Centennial in 1876, but it was delayed because France was involved in a war with Prussia. Frédéric Bartholdi designed and sculpted the statue. He was sent to America to complete his plans. As he sailed into the harbor at Bedloe's Island, he knew that was where the statue should be. He decided to make the statue a lady as a symbol of liberty and that she would face the ocean with a greeting and a promise. He decided to call it Liberty Enlightening the World. Bartholdi talked to President Grant, and it was agreed that France would built the statue and the United States would build the base and pedestal.

The seven spikes in the statue's crown reach out to the seven seas and the seven continents. The seven spikes also stand for seven liberties.

A. These words were used in the selection you just read. Match the words from the list on the left with their proper meanings.

_____ 1. immigrants   a. long, pointed piece of metal or wood

_____ 2. sculpted   b. people from another country

_____ 3. statue   c. rights or freedoms

_____ 4. spikes   d. shaped or designed

_____ 5. liberties   e. likeness of something that has been sculpted out of another material such as clay

B. Use the back of this paper to answer the following exercises.

1. What does the Statue of Liberty symbolize?

2. Who gave the United States the statue and when?

3. Who designed it?

4. What did the designer decide to name the statue?

5. What do the seven spikes in the crown stand for?

A. A. Milne

Preview the words in exercise A before reading the following selection. Then complete the exercises below.

Alan Alexander Milne, better known as A. A. Milne, is the author of Winnie-the-Pooh stories for children. He was born on January 18, 1882, in London, England, and was the youngest of three boys. An unambitious student, he discovered writing when his brother bet him he couldn't compose a verse as well as he could. But Milne surprised his brother with a well-written poem, and the two collaborated on verse for a couple of years.

During World War I Milne joined the Royal Warwickshire Regiment, a reserve battalion, and served in France. In his spare time he was able to write his first children's book and a play to entertain the troops. When he returned to civilian life, he continued with his writing career. On August 21, 1920, his only son, Christopher Robin, was born. The book that established him as a major children's author was the 1926 story *Winnie-the-Pooh*.

Winnie, Eeyore, and Christopher Robin have become some of children's favorite storybook characters. In recent years they were immortalized on screen by the Walt Disney Company, which made its first motion picture about *Winnie-the-Pooh* in 1965.

A. These words were used in the selection you just read. Match the words from the list on the left with their proper meanings.

_____ 1. unambitious   a. groups of soldiers

_____ 2. collaborated   b. one section of a poem or song

_____ 3. verse   c. not eager to succeed

_____ 4. entertain   d. worked with someone on a project

_____ 5. troops   e. to hold someone's attention

B. Use the back of this paper to answer the following questions.

1. How did A. A. Milne became a writer?

2. During World War I, what did he do in his spare time?

3. What book did he write in 1926?

4. Who made the first motion picture about the book written in 1926?

5. What would happen if *Winnie-the-Pooh* took place in Japan? Explain your answer.

Constellations

Preview the words in exercise A before reading the following selection. Then complete the exercises below.

People have been using stars to guide their way and lives for centuries. Without the use of landmarks, mariners of old depended solely upon compass and stars to direct their ships. Since the stars served such an important role for people, names were given to groups of stars to help chart the night sky. We call these star groupings constellations. The constellations have been known by many different names by different groups of people. A good example of this is the Big Dipper. The Big Dipper is known as the Bear by the ancient Greeks, the Wagon by the ancient Romans, and the Plow by many European people today. To the Hindus, the Big Dipper represents the Seven Rishis.

Many of the constellation names were based on ancient stories and myths. The following is a story from Greek mythology which explains the constellation Cassiopeia.

Cassiopeia claimed that she was more beautiful than the lovely sea nymphs. The nymphs became angry and complained to Poseidon, god of the sea. Poseidon decided to punish Cassiopeia for her vanity by sending a sea monster to destroy her kingdom. He then demanded that Cassiopeia's daughter be sacrificed to the sea monster. Fortunately, the young girl was rescued by Perseus before the sea monster could kill her. Cassiopeia was changed into a constellation at her death and was placed into the night sky for all to remember.

A. These words were used in the selection you just read. Match the words from the list on the left with their proper meanings.

_____ 1. mariners   a. to rely upon

_____ 2. compass   b. ones who navigate a ship

_____ 3. European   c. natives of India who believes in Hinduism

_____ 4. Hindu   d. instrument used to tell geographic locations

_____ 5. depended   e. from Europe

_____ 6. nymphs   f. female spirits who live in woods or water

B. Use the back of this paper to answer the following questions.

1. What did ancient people use the stars for?

2. What do we call star groupings?

3. What is the name of one of the constellations written about in the article?

4. What were many of the stars' names based on?

5. What did Cassiopeia think about herself?

Hercules

Preview the words in exercise A before reading the following selection. Then complete the exercises below.

Hercules is a great hero in Greek mythology. He was the son of Zeus, king of the gods of Olympia.

When Hercules was just a baby, he began showing that he had great strength by killing two serpents who were about to attack him. As he grew up, he became famous for his strength and his kindness to those in need. He learned wrestling, archery, and fencing. Although Hercules was basically a good person, he had one serious problem. He had a terrible temper. His temper was so uncontrollable that he had been banished from Thebes. Hercules was told that the only way he could make up for his behavior was to serve King Eurystheus for 12 years. During this time, Hercules was given many difficult tasks to accomplish. With strong determination, he was able to accomplish all of them

A. These words were used in the selection you just read. Match the words from the list on the left with their proper meanings.

_____ 1. banished

_____ 2. accomplish

_____ 3. mythology

_____ 4. temper

_____ 5. fencing

a. tendency to become angry

b. sport using swords

c. to carry out

d. made-up stories about people, gods, and ancestors

e. forced to leave

B. Use the back of this paper to answer the following questions.

1. Who was Hercules' father?

2. What unusual thing did Hercules do when he was just a baby?

3. What are the names of two activities that he liked to do when he was growing up?

4. Why was he banished from Thebes?

5. What did he have to do to make up for his bad behavior?

6. What lesson do you think Hercules learned from his 12-year experience?

Neil Armstrong

Preview the words in exercise A before reading the following selection. Then complete the exercises below.

Neil Alden Armstrong was born in 1930 in Wapakoneta, Ohio. During the Korean War, Armstrong was a pilot for the United States Navy. After the war, he studied at Purdue University where he graduated in 1955. Then Armstrong became a civilian test pilot for what is now called the National Aeronautics and Space Administration (NASA). In 1962, Armstrong started training to be an astronaut, making him the first civilian to join the program.

In 1966, Armstrong climbed aboard Gemini 8 to make his first flight into space. Although the mission was a success, it did encounter a serious problem. After docking the two spacecrafts, it went into a violent roll. Fortunately, he and his partner were able to deal with the crisis and safely return to Earth.

In July 1969, Armstrong was chosen as the commander of the Apollo 11 mission. People from all around the world watched as Armstrong made history on July 20, 1969, by being the first person to walk on the moon.

Armstrong retired from NASA in 1971 to become an aerospace engineering professor.

A. These words were used in the selection you just read. Match the words from the list on the left with their proper meanings.

_____ 1. aerospace   a. to meet unexpectedly

_____ 2. civilian   b. a crucial situation

_____ 3. docking   c. science that deals with space flight

_____ 4. crisis   d. guiding or coming to a dock

_____ 5. encounter   e. a person not in the armed forces

B. Use the back of this paper to answer the following questions.

1. What job did Neil Armstrong do for the Navy?

2. What was the name of the first flight that he took?

3. What was the problem they faced on the Gemini 8 flight?

4. When did he retire, and what did he do?

5. How do you think Armstrong felt about being the first person to walk on the moon? Explain your answer.

Babe Ruth

Preview the words in exercise A before reading the following
selection. Then complete the exercises below.

Born in 1895, George Herman Ruth grew up on the streets of
Baltimore, fending for himself, and by the age of eight had gotten
into trouble. Young George was sent to a Catholic boys' home,
where he played baseball. An invaluable team member, he could
play just about any position.

In 1914 Ruth began his career with the Baltimore Orioles, at that
time a minor league team. Later that year, Ruth joined the
Boston Red Sox. There he served as a pitcher while also
showing his prowess as a hitter. Because he could hit the ball
harder and farther than any other team member, he held two positions—in some games he
pitched and in other games he played in the outfield. By 1918, Babe Ruth was recognized as
the best left-handed pitcher in baseball. He also led the American League in home runs.
Boston's owner, in need of money, sold Ruth to the New York Yankees after the 1919 season.
As a Yankee, Ruth concentrated solely on hitting and playing the outfield, and immediately, he
shattered a number of records and brought baseball to a new level.

Formerly, baseball had been a pitcher's game, but Ruth changed all that; now it was a hitter's
game. Ruth set many records that stood unchanged for years. In 1920 he broke the 1884
record of 24 home runs in one season by hitting 54. The next year he hit 59 homers and
scored a total of 177 runs. In 1927 Ruth hit 60 home runs, a record that stood for 34 years.
Attendance at games increased so much that the Yankees built Yankee Stadium, sometimes
known as "the house that Ruth built."

A. These words were used in the selection you just read. Match the words from the list on
   the left with their proper meanings.

   _____ 1. fending   a. superior skill or ability
   _____ 2. invaluable   b. to provide for
   _____ 3. concentrated   c. home runs
   _____ 4. attendance   d. priceless
   _____ 5. prowess   e. focused
   _____ 6. homers   f. number of people at an event

B. Use the back of this paper to answer the following questions.

   1. Where was George Herman Ruth born?
   2. What was his childhood like?
   3. During his lifetime, what positions did he play?
   4. What record did he break in 1920?
   5. What was the other name for Yankee Stadium?
   6. If you met him on the street today, what would you say to him?

Elvis Presley

Preview the words in exercise A before reading the following selection. Then complete the exercises below.

Elvis Presley has been called the King of rock and roll. Born on January 8, 1935, in Tupelo, Mississippi, Presley won his first talent contest when he was just eight years old. In 1954, he recorded his first song as a present for his mother. The owner of the recording service had recently started his own record company, Sun, and signed Presley as a new talent. Presley did not have much success with Sun and after a year left for RCA. Thanks in large part to television and appearances on programs such as *The Ed Sullivan Show*, Presley became a huge star all across America.

In 1955, Colonel Tom Parker became Presley's manager and signed him to RCA Records at a cost of $40,000. One year later, Presley had a number-one hit with "Heartbreak Hotel." A string of hits continued with "Hound Dog," "Don't Be Cruel," and "Love Me Tender."

Presley entered the film industry and starred in a number of musicals until he was drafted by the U.S. Army. For two years he served his country, and he was proud to do so. His return to civilian life meant a return to acting, but his singing career was not as hot as it once was. Pop artists of the sixties began to replace his now-dated style.

During the seventies, Presley started live tours, and his singing career picked up. On August 16, 1977, Elvis Presley died. He left behind an impressive 94 gold singles and over 40 gold albums. Today, he remains one of the biggest influences on 20th century pop culture and is an enduring idol in the world of rock and roll.

A. These words were used in the selection you just read. Match the words from the list on the left with their proper meanings.

1. success   a. making a strong impression
2. enduring   b. long lasting
3. manager   c. popular singers
4. drafted   d. to be selected for military service
5. pop artists   e. having achieved something
6. impressive   f. a person who is in charge of a business or person

B. Use the back of this paper to answer the following questions.

1. What did Elvis win when he was eight years old?
2. Why did he record his first song?
3. Why did he stop starring in movies?
4. How did Elvis help his career in the seventies?
5. How many albums did he make in his lifetime?
6. If Elvis were alive today, do you think you would like to go to see him in a concert? Explain your answer.

Orel Hershiser

Preview the words in exercise A before reading the following selection. Then complete the exercises below.

When Orel Hershiser was young, he enjoyed playing a variety of sports, such as racquetball, tennis, golf, and hockey. However, baseball was his favorite. At the age of eight, Hershiser entered a contest that was held in Yankee Stadium in New York. In the contest, he had to throw, hit, and run. He completed against boys from all across America. Hershiser came in third place.

Hershiser had a great deal of difficulty playing baseball in high school and college. In high school, he started out playing, but he was cut from the team. In college, he was not allowed to join the baseball team because his grades and his playing were not good enough. Rather than give up, Hershiser worked to improve his grades and his baseball skills. His grades went up, and he increased the speed of his pitch by five miles per hour. As a result, he made the college team.

Hershiser started playing professional baseball as a pitcher for the Los Angeles Dodgers' minor-league team. His playing ability was only fair, and he often felt discouraged. However, his coach, trainer, and manager felt Hershiser had potential so they convinced him to keep working on his pitch. That is exactly what Hershiser did, and eventually he became a starring pitcher for the major leagues.

A. These words were used in the selection you just read. Match the words from the list on the left with their proper meanings.

_____ 1. convinced   a. possibility; promise

_____ 2. variety   b. number of different kinds

_____ 3. ability   c. persuaded to do something

_____ 4. potential   d. skill

_____ 5. discouraged   e. to lack confidence or hope

B. Use the back of this paper to answer the following questions.

1. What was Orel's favorite sport as a child?

2. Did he play baseball in college?

3. Where did he start playing professional baseball?

4. Was baseball easy for him as an adult? Explain your answer.

5. Why do you think he kept on playing baseball even though he was not a great player and was often discouraged?

King Arthur

Read the following story and then complete the exercises on page 67.

King Arthur was and continues to be one of the great British heros of medieval times. Although it is believed that there really was an Arthur, the adventure stories that have been told about him for nearly 1,000 years are generally thought to be legend. According to the Latin versions of the story, King Uther Pendragon, Arthur's father was not allowed to raise Arthur himself because he had made a special pact with Merlin, a magician. As a result, Merlin raised Arthur as his own son and never told him that his father was a king.

According to the legend, there was a sword embedded in a stone that was located in a churchyard. The sword, called Excalibur, was said to be magical, and anyone who could remove it from the stone would become the king of Britain. Many nobles and knights tried to remove it, but they could not. Then Arthur tried and easily pulled Excalibur

from the stone. This amazing feat proved that he was royalty, so he became Britain's king. At some point after Arthur became king, he fell in love with Princess Guinevere and married her. Although they had several castles to choose from, Arthur preferred to stay at Camelot, which was located somewhere in southern England.

Arthur tried to rule with fairness and wisdom. As a result, most knights greatly respected Arthur and wanted to serve him. They came from many countries in hopes of being chosen as a knight of the Round Table. This table was round in shape and could seat 1,600 knights without any one knight having a better seat than the others. Arthur felt that this was the best way to prevent his knights from arguing.

The legend of King Arthur tells about his many heroic adventures. He is said to have conquered most of western Europe by defeating the Roman Empire. Unfortunately, while he was away, his nephew, Mordred, captured his kingdom. When Arthur returned home, he fought and killed Mordred. Although he was victorious, he received wounds during this battle and later died. Some say that Arthur never died but was taken to the mystical island of Avalon so that his wounds would heal. Many believe that he will return someday.

King Arthur (cont.)

A. These words were used in the selection you just read. Match the words from the list on the left with their proper meanings.

_____ 1. British	a.	very brave or daring
_____ 2. legend	b.	the people of Great Britain
_____ 3. medieval	c.	members of a royal family (i.e., king or queen)
_____ 4. embedded	d.	story handed down from earlier times
_____ 5. royalty	e.	relating to the Middle Ages
_____ 6. heroic	f.	firmly enclosed

B. Use the space below and on the back of this paper to answer the following questions.

1. According to legend, who raised King Arthur as his own son?

2. What did Arthur do with the sword embedded in the stone?

3. What kind of ruler was King Arthur?

4. Describe the table that he had built and why he chose the shape that he did?

5. What circumstances could have caused his death?

6. What would you have done if you had been able to pull Excalibur from the stone?

_____

_____

_____

_____

_____

_____

_____

Ludwig van Beethoven

Read the selection below. When you are finished, answer the questions on page 69 and complete the activities on pages 70–72.

Ludwig van Beethoven was born in Bonn, Germany, in 1770. When he was only four years old, he was practicing on the violin and the clavier (a keyboard) for many hours each day. His father was determined to turn the boy into a musician.

He learned so quickly that he went on his first concert tour at the age of 11. When Beethoven was 17, Mozart, a great musician and composer of the time, heard him play and was impressed with his ability.

A few years later, Beethoven went to Vienna, Austria, to study with Haydn, another great musician and composer. It was not long before Beethoven was writing music, too. In his lifetime, he wrote about 300 pieces of music. Beethoven's compositions included sonatas, symphonies, concertos, and operas. (Sonatas are long musical compositions that are divided into several parts or "movements." Symphonies are sonatas written for the orchestra. Concertos are sonatas written for an instrument soloist and orchestra. Operas are plays in which the words are sung to music.)

After an illness at the age of 31, Beethoven gradually lost his hearing. Despite this terrible tragedy, he was somehow able to keep the melody or tune, the harmony of the chords, and the tempo or beat of the music inside his head. He wrote some of his most beautiful music after that time. Yet, he was never able to hear what he had written!

Toward the end of his life, Beethoven had to be turned toward the audience to see the applause because he could not hear it. He died in 1827 at the age of 57 and is considered one of the greatest composers who ever lived.

Ludwig van Beethoven (cont.)

What did you learn about Ludwig van Beethoven? Answer the following questions in complete sentences.

1. Where and when was Beethoven born? _____

2. How old was he when he began to study music?

   _____

3. Who wanted him to be a musician?

   _____

4. How old was Beethoven when he went on his first concert tour?

   _____

5. How old was Beethoven when Mozart heard him play?

   _____

6. Where did Beethoven go to study music?

   _____

7. With whom did he study?

   _____

8. About how many musical compositions did Beethoven write?

   _____

9. What types of compositions did he write?

   _____

10. What great tragedy befell Beethoven?

   _____

Ludwig van Beethoven (cont.)

It is important to be able to read and spell the different words connected with the study of Beethoven. Here are some of the words you might be using.

composer	symphony	Mozart	violin
Austria	melody	concerto	Haydn
Bonn	composition	harmony	sonata
orchestra	Germany	notation	tempo
opera	piano	Vienna	musician

Using words in different ways helps you learn to read them and to spell them. Practice these skills by writing the words in alphabetical order on the lines below.

1. _____

2. _____

3. _____

4. _____

5. _____

6. _____

7. _____

8. _____

9. _____

10. _____

11. _____

12. _____

13. _____

14. _____

15. _____

16. _____

17. _____

18. _____

19. _____

20. _____

Ludwig van Beethoven (cont.)

Use these words to solve the word search.

composer	symphony	Mozart	violin
Austria	melody	concerto	Haydn
Bonn	composition	harmony	sonata
orchestra	Germany	notation	tempo
opera	piano	Vienna	musician

```
S D F G H J K P Q W E A U S T R I A X C
A C O M P O S I T I O N Z X C S T V O P
M O O N B V C A C E X Z O V I O L I N I
L M K N J H G N G F M D S T A N Q E E R
U P Y T C T R O S E R P F G A A H N H U
B O N N M E L O D Y A S O D F T H N A Y
G S T O P E R A R G M E D C V A I A Y T
A E S D F G H T K L E P M N B V C O D A
Q R W E R T Y O O I O R H P L K J H N C
A M U S I C I A N Q U I M O Z A R T S D
A S D F G H J K L P O I U A N Y T R E W
O R C H E S T R A H A R M O N Y A S D F
Q A Z X S W E D C V F R T G B Y J U I L
```

Ludwig van Beethoven (cont.)

Imagine that you are Beethoven, the great composer. Use what you have learned from the previous selection and activities to complete this writing exercise. Write a letter to your best friend, expressing your feelings about losing your hearing while you still have so much more music to write.

Use the correct form for a personal letter and your best writing skills—grammar, punctuation, and spelling—so your readers will understand and enjoy what you have written.

Date your letter sometime in 1801, the year Beethoven suffered the loss of his hearing.

_____

_____

_____

_____

_____

_____

_____

_____

_____

_____

_____

_____

_____

_____

The Summer of the Swans

The following questions are based on the book, *The Summer of the Swans* by Betsy Byers (Scholastic, 1970).

Read the book in chapter groups as follows: 1-4, 5-9, 10-14, 15-18, and 19-20. Stop after each group of chapters to answer the questions below and on pages 74 and 75.

After you have completed the book, answer the book review questions on page 76.

Chapters 1-4

1. Why is Sara so negative about herself?

_____

_____

_____

2. Who is Charlie?

_____

_____

3. Why does Aunt Willie live with and care for Sara, Charlie, and Wanda?

_____

_____

_____

4. What does Sara compare her life to and why?

_____

_____

_____

_____

5. What is Sara's main frustration with her siblings?

_____

_____

_____

The Summer of the Swans (cont.)

━━━━━━━━━━━━━━━━━━━━━Chapters 5-9━━━━━━━━━━━━━━━━━━━

1. Why is Charlie's wristwatch such a pleasure for him?

_____

2. How does Charlie indicate that he sees the swans?

_____

_____

3. Where do the swans live most of the time?

_____

4. Why does Sara say she dislikes Frank? What might be another reason?

_____

_____

━━━━━━━━━━━━━━━━━━━━━Chapters 10-14 ━━━━━━━━━━━━━━━━

1. Why does Sara go back to the lake?

_____

_____

2. How does Sara feel when she does not find Charlie with the swans?

_____

_____

3. What promise did Aunt Willie make to the children's mother?

_____

4. Why does Sara feel that she has lost her father, too?

_____

_____

5. How do we know that Sara is really a fair person?

_____

_____

The Summer of the Swans (cont.)

Chapters 15-18

1. How does Sara find out she is wrong about Joe Melby?

_____

2. Why does Sara want to run away when she sees Joe Melby coming?

_____

_____

3. How does Joe make it easier for Sara to apologize?

_____

4. What causes Charlie even more stress, and how does he handle it?

_____

5. How does Joe prove what a good friend he is?

_____

_____

Chapters 19-20

1. What does Sara do to help relieve her anxiety?

_____

_____

2. What makes Charlie feel safe and well?

_____

3. How does Joe help comfort Charlie?

_____

4. How can we tell Charlie loves Aunt Willie?

_____

5. In what ways does Sara change over this summer?

_____

_____

The Summer of the Swans (cont.)

Book Review

Matching: Match the descriptions with the correct people.

_____ 1. Sara

_____ 2. Sam

_____ 3. Charlie

_____ 4. Aunt Willie

_____ 5. Wanda

a. raises three children.

b. works in Ohio.

c. is called "Little One."

d. is unhappy with her life.

e. gets lost.

True or False: Write true or false next to each statement below.

_____ 1. Charlie follows the swans and gets lost.

_____ 2. Sara has low self-esteem.

_____ 3. Aunt Willie likes to ride Frank's motor scooter.

_____ 4. Wanda works as a teacher's guide.

_____ 5. Mary is more worried about the party than finding Charlie.

Short Answer: Answer these questions using complete sentences.

1. How do you know how Sara feels about herself?

   _____

2. Why does Aunt Willie live with the children?

   _____

3. What happened to Charlie when he was only three years old?

   _____

4. What things about her family cause Sara distress and dissatisfaction?

   _____

5. Why is apologizing to Joe Melby so hard for Sara?

   _____

Shiloh

The following questions are based on the book *Shiloh* by Phyllis Reynolds Naylor (Dell, 1991).
Read the book in chapter groups as follows: 1-3, 4-7, 8-11, and 12-15.
Stop after each group of chapters to answer the questions below and on pages 78 and 79.
After you have completed the book, answer the book review questions on page 80.

Chapters 1-3

1. Briefly describe how Marty and Shiloh first meet. How does Shiloh behave?

_____

_____

_____

_____

2. List the names of the three Preston children and their ages.

_____

_____

_____

3. In what town and state does the story take place? What season is it?

_____

_____

4. How does Judd treat Shiloh after Marty returns him? How does Marty respond?

_____

_____

_____

_____

5. How does Marty try to raise money?

_____

_____

_____

_____

Shiloh (cont.)

Chapters 4-7

1. What promise does Marty make to Shiloh?

_____

2. How does Marty keep Dara Lynn off the hill where he is hiding Shiloh?

_____

3. What do we learn about Judd Travers' childhood?

_____

_____

4. What does Marty purchase at Mr. Wallace's corner store and why?

_____

5. Although he feels badly about it, Marty must lie in order to keep Shiloh safe. List at least three different lies Marty tells in Chapter 4-7.

_____

_____

Chapters 8-11

1. After Mrs. Preston discovers Shiloh, Marty comes up with a plan to find his beloved beagle a safe home. What is his plan?

_____

_____

2. Briefly describe how Shiloh gets hurt.

_____

_____

3. Describe what takes place at Doc Murphy's house.

_____

_____

4. How does Marty feel after he tells David Howard the truth about Shiloh? How does David respond?

_____

_____

5. What agreement do the Prestons make with Judd concerning Shiloh?

_____

Shiloh (cont.)

Chapters 12-15

1. All along, Marty is certain Judd mistreats his animals. Why not, then, just report Judd to the proper authorities?

_____

_____

_____

_____

2. Judd works Marty very hard. List three of Marty's chores.

_____

_____

_____

3. What word does Judd leave out of the contract? Why does Marty insist that he include it?

_____

_____

_____

_____

4. According to Judd, the contract between him and Marty is no good. Why not?

_____

_____

_____

_____

5. After Marty completes his side of the bargain, Judd presents him with a gift. What does he give him? Why is it an important gesture?

_____

_____

_____

_____

Shiloh (cont.)

Book Review

Matching: Match the descriptions of the characters with their names.

1. Marty Preston	a. gentle but frank mother of three
2. Mrs. Preston	b. Marty's friend from Friendly
3. Mr. Preston	c. grocery story owner
4. Judd Travers	d. a teacher, likes to talk about politics
5. Mr. Wallace	e. 11-year-old boy in love with a beagle
6. Doc Murphy	f. 7 years old, curious but afraid of snakes
7. David Howard	g. Shiloh's personal veterinarian
8. Mrs. Howard	h. chews tobacco, had a tough childhood
9. Dara Lynn	i. youngest of the Prestons
10. Becky	j. postman, hardworking father of three

True or False: Answer true or false in the blanks below.

_____ 1. The Prestons live in North Carolina.

_____ 2. Shiloh is a hunting dog.

_____ 3. Judd and Marty's relationship ends on a sour note.

_____ 4. David Howard has a pet hermit crab.

_____ 5. The Prestons have street lights near their home.

Sequence: Arrange these events in order by writing numbers 1 to 5 on the lines.

_____ Marty's mom catches Marty and Shiloh.

_____ Judd gives Marty a dog collar.

_____ Marty builds the pen for Shiloh.

_____ Mr. Baker's German shepherd attacks Shiloh.

_____ Marty goes on the postal route with his dad.

Short Answer: On the back of this paper, write a brief response to each question.

1. Name a three of the towns in Tyler County.

2. What will Marty do if Shiloh is not allowed in heaven?

3. To what call does Shiloh respond when Marty finds him?

Addition Facts Timed Practice

When you practice basic addition facts for speed and accuracy, you improve your ability to solve problems in which addition computations are needed.

You will need a pencil and a timer with a second hand.   Set the timer . . . and go.

1. $\begin{array}{r} 6 \\ +\,9 \\ \hline \end{array}$	2. $\begin{array}{r} 8 \\ +\,1 \\ \hline \end{array}$	3. $\begin{array}{r} 8 \\ +\,9 \\ \hline \end{array}$	4. $\begin{array}{r} 9 \\ +\,4 \\ \hline \end{array}$	5. $\begin{array}{r} 5 \\ +\,0 \\ \hline \end{array}$
6. $\begin{array}{r} 8 \\ +\,0 \\ \hline \end{array}$	7. $\begin{array}{r} 5 \\ +\,9 \\ \hline \end{array}$	8. $\begin{array}{r} 6 \\ +\,1 \\ \hline \end{array}$	9. $\begin{array}{r} 8 \\ +\,8 \\ \hline \end{array}$	10. $\begin{array}{r} 5 \\ +\,5 \\ \hline \end{array}$
11. $\begin{array}{r} 7 \\ +\,6 \\ \hline \end{array}$	12. $\begin{array}{r} 5 \\ +\,1 \\ \hline \end{array}$	13. $\begin{array}{r} 0 \\ +\,6 \\ \hline \end{array}$	14. $\begin{array}{r} 4 \\ +\,1 \\ \hline \end{array}$	15. $\begin{array}{r} 4 \\ +\,4 \\ \hline \end{array}$
16. $\begin{array}{r} 3 \\ +\,1 \\ \hline \end{array}$	17. $\begin{array}{r} 6 \\ +\,5 \\ \hline \end{array}$	18. $\begin{array}{r} 6 \\ +\,4 \\ \hline \end{array}$	19. $\begin{array}{r} 7 \\ +\,0 \\ \hline \end{array}$	20. $\begin{array}{r} 9 \\ +\,3 \\ \hline \end{array}$
21. $\begin{array}{r} 5 \\ +\,2 \\ \hline \end{array}$	22. $\begin{array}{r} 9 \\ +\,9 \\ \hline \end{array}$	23. $\begin{array}{r} 4 \\ +\,2 \\ \hline \end{array}$	24. $\begin{array}{r} 3 \\ +\,5 \\ \hline \end{array}$	25. $\begin{array}{r} 6 \\ +\,6 \\ \hline \end{array}$
26. $\begin{array}{r} 6 \\ +\,7 \\ \hline \end{array}$	27. $\begin{array}{r} 6 \\ +\,8 \\ \hline \end{array}$	28. $\begin{array}{r} 5 \\ +\,6 \\ \hline \end{array}$	29. $\begin{array}{r} 0 \\ +\,7 \\ \hline \end{array}$	30. $\begin{array}{r} 4 \\ +\,6 \\ \hline \end{array}$
31. $\begin{array}{r} 9 \\ +\,6 \\ \hline \end{array}$	32. $\begin{array}{r} 2 \\ +\,2 \\ \hline \end{array}$	33. $\begin{array}{r} 9 \\ +\,0 \\ \hline \end{array}$	34. $\begin{array}{r} 9 \\ +\,5 \\ \hline \end{array}$	35. $\begin{array}{r} 0 \\ +\,1 \\ \hline \end{array}$
36. $\begin{array}{r} 7 \\ +\,7 \\ \hline \end{array}$	37. $\begin{array}{r} 3 \\ +\,6 \\ \hline \end{array}$	38. $\begin{array}{r} 9 \\ +\,8 \\ \hline \end{array}$	39. $\begin{array}{r} 7 \\ +\,3 \\ \hline \end{array}$	40. $\begin{array}{r} 4 \\ +\,9 \\ \hline \end{array}$
41. $\begin{array}{r} 9 \\ +\,1 \\ \hline \end{array}$	42. $\begin{array}{r} 0 \\ +\,9 \\ \hline \end{array}$	43. $\begin{array}{r} 3 \\ +\,9 \\ \hline \end{array}$	44. $\begin{array}{r} 7 \\ +\,2 \\ \hline \end{array}$	45. $\begin{array}{r} 3 \\ +\,0 \\ \hline \end{array}$
46. $\begin{array}{r} 6 \\ +\,0 \\ \hline \end{array}$	47. $\begin{array}{r} 5 \\ +\,3 \\ \hline \end{array}$	48. $\begin{array}{r} 8 \\ +\,5 \\ \hline \end{array}$	49. $\begin{array}{r} 9 \\ +\,7 \\ \hline \end{array}$	50. $\begin{array}{r} 4 \\ +\,7 \\ \hline \end{array}$

Practice and Learn—Fifth Grade

Addition Facts Timed Practice (cont.)

51. $\begin{array}{r} 7 \\ +\ 1 \\ \hline \end{array}$	52. $\begin{array}{r} 8 \\ +\ 3 \\ \hline \end{array}$	53. $\begin{array}{r} 4 \\ +\ 10 \\ \hline \end{array}$	54. $\begin{array}{r} 4 \\ +\ 3 \\ \hline \end{array}$	55. $\begin{array}{r} 1 \\ +\ 3 \\ \hline \end{array}$
56. $\begin{array}{r} 2 \\ +\ 0 \\ \hline \end{array}$	57. $\begin{array}{r} 7 \\ +\ 8 \\ \hline \end{array}$	58. $\begin{array}{r} 3 \\ +\ 3 \\ \hline \end{array}$	59. $\begin{array}{r} 1 \\ +\ 1 \\ \hline \end{array}$	60. $\begin{array}{r} 6 \\ +\ 2 \\ \hline \end{array}$
61. $\begin{array}{r} 5 \\ +\ 7 \\ \hline \end{array}$	62. $\begin{array}{r} 2 \\ +\ 7 \\ \hline \end{array}$	63. $\begin{array}{r} 1 \\ +\ 2 \\ \hline \end{array}$	64. $\begin{array}{r} 8 \\ +\ 4 \\ \hline \end{array}$	65. $\begin{array}{r} 7 \\ +\ 9 \\ \hline \end{array}$
66. $\begin{array}{r} 0 \\ +\ 5 \\ \hline \end{array}$	67. $\begin{array}{r} 4 \\ +\ 5 \\ \hline \end{array}$	68. $\begin{array}{r} 7 \\ +\ 4 \\ \hline \end{array}$	69. $\begin{array}{r} 3 \\ +\ 2 \\ \hline \end{array}$	70. $\begin{array}{r} 1 \\ +\ 8 \\ \hline \end{array}$
71. $\begin{array}{r} 1 \\ +\ 6 \\ \hline \end{array}$	72. $\begin{array}{r} 1 \\ +\ 9 \\ \hline \end{array}$	73. $\begin{array}{r} 0 \\ +\ 4 \\ \hline \end{array}$	74. $\begin{array}{r} 8 \\ +\ 6 \\ \hline \end{array}$	75. $\begin{array}{r} 2 \\ +\ 9 \\ \hline \end{array}$
76. $\begin{array}{r} 2 \\ +\ 3 \\ \hline \end{array}$	77. $\begin{array}{r} 4 \\ +\ 8 \\ \hline \end{array}$	78. $\begin{array}{r} 5 \\ +\ 4 \\ \hline \end{array}$	79. $\begin{array}{r} 8 \\ +\ 2 \\ \hline \end{array}$	80. $\begin{array}{r} 1 \\ +\ 4 \\ \hline \end{array}$
81. $\begin{array}{r} 0 \\ +\ 0 \\ \hline \end{array}$	82. $\begin{array}{r} 3 \\ +\ 4 \\ \hline \end{array}$	83. $\begin{array}{r} 8 \\ +\ 7 \\ \hline \end{array}$	84. $\begin{array}{r} 3 \\ +\ 7 \\ \hline \end{array}$	85. $\begin{array}{r} 2 \\ +\ 1 \\ \hline \end{array}$
86. $\begin{array}{r} 0 \\ +\ 2 \\ \hline \end{array}$	87. $\begin{array}{r} 6 \\ +\ 3 \\ \hline \end{array}$	88. $\begin{array}{r} 1 \\ +\ 7 \\ \hline \end{array}$	89. $\begin{array}{r} 2 \\ +\ 4 \\ \hline \end{array}$	90. $\begin{array}{r} 3 \\ +\ 8 \\ \hline \end{array}$
91. $\begin{array}{r} 5 \\ +\ 8 \\ \hline \end{array}$	92. $\begin{array}{r} 2 \\ +\ 6 \\ \hline \end{array}$	93. $\begin{array}{r} 0 \\ +\ 3 \\ \hline \end{array}$	94. $\begin{array}{r} 1 \\ +\ 9 \\ \hline \end{array}$	95. $\begin{array}{r} 2 \\ +\ 5 \\ \hline \end{array}$
96. $\begin{array}{r} 0 \\ +\ 8 \\ \hline \end{array}$	97. $\begin{array}{r} 1 \\ +\ 5 \\ \hline \end{array}$	98. $\begin{array}{r} 2 \\ +\ 8 \\ \hline \end{array}$	99. $\begin{array}{r} 0 \\ +\ 2 \\ \hline \end{array}$	100. $\begin{array}{r} 7 \\ +\ 5 \\ \hline \end{array}$

How long did it take you to complete the page? _____

How many did you get correct? _____

Single-Digit Addition: Three Rows

1.
$$\begin{array}{r} 1 \\ 2 \\ +\ 3 \\ \hline \end{array}$$

2.
$$\begin{array}{r} 1 \\ 2 \\ +\ 9 \\ \hline \end{array}$$

3.
$$\begin{array}{r} 3 \\ 1 \\ +\ 1 \\ \hline \end{array}$$

4.
$$\begin{array}{r} 6 \\ 6 \\ +\ 1 \\ \hline \end{array}$$

5.
$$\begin{array}{r} 1 \\ 6 \\ +\ 3 \\ \hline \end{array}$$

6.
$$\begin{array}{r} 3 \\ 2 \\ +\ 6 \\ \hline \end{array}$$

7.
$$\begin{array}{r} 5 \\ 8 \\ +\ 4 \\ \hline \end{array}$$

8.
$$\begin{array}{r} 7 \\ 3 \\ +\ 9 \\ \hline \end{array}$$

9.
$$\begin{array}{r} 8 \\ 5 \\ +\ 2 \\ \hline \end{array}$$

10.
$$\begin{array}{r} 5 \\ 8 \\ +\ 3 \\ \hline \end{array}$$

11.
$$\begin{array}{r} 8 \\ 6 \\ +\ 0 \\ \hline \end{array}$$

12.
$$\begin{array}{r} 9 \\ 3 \\ +\ 7 \\ \hline \end{array}$$

13.
$$\begin{array}{r} 1 \\ 7 \\ +\ 2 \\ \hline \end{array}$$

14.
$$\begin{array}{r} 7 \\ 0 \\ +\ 5 \\ \hline \end{array}$$

15.
$$\begin{array}{r} 9 \\ 6 \\ +\ 5 \\ \hline \end{array}$$

16.
$$\begin{array}{r} 5 \\ 2 \\ +\ 9 \\ \hline \end{array}$$

Single-Digit Addition: Four Rows

1.
```
    7
    9
    5
+   5
────
```

2.
```
    1
    2
    2
+   1
────
```

3.
```
    5
    4
    8
+   1
────
```

4.
```
    5
    6
    0
+   4
────
```

5.
```
    1
    7
    0
+   1
────
```

6.
```
    4
    5
    7
+   1
────
```

7.
```
    3
    6
    5
+   1
────
```

8.
```
    7
    3
    7
+   5
────
```

9.
```
    1
    7
    5
+   5
────
```

10.
```
    6
    8
    8
+   1
────
```

11.
```
    2
    6
    9
+   3
────
```

12.
```
    8
    4
    6
+   2
────
```

Single-Digit Addition: Eight Rows

1.	7 3 5 7 9 5 9 + 7	2.	6 8 5 3 6 8 5 + 8	3.	8 7 4 7 9 6 8 + 3	4.	1 3 6 3 3 9 5 + 8

5.	3 1 8 4 5 6 3 + 3	6.	3 8 3 7 2 1 4 + 7	7.	4 9 5 2 6 2 7 + 7	8.	7 5 3 8 6 6 5 + 6

9.	9 1 9 9 2 4 7 + 9	10.	2 7 8 6 5 1 7 + 2	11.	8 6 4 8 7 1 8 + 4	12.	2 8 2 1 7 8 1 + 2

13.	6 2 3 3 6 4 9 + 4	14.	8 7 1 3 6 7 4 + 4	15.	3 2 5 0 1 3 8 + 0	14.	9 0 5 2 3 0 1 + 7

Two Digits Plus One Digit

1. 14
    + 5

2. 16
    + 4

3. 14
    + 3

4. 47
    + 2

5. 55
    + 5

6. 52
    + 1

7. 26
    + 4

8. 68
    + 7

9. 75
    + 3

10. 82
    + 5

11. 39
    + 6

12. 60
    + 1

13. 52
    + 6

14. 20
    + 2

15. 61
    + 2

16. 15
    + 4

17. 29
    + 6

18. 79
    + 8

19. 78
    + 9

20. 48
    + 2

21. 51
    + 6

22. 37
    + 5

23. 96
    + 1

24. 48
    + 8

25. 91
    + 7

Two-Digit Addition: Two Rows

1. $\begin{array}{r} 36 \\ + 85 \\ \hline \end{array}$
2. $\begin{array}{r} 59 \\ + 95 \\ \hline \end{array}$
3. $\begin{array}{r} 88 \\ + 43 \\ \hline \end{array}$
4. $\begin{array}{r} 54 \\ + 40 \\ \hline \end{array}$
5. $\begin{array}{r} 55 \\ + 26 \\ \hline \end{array}$

6. $\begin{array}{r} 57 \\ + 32 \\ \hline \end{array}$
7. $\begin{array}{r} 28 \\ + 16 \\ \hline \end{array}$
8. $\begin{array}{r} 79 \\ + 41 \\ \hline \end{array}$
9. $\begin{array}{r} 35 \\ + 56 \\ \hline \end{array}$
10. $\begin{array}{r} 14 \\ + 25 \\ \hline \end{array}$

11. $\begin{array}{r} 38 \\ + 86 \\ \hline \end{array}$
12. $\begin{array}{r} 34 \\ + 13 \\ \hline \end{array}$
13. $\begin{array}{r} 65 \\ + 60 \\ \hline \end{array}$
14. $\begin{array}{r} 76 \\ + 62 \\ \hline \end{array}$
15. $\begin{array}{r} 71 \\ + 36 \\ \hline \end{array}$

16. $\begin{array}{r} 99 \\ + 97 \\ \hline \end{array}$
17. $\begin{array}{r} 43 \\ + 68 \\ \hline \end{array}$
18. $\begin{array}{r} 21 \\ + 46 \\ \hline \end{array}$
19. $\begin{array}{r} 15 \\ + 39 \\ \hline \end{array}$
20. $\begin{array}{r} 82 \\ + 45 \\ \hline \end{array}$

21. $\begin{array}{r} 73 \\ + 47 \\ \hline \end{array}$
22. $\begin{array}{r} 66 \\ + 53 \\ \hline \end{array}$
23. $\begin{array}{r} 64 \\ + 96 \\ \hline \end{array}$
24. $\begin{array}{r} 58 \\ + 77 \\ \hline \end{array}$
25. $\begin{array}{r} 61 \\ + 12 \\ \hline \end{array}$

Two-Digit Addition: Three Rows

1.   76
        16
     + 77
     _____

2.   79
        40
     + 98
     _____

3.   64
        93
     + 34
     _____

4.   78
        67
     + 12
     _____

5.   42
        72
     + 18
     _____

6.   99
        21
     + 59
     _____

7.   48
        29
     + 34
     _____

8.   54
        45
     + 49
     _____

9.   12
        85
     + 91
     _____

10.   19
        98
     + 78
     _____

11.   82
        70
     + 29
     _____

12.   14
        16
     + 51
     _____

13.   69
        81
     + 68
     _____

14.   54
        57
     + 81
     _____

15.   68
        41
     + 78
     _____

16.   78
        16
     + 82
     _____

Two-Digit Addition: Four Rows

1.　　55
　　　77
　　　71
　　+ 63
　　──────

2.　　75
　　　72
　　　82
　　+ 71
　　──────

3.　　58
　　　16
　　　96
　　+ 12
　　──────

4.　　61
　　　52
　　　79
　　+ 73
　　──────

5.　　53
　　　36
　　　48
　　+ 45
　　──────

6.　　73
　　　87
　　　50
　　+ 36
　　──────

7.　　65
　　　62
　　　69
　　+ 16
　　──────

8.　　15
　　　71
　　　20
　　+ 42
　　──────

9.　　91
　　　99
　　　82
　　+ 86
　　──────

10.　　31
　　　88
　　　98
　　+ 86
　　──────

11.　　76
　　　96
　　　64
　　+ 12
　　──────

12.　　45
　　　17
　　　13
　　+ 16
　　──────

Three-Digit Addition: Two Rows

1.   286
  + 612

2.   442
  + 383

3.   141
  + 931

4.   321
  + 552

5.   313
  + 675

6.   182
  + 837

7.   445
  + 891

8.   158
  + 703

9.   146
  + 243

10.   794
  + 323

11.   694
  + 396

12.   323
  + 298

13.   197
  + 646

14.   795
  + 607

15.   661
  + 351

16.   693
  + 977

17.   594
  + 229

18.   894
  + 928

19.   621
  + 346

20.   321
  + 617

21.   756
  + 492

22.   324
  + 601

23.   388
  + 235

24.   824
  + 123

25.   575
  + 739

Three-Digit Addition: Three Rows

1.   779
       864
    + 392

2.   156
       732
    + 991

3.   297
       948
    + 915

4.   862
       734
    + 367

5.   887
       228
    + 316

6.   875
       593
    + 294

7.   483
       114
    + 663

8.   879
       814
    + 582

9.   423
       384
    + 854

10.   986
       382
    + 376

11.   918
       782
    + 294

12.   893
       453
    + 276

13.   544
       218
    + 938

14.   587
       293
    + 952

15.   493
       571
    + 949

16.   224
       688
    + 111

Three-Digit Addition: Four Rows

1.   757
       213
       141
   +   293
   _____

2.   414
       563
       951
   +   747
   _____

3.   486
       152
       342
   +   116
   _____

4.   775
       256
       675
   +   118
   _____

5.   954
       913
       529
   +   788
   _____

6.   495
       394
       525
   +   411
   _____

7.   994
       292
       197
   +   188
   _____

8.   181
       579
       957
   +   493
   _____

9.   555
       923
       986
   +   592
   _____

10.   288
       953
       842
   +   276
   _____

11.   885
       563
       836
   +   394
   _____

12.   384
       925
       881
   +   171
   _____

Four-Digit Addition: Two Rows

1. 7418
   + 9921

2. 5335
   + 9155

3. 5721
   + 9778

4. 4199
   + 1538

5. 7932
   + 5284

6. 4141
   + 6194

7. 5425
   + 1444

8. 6422
   + 9623

9. 1274
   + 3411

10. 7983
    + 6375

11. 3323
    + 7196

12. 2497
    + 4839

13. 5489
    + 3121

14. 6758
    + 1565

15. 7788
    + 4456

16. 2626
    + 5161

17. 1457
    + 6296

18. 6582
    + 1458

19. 3951
    + 5146

20. 7835
    + 4196

21. 5476
    + 2939

22. 1942
    + 8844

23. 9255
    + 7622

24. 2558
    + 4571

25. 2719
    + 2447

Four-Digit Addition: Three Rows

1.　 1865
　　 8935
　 + 8755

2.　 2315
　　 9165
　 + 2537

3.　 4978
　　 1918
　 + 2259

4.　 6731
　　 6579
　 + 2253

5.　 4732
　　 9287
　 + 2133

6.　 5772
　　 9105
　 + 2675

7.　 2843
　　 7503
　 + 6823

8.　 2459
　　 7737
　 + 5192

9.　 5874
　　 3316
　 + 6627

10.　 7664
　　 3491
　 + 1638

11.　 4178
　　 2877
　 + 7131

12.　 6772
　　 7966
　 + 9466

13.　 8473
　　 6825
　 + 9351

14.　 8245
　　 3306
　 + 6149

15.　 9341
　　 8816
　 + 6919

16.　 8741
　　 3687
　 + 1393

Four-Digit Addition: Four Rows

1.	5263 5752 7852 + 8921	2.	7446 2885 7729 + 9767	3.	6788 4986 2338 + 9924	4.	8354 2276 8213 + 6972
5.	6194 1685 3392 + 1543	6.	8356 9424 3734 + 7751	7.	3355 8421 5896 + 7818	8.	7148 5845 2516 + 8148
9.	9972 4365 7942 + 5965	10.	1744 5556 1545 + 3956	11.	3417 7299 8892 + 5524	12.	6459 5281 4952 + 1446

Mixed Addition Practice

1.　　55
　　+ 21
　　_____

2.　　　5
　　+ 6
　　_____

3.　　83
　　+ 37
　　_____

4.　　　5
　　+ 4
　　_____

5.　　　8
　　+ 7
　　_____

6.　4662
　　+ 8
　　_____

7.　　18
　　+ 21
　　_____

8.　　　9
　　+ 8
　　_____

9.　　85
　　+ 96
　　_____

10.　1769
　　+ 9
　　_____

11.　　92
　　+ 48
　　_____

12.　　　5
　　+ 14
　　_____

13.　　85
　　+ 95
　　_____

14.　1839
　　+ 4
　　_____

15.　　　7
　　+ 11
　　_____

16.　　　7
　　+ 9
　　_____

17.　　79
　　+ 79
　　_____

18.　　88
　　+ 13
　　_____

19.　3445
　　+ 4
　　_____

20.　　63
　　+ 47
　　_____

Subtraction Facts Timed Practice

When you practice your basic subtraction facts for speed and accuracy, you improve your ability to solve problems in which subtraction computations are needed.

You will need a pencil and a timer with a second hand. Set the timer . . . and go.

1. $13 - 4$	2. $17 - 9$	3. $9 - 1$	4. $15 - 9$	5. $5 - 0$
6. $8 - 0$	7. $14 - 9$	8. $7 - 1$	9. $16 - 8$	10. $10 - 5$
11. $13 - 6$	12. $6 - 1$	13. $6 - 6$	14. $5 - 1$	15. $8 - 4$
16. $4 - 1$	17. $11 - 5$	18. $10 - 4$	19. $7 - 0$	20. $12 - 3$
21. $7 - 2$	22. $18 - 9$	23. $6 - 2$	24. $8 - 5$	25. $12 - 6$
26. $13 - 7$	27. $14 - 8$	28. $11 - 6$	29. $7 - 0$	30. $10 - 6$
31. $15 - 6$	32. $4 - 2$	33. $9 - 0$	34. $14 - 5$	35. $1 - 0$
36. $14 - 7$	37. $9 - 6$	38. $17 - 8$	39. $10 - 3$	40. $13 - 9$
41. $10 - 1$	42. $9 - 9$	43. $12 - 9$	44. $9 - 2$	45. $3 - 0$
46. $6 - 0$	47. $8 - 3$	48. $13 - 5$	49. $16 - 7$	50. $11 - 7$

Subtraction Facts Timed Practice (cont.)

51.	8 − 1	52.	11 − 3	53.	4 − 0	54.	7 − 3	55.	4 − 3
56.	2 − 0	57.	15 − 8	58.	6 − 3	59.	2 − 1	60.	8 − 2
61.	12 − 7	62.	9 − 7	63.	3 − 2	64.	12 − 4	65.	16 − 9
66.	5 − 5	67.	9 − 5	68.	11 − 4	69.	5 − 2	70.	9 − 8
71.	7 − 6	72.	10 − 9	73.	4 − 4	74.	14 − 6	75.	11 − 9
76.	5 − 3	77.	12 − 8	78.	9 − 4	79.	10 − 2	80.	5 − 4
81.	0 − 0	82.	7 − 4	83.	15 − 7	84.	10 − 7	85.	3 − 1
86.	11 − 2	87.	9 − 3	88.	8 − 7	89.	6 − 4	90.	11 − 8
91.	13 − 8	92.	8 − 6	93.	3 − 3	94.	1 − 0	95.	7 − 5
96.	8 − 8	97.	6 − 5	98.	10 − 8	99.	2 − 2	100.	12 − 5

How long did it take to complete the page? _____

How many did you get correct? _____

Two Digits Minus One Digit

1. $\begin{array}{r} 41 \\ -\ 6 \\ \hline \end{array}$
2. $\begin{array}{r} 21 \\ -\ 7 \\ \hline \end{array}$
3. $\begin{array}{r} 41 \\ -\ 7 \\ \hline \end{array}$
4. $\begin{array}{r} 51 \\ -\ 7 \\ \hline \end{array}$
5. $\begin{array}{r} 47 \\ -\ 6 \\ \hline \end{array}$

6. $\begin{array}{r} 84 \\ -\ 9 \\ \hline \end{array}$
7. $\begin{array}{r} 17 \\ -\ 4 \\ \hline \end{array}$
8. $\begin{array}{r} 83 \\ -\ 2 \\ \hline \end{array}$
9. $\begin{array}{r} 98 \\ -\ 7 \\ \hline \end{array}$
10. $\begin{array}{r} 93 \\ -\ 8 \\ \hline \end{array}$

11. $\begin{array}{r} 97 \\ -\ 9 \\ \hline \end{array}$
12. $\begin{array}{r} 48 \\ -\ 2 \\ \hline \end{array}$
13. $\begin{array}{r} 99 \\ -\ 5 \\ \hline \end{array}$
14. $\begin{array}{r} 58 \\ -\ 8 \\ \hline \end{array}$
15. $\begin{array}{r} 57 \\ -\ 4 \\ \hline \end{array}$

16. $\begin{array}{r} 71 \\ -\ 1 \\ \hline \end{array}$
17. $\begin{array}{r} 47 \\ -\ 6 \\ \hline \end{array}$
18. $\begin{array}{r} 27 \\ -\ 6 \\ \hline \end{array}$
19. $\begin{array}{r} 68 \\ -\ 1 \\ \hline \end{array}$
20. $\begin{array}{r} 59 \\ -\ 6 \\ \hline \end{array}$

21. $\begin{array}{r} 38 \\ -\ 6 \\ \hline \end{array}$
22. $\begin{array}{r} 88 \\ -\ 9 \\ \hline \end{array}$
23. $\begin{array}{r} 14 \\ -\ 6 \\ \hline \end{array}$
24. $\begin{array}{r} 99 \\ -\ 9 \\ \hline \end{array}$
25. $\begin{array}{r} 29 \\ -\ 4 \\ \hline \end{array}$

Three Digits Minus Two Digits

1.   411
    − 51

2.   666
    − 41

3.   256
    − 37

4.   417
    − 68

5.   613
    − 32

6.   879
    − 56

7.   595
    − 62

8.   319
    − 72

9.   571
    − 37

10.   439
    − 99

11.   174
    − 56

12.   462
    − 81

13.   551
    − 94

14.   293
    − 31

15.   958
    − 28

16.   831
    − 67

17.   352
    − 13

18.   967
    − 88

19.   577
    − 44

20.   617
    − 22

21.   773
    − 95

22.   382
    − 25

23.   732
    − 75

24.   879
    − 53

25.   575
    − 22

Three Digits Minus Two Digits (cont.)

1. $\begin{array}{r} 917 \\ -\ 72 \\ \hline \end{array}$
2. $\begin{array}{r} 241 \\ -\ 82 \\ \hline \end{array}$
3. $\begin{array}{r} 335 \\ -\ 78 \\ \hline \end{array}$
4. $\begin{array}{r} 918 \\ -\ 97 \\ \hline \end{array}$
5. $\begin{array}{r} 952 \\ -\ 64 \\ \hline \end{array}$

6. $\begin{array}{r} 274 \\ -\ 73 \\ \hline \end{array}$
7. $\begin{array}{r} 246 \\ -\ 13 \\ \hline \end{array}$
8. $\begin{array}{r} 783 \\ -\ 24 \\ \hline \end{array}$
9. $\begin{array}{r} 498 \\ -\ 92 \\ \hline \end{array}$
10. $\begin{array}{r} 485 \\ -\ 24 \\ \hline \end{array}$

11. $\begin{array}{r} 543 \\ -\ 11 \\ \hline \end{array}$
12. $\begin{array}{r} 568 \\ -\ 13 \\ \hline \end{array}$
13. $\begin{array}{r} 188 \\ -\ 21 \\ \hline \end{array}$
14. $\begin{array}{r} 237 \\ -\ 14 \\ \hline \end{array}$
15. $\begin{array}{r} 755 \\ -\ 47 \\ \hline \end{array}$

16. $\begin{array}{r} 681 \\ -\ 96 \\ \hline \end{array}$
17. $\begin{array}{r} 923 \\ -\ 36 \\ \hline \end{array}$
18. $\begin{array}{r} 266 \\ -\ 33 \\ \hline \end{array}$
19. $\begin{array}{r} 876 \\ -\ 36 \\ \hline \end{array}$
20. $\begin{array}{r} 864 \\ -\ 48 \\ \hline \end{array}$

21. $\begin{array}{r} 178 \\ -\ 32 \\ \hline \end{array}$
22. $\begin{array}{r} 834 \\ -\ 86 \\ \hline \end{array}$
23. $\begin{array}{r} 326 \\ -\ 76 \\ \hline \end{array}$
24. $\begin{array}{r} 779 \\ -\ 71 \\ \hline \end{array}$
25. $\begin{array}{r} 484 \\ -\ 41 \\ \hline \end{array}$

Four Digits Minus Three Digits

1. 4556
    − 343

2. 3722
    − 411

3. 2983
    − 661

4. 4349
    − 122

5. 4986
    − 813

6. 2991
    − 131

7. 4965
    − 714

8. 9589
    − 257

9. 1757
    − 145

10. 1995
    − 164

11. 5375
    − 213

12. 2558
    − 427

13. 6649
    − 344

14. 9371
    − 321

15. 7978
    − 848

16. 9356
    − 123

17. 7955
    − 321

18. 3796
    − 166

19. 7379
    − 133

20. 8976
    − 734

21. 2566
    − 332

22. 8759
    − 647

23. 7887
    − 317

24. 9998
    − 358

25. 1499
    − 328

Four Digits Minus Three Digits (cont.)

1. 9487
   − 156

2. 1896
   − 653

3. 9238
   − 121

4. 5886
   − 235

5. 8736
   − 424

6. 4648
   − 523

7. 2698
   − 247

8. 7774
   − 651

9. 9953
   − 112

10. 6697
    − 544

11. 4776
    − 735

12. 3598
    − 352

13. 1894
    − 361

14. 4758
    − 248

15. 5678
    − 348

16. 8268
    − 253

17. 6553
    − 242

18. 3497
    − 226

19. 7488
    − 314

20. 6646
    − 242

21. 4598
    − 445

22. 1416
    − 657

23. 2413
    − 766

24. 4515
    − 249

25. 7279
    − 646

Mixed Subtraction Practice

1. $\begin{array}{r} 68 \\ -\ 6 \\ \hline \end{array}$ 2. $\begin{array}{r} 53 \\ -\ 29 \\ \hline \end{array}$ 3. $\begin{array}{r} 334 \\ -\ 4 \\ \hline \end{array}$ 4. $\begin{array}{r} 794 \\ -\ 9 \\ \hline \end{array}$

5. $\begin{array}{r} 7192 \\ -\ 46 \\ \hline \end{array}$ 6. $\begin{array}{r} 8495 \\ -\ 47 \\ \hline \end{array}$ 7. $\begin{array}{r} 84 \\ -\ 9 \\ \hline \end{array}$ 8. $\begin{array}{r} 2794 \\ -\ 6 \\ \hline \end{array}$

9. $\begin{array}{r} 9689 \\ -\ 84 \\ \hline \end{array}$ 10. $\begin{array}{r} 8927 \\ -\ 5 \\ \hline \end{array}$ 11. $\begin{array}{r} 186 \\ -\ 61 \\ \hline \end{array}$ 12. $\begin{array}{r} 7851 \\ -\ 84 \\ \hline \end{array}$

13. $\begin{array}{r} 15 \\ -\ 7 \\ \hline \end{array}$ 14. $\begin{array}{r} 6688 \\ -\ 94 \\ \hline \end{array}$ 15. $\begin{array}{r} 1157 \\ -\ 9 \\ \hline \end{array}$ 16. $\begin{array}{r} 823 \\ -\ 8 \\ \hline \end{array}$

17. $\begin{array}{r} 45 \\ -\ 5 \\ \hline \end{array}$ 18. $\begin{array}{r} 861 \\ -\ 7 \\ \hline \end{array}$ 19. $\begin{array}{r} 38 \\ -\ 9 \\ \hline \end{array}$ 20. $\begin{array}{r} 76 \\ -\ 8 \\ \hline \end{array}$

Mixed Subtraction Practice (cont.)

1.
$$\begin{array}{r} 5 \\ -\ 5 \\ \hline \end{array}$$

2.
$$\begin{array}{r} 355 \\ -\ 186 \\ \hline \end{array}$$

3.
$$\begin{array}{r} 5 \\ -\ 3 \\ \hline \end{array}$$

4.
$$\begin{array}{r} 876 \\ -\ 344 \\ \hline \end{array}$$

5.
$$\begin{array}{r} 5 \\ -\ 3 \\ \hline \end{array}$$

6.
$$\begin{array}{r} 2312 \\ -\ 479 \\ \hline \end{array}$$

7.
$$\begin{array}{r} 9224 \\ -\ 667 \\ \hline \end{array}$$

8.
$$\begin{array}{r} 5792 \\ -\ 9 \\ \hline \end{array}$$

9.
$$\begin{array}{r} 433 \\ -\ 318 \\ \hline \end{array}$$

10.
$$\begin{array}{r} 7 \\ -\ 2 \\ \hline \end{array}$$

11.
$$\begin{array}{r} 333 \\ -\ 124 \\ \hline \end{array}$$

12.
$$\begin{array}{r} 7 \\ -\ 2 \\ \hline \end{array}$$

13.
$$\begin{array}{r} 742 \\ -\ 553 \\ \hline \end{array}$$

14.
$$\begin{array}{r} 3211 \\ -\ 7 \\ \hline \end{array}$$

15.
$$\begin{array}{r} 4718 \\ -\ 266 \\ \hline \end{array}$$

16.
$$\begin{array}{r} 888 \\ -\ 364 \\ \hline \end{array}$$

17.
$$\begin{array}{r} 5261 \\ -\ 5143 \\ \hline \end{array}$$

18.
$$\begin{array}{r} 9 \\ -\ 6 \\ \hline \end{array}$$

19.
$$\begin{array}{r} 3918 \\ -\ 2 \\ \hline \end{array}$$

20.
$$\begin{array}{r} 6766 \\ -\ 8 \\ \hline \end{array}$$

Multiplication Facts Timed Practice

When you practice basic multiplication facts for speed and accuracy, you improve your ability to solve problems in which multiplication computations are needed.

You will need a pencil and a timer with a second hand. Set the timer . . . and go.

1. 9 X 4	2. 3 X 0	3. 7 X 3	4. 7 X 4	5. 8 X 9
6. 6 X 8	7. 5 X 7	8. 4 X 3	9. 0 X 5	10. 6 X 5
11. 8 X 1	12. 6 X 6	13. 7 X 2	14. 3 X 2	15. 4 X 2
16. 6 X 2	17. 0 X 4	18. 3 X 5	19. 5 X 1	20. 6 X 9
21. 1 X 7	22. 4 X 4	23. 3 X 7	24. 7 X 1	25. 5 X 6
26. 4 X 5	27. 7 X 6	28. 6 X 7	29. 9 X 6	30. 1 X 2
31. 5 X 5	32. 7 X 8	33. 2 X 7	34. 6 X 0	35. 3 X 1
36. 9 X 9	37. 1 X 9	38. 6 X 3	39. 8 X 3	40. 4 X 9
41. 0 X 7	42. 1 X 8	43. 3 X 9	44. 4 X 0	45. 3 X 3
46. 5 X 3	47. 2 X 3	48. 5 X 2	49. 9 X 7	50. 2 X 4

Multiplication Facts Timed Practice (cont.)

51.　　1
　　×　1

52.　　8
　　×　7

53.　　8
　　×　8

54.　　8
　　×　6

55.　　3
　　×　6

56.　　9
　　×　0

57.　　1
　　×　6

58.　　4
　　×　1

59.　　2
　　×　2

60.　　0
　　×　9

61.　　8
　　×　0

62.　　2
　　×　6

63.　　4
　　×　7

64.　　3
　　×　4

65.　　5
　　×　8

66.　　9
　　×　5

67.　　7
　　×　9

68.　　7
　　×　0

69.　　0
　　×　6

70.　　9
　　×　3

71.　　1
　　×　3

72.　　9
　　×　1

73.　　2
　　×　9

74.　　6
　　×　4

75.　　4
　　×　6

76.　　8
　　×　4

77.　　3
　　×　8

78.　　7
　　×　7

79.　　5
　　×　9

80.　　8
　　×　5

81.　　5
　　×　0

82.　　6
　　×　1

83.　　2
　　×　0

84.　　9
　　×　8

85.　　1
　　×　0

86.　　0
　　×　3

87.　　1
　　×　4

88.　　8
　　×　2

89.　　5
　　×　4

90.　　4
　　×　8

91.　　0
　　×　0

92.　　0
　　×　1

93.　　9
　　×　2

94.　　1
　　×　1

95.　　7
　　×　5

96.　　0
　　×　2

97.　　2
　　×　8

98.　　1
　　×　5

99.　　0
　　×　8

100.　　2
　　×　5

How long did it take you to complete the pages? _____

How many did you get correct? _____

　　　　　　107　　　　　　*Practice and Learn—Fifth Grade*

Two Digits Times One Digit

1. 42
    X 9

2. 99
    X 8

3. 32
    X 9

4. 15
    X 6

5. 73
    X 8

6. 81
    X 5

7. 45
    X 1

8. 88
    X 7

9. 88
    X 2

10. 33
     X 7

11. 75
     X 5

12. 92
     X 6

13. 18
     X 2

14. 76
     X 4

15. 81
     X 7

16. 25
     X 9

17. 18
     X 6

18. 18
     X 2

19. 48
     X 3

20. 35
     X 2

21. 18
     X 5

22. 98
     X 5

23. 96
     X 9

24. 25
     X 6

25. 68
     X 4

Two Digits Times One Digit (cont.)

1. $\begin{array}{r} 11 \\ \times\ 4 \\ \hline \end{array}$
2. $\begin{array}{r} 91 \\ \times\ 3 \\ \hline \end{array}$
3. $\begin{array}{r} 69 \\ \times\ 4 \\ \hline \end{array}$
4. $\begin{array}{r} 59 \\ \times\ 5 \\ \hline \end{array}$
5. $\begin{array}{r} 26 \\ \times\ 4 \\ \hline \end{array}$

6. $\begin{array}{r} 17 \\ \times\ 3 \\ \hline \end{array}$
7. $\begin{array}{r} 42 \\ \times\ 6 \\ \hline \end{array}$
8. $\begin{array}{r} 97 \\ \times\ 3 \\ \hline \end{array}$
9. $\begin{array}{r} 22 \\ \times\ 2 \\ \hline \end{array}$
10. $\begin{array}{r} 71 \\ \times\ 4 \\ \hline \end{array}$

11. $\begin{array}{r} 12 \\ \times\ 7 \\ \hline \end{array}$
12. $\begin{array}{r} 26 \\ \times\ 3 \\ \hline \end{array}$
13. $\begin{array}{r} 25 \\ \times\ 7 \\ \hline \end{array}$
14. $\begin{array}{r} 85 \\ \times\ 3 \\ \hline \end{array}$
15. $\begin{array}{r} 58 \\ \times\ 5 \\ \hline \end{array}$

16. $\begin{array}{r} 97 \\ \times\ 4 \\ \hline \end{array}$
17. $\begin{array}{r} 18 \\ \times\ 9 \\ \hline \end{array}$
18. $\begin{array}{r} 33 \\ \times\ 1 \\ \hline \end{array}$
19. $\begin{array}{r} 86 \\ \times\ 3 \\ \hline \end{array}$
20. $\begin{array}{r} 16 \\ \times\ 6 \\ \hline \end{array}$

21. $\begin{array}{r} 65 \\ \times\ 7 \\ \hline \end{array}$
22. $\begin{array}{r} 38 \\ \times\ 7 \\ \hline \end{array}$
23. $\begin{array}{r} 43 \\ \times\ 8 \\ \hline \end{array}$
24. $\begin{array}{r} 24 \\ \times\ 8 \\ \hline \end{array}$
25. $\begin{array}{r} 95 \\ \times\ 3 \\ \hline \end{array}$

Two Digits Times Two Digits

1.   35
    X 22

2.   23
    X 77

3.   11
    X 44

4.   58
    X 53

5.   94
    X 55

6.   48
    X 67

7.   74
    X 35

8.   91
    X 88

9.   11
    X 51

10.   53
    X 73

11.   93
    X 34

12.   99
    X 82

13.   47
    X 62

14.   12
    X 93

15.   28
    X 45

16.   78
    X 99

17.   87
    X 29

18.   32
    X 76

19.   71
    X 66

20.   39
    X 28

21.   18
    X 29

22.   61
    X 56

23.   31
    X 23

24.   59
    X 22

25.   75
    X 97

Two Digits Times Two Digits (cont.)

1.   16   2.   44   3.   36   4.   98   5.   16
   X 98   X 88   X 74   X 31   X 36

6.   37   7.   77   8.   29   9.   47   10.   92
   X 98   X 54   X 49   X 82   X 19

11.   67   12.   39   13.   82   14.   59   15.   96
   X 56   X 76   X 34   X 44   X 24

16.   91   17.   73   18.   22   19.   29   20.   98
   X 71   X 77   X 87   X 77   X 48

21.   95   22.   36   23.   58   24.   73   25.   82
   X 31   X 75   X 71   X 95   X 52

Three Digits Times One Digit

1. 385
    X 8

2. 775
    X 5

3. 252
    X 5

4. 617
    X 9

5. 599
    X 9

6. 467
    X 6

7. 214
    X 6

8. 991
    X 2

9. 155
    X 6

10. 202
    X 5

11. 641
    X 6

12. 869
    X 2

13. 908
    X 2

14. 854
    X 5

15. 144
    X 6

16. 588
    X 6

17. 301
    X 2

18. 683
    X 9

19. 331
    X 8

20. 458
    X 8

21. 532
    X 9

22. 121
    X 9

23. 957
    X 7

24. 859
    X 2

25. 474
    X 5

Three Digits Times One Digit (cont.)

1.   283
   X 7

2.   346
   X 6

3.   923
   X 8

4.   796
   X 2

5.   596
   X 4

6.   811
   X 5

7.   231
   X 8

8.   206
   X 6

9.   179
   X 6

10.   853
   X 3

11.   682
   X 8

12.   117
   X 9

13.   636
   X 2

14.   884
   X 9

15.   929
   X 4

16.   393
   X 1

17.   346
   X 7

18.   802
   X 5

19.   597
   X 1

20.   955
   X 8

21.   864
   X 2

22.   832
   X 4

23.   273
   X 8

24.   375
   X 3

25.   681
   X 5

Three Digits Times One Digit (cont.)

1. 283 X 9	2. 746 X 6	3. 985 X 1	4. 123 X 6	5. 224 X 4
6. 783 X 7	7. 486 X 9	8. 735 X 3	9. 797 X 8	10. 453 X 4
11. 514 X 2	12. 733 X 6	13. 709 X 6	14. 998 X 6	15. 261 X 1
16. 536 X 5	17. 228 X 1	18. 651 X 5	19. 192 X 3	20. 765 X 6
21. 166 X 3	22. 572 X 7	23. 109 X 1	24. 641 X 9	25. 646 X 7

Three Digits Times Two Digits (cont.)

1. 911
    X 41

2. 748
    X 63

3. 128
    X 41

4. 667
    X 36

5. 843
    X 38

6. 156
    X 76

7. 497
    X 22

8. 898
    X 33

9. 473
    X 72

10. 444
     X 86

11. 971
     X 24

12. 691
     X 84

13. 903
     X 93

14. 621
     X 85

15. 692
     X 45

16. 459
     X 56

17. 133
     X 69

18. 333
     X 15

19. 794
     X 17

20. 638
     X 25

21. 775
     X 27

22. 315
     X 43

23. 671
     X 52

24. 489
     X 52

25. 592
     X 13

Three Digits Times Two Digits (cont.)

1. 261
    X 71

2. 243
    X 17

3. 951
    X 31

4. 785
    X 66

5. 864
    X 25

6. 232
    X 19

7. 235
    X 69

8. 871
    X 92

9. 785
    X 98

10. 637
    X 44

11. 693
    X 77

12. 967
    X 27

13. 928
    X 37

14. 822
    X 51

15. 346
    X 46

16. 165
    X 81

17. 724
    X 45

18. 644
    X 84

19. 783
    X 63

20. 278
    X 26

21. 323
    X 32

22. 937
    X 15

23. 827
    X 31

24. 812
    X 39

25. 372
    X 55

Mixed Multiplication Practice

1. $\begin{array}{r} 9 \\ \times\ 5 \\ \hline \end{array}$
2. $\begin{array}{r} 27 \\ \times\ 6 \\ \hline \end{array}$
3. $\begin{array}{r} 46 \\ \times\ 8 \\ \hline \end{array}$
4. $\begin{array}{r} 9 \\ \times\ 3 \\ \hline \end{array}$

5. $\begin{array}{r} 32 \\ \times\ 69 \\ \hline \end{array}$
6. $\begin{array}{r} 3 \\ \times\ 2 \\ \hline \end{array}$
7. $\begin{array}{r} 5 \\ \times\ 54 \\ \hline \end{array}$
8. $\begin{array}{r} 31 \\ \times\ 5 \\ \hline \end{array}$

9. $\begin{array}{r} 4 \\ \times\ 15 \\ \hline \end{array}$
10. $\begin{array}{r} 4 \\ \times\ 97 \\ \hline \end{array}$
11. $\begin{array}{r} 76 \\ \times\ 92 \\ \hline \end{array}$
12. $\begin{array}{r} 46 \\ \times\ 5 \\ \hline \end{array}$

13. $\begin{array}{r} 5 \\ \times\ 34 \\ \hline \end{array}$
14. $\begin{array}{r} 1 \\ \times\ 9 \\ \hline \end{array}$
15. $\begin{array}{r} 47 \\ \times\ 79 \\ \hline \end{array}$
16. $\begin{array}{r} 28 \\ \times\ 5 \\ \hline \end{array}$

17. $\begin{array}{r} 8 \\ \times\ 11 \\ \hline \end{array}$
18. $\begin{array}{r} 8 \\ \times\ 7 \\ \hline \end{array}$
19. $\begin{array}{r} 57 \\ \times\ 2 \\ \hline \end{array}$
20. $\begin{array}{r} 5 \\ \times\ 7 \\ \hline \end{array}$

Mixed Multiplication Practice (cont.)

1. 125
    X 69

2. 28
    X 91

3. 783
    X 62

4. 8
    X 7

5. 5
    X 5

6. 347
    X 3171

7. 238
    X 98

8. 878
    X 98

9. 55
    X 35

10. 718
     X 61

11. 4883
     X 737

12. 269
     X 47

13. 9
     X 6

14. 81
     X 89

15. 9
     X 3

16. 43
     X 68

17. 378
     X 99

18. 4
     X 3

19. 3
     X 4

20. 5
     X 9

Division Facts Timed Practice

When you practice basic division facts for speed and accuracy, you improve your ability to solve problems in which division computations are needed.

You will need a pencil and a timer with a second hand. Set the timer . . . and go.

1. $1\overline{)5}$ 2. $8\overline{)56}$ 3. $2\overline{)16}$ 4. $3\overline{)21}$ 5. $6\overline{)30}$

6. $9\overline{)72}$ 7. $9\overline{)54}$ 8. $3\overline{)9}$ 9. $4\overline{)20}$ 10. $6\overline{)0}$

11. $7\overline{)28}$ 12. $5\overline{)40}$ 13. $2\overline{)10}$ 14. $4\overline{)28}$ 15. $1\overline{)4}$

16. $2\overline{)18}$ 17. $5\overline{)0}$ 18. $8\overline{)48}$ 19. $2\overline{)14}$ 20. $5\overline{)25}$

21. $3\overline{)6}$ 22. $6\overline{)42}$ 23. $3\overline{)27}$ 24. $6\overline{)54}$ 25. $7\overline{)14}$

26. $2\overline{)12}$ 27. $8\overline{)64}$ 28. $6\overline{)24}$ 29. $8\overline{)0}$ 30. $1\overline{)3}$

31. $5\overline{)45}$ 32. $2\overline{)8}$ 33. $8\overline{)32}$ 34. $4\overline{)12}$ 35. $9\overline{)81}$

36. $3\overline{)18}$ 37. $8\overline{)72}$ 38. $7\overline{)63}$ 39. $9\overline{)45}$ 40. $9\overline{)63}$

Division Facts Timed Practice (cont.)

41. 8) 8   42. 9) 36   43. 4) 32   44. 1) 1   45. 5) 15

46. 6) 18   47. 7) 7   48. 5) 30   49. 2) 0   50. 5) 10

51. 8) 24   52. 1) 9   53. 1) 3   54. 7) 35   55. 4) 16

56. 3) 0   57. 4) 24   58. 1) 0   59. 6) 36   60. 4) 8

61. 5) 35   62. 4) 36   63. 9) 27   64. 3) 12   65. 2) 6

66. 4) 0   67. 6) 12   68. 1) 6   69. 6) 48   70. 3) 3

71. 7) 0   72. 9) 9   73. 7) 56   74. 8) 40   75. 7) 42

76. 1) 7   77. 8) 16   78. 5) 20   79. 3) 24   80. 3) 15

81. 7) 21   82. 1) 8   83. 9) 18   84. 5) 5   85. 6) 6

86. 4) 4   87. 9) 0   88. 2) 4   89. 7) 49   90. 2) 2

How long did it take you to complete this practice? _____

How many did you get correct? _____

One Digit Divided by One Digit

1. $2\overline{)7}$

2. $5\overline{)7}$

3. $3\overline{)4}$

4. $1\overline{)5}$

5. $3\overline{)6}$

6. $3\overline{)8}$

7. $2\overline{)4}$

8. $3\overline{)4}$

9. $6\overline{)9}$

10. $4\overline{)9}$

11. $3\overline{)7}$

12. $1\overline{)4}$

13. $5\overline{)6}$

14. $1\overline{)6}$

15. $3\overline{)9}$

16. $5\overline{)8}$

17. $4\overline{)4}$

18. $4\overline{)7}$

19. $2\overline{)2}$

20. $1\overline{)9}$

One Digit Divided by One Digit (cont.)

1. $1 \overline{)4}$ 2. $3 \overline{)8}$ 3. $7 \overline{)7}$ 4. $2 \overline{)8}$

5. $5 \overline{)7}$ 6. $5 \overline{)8}$ 7. $2 \overline{)7}$ 8. $3 \overline{)6}$

9. $7 \overline{)9}$ 10. $4 \overline{)6}$ 11. $1 \overline{)7}$ 12. $6 \overline{)9}$

13. $4 \overline{)7}$ 14. $3 \overline{)7}$ 15. $4 \overline{)9}$ 16. $7 \overline{)8}$

17. $1 \overline{)4}$ 18. $1 \overline{)6}$ 19. $2 \overline{)3}$ 20. $3 \overline{)5}$

Two Digits Divided by One Digit

1. $1\overline{)19}$ 2. $5\overline{)56}$ 3. $3\overline{)81}$ 4. $8\overline{)77}$

5. $3\overline{)32}$ 6. $4\overline{)85}$ 7. $4\overline{)24}$ 8. $1\overline{)93}$

9. $7\overline{)38}$ 10. $2\overline{)54}$ 11. $4\overline{)67}$ 12. $3\overline{)62}$

13. $6\overline{)94}$ 14. $2\overline{)42}$ 15. $7\overline{)66}$ 16. $2\overline{)44}$

17. $9\overline{)13}$ 18. $4\overline{)58}$ 19. $9\overline{)82}$ 20. $5\overline{)67}$

Two Digits Divided by One Digit (cont.)

1. $5\overline{)25}$ 2. $4\overline{)19}$ 3. $8\overline{)94}$ 4. $9\overline{)97}$

5. $5\overline{)44}$ 6. $4\overline{)61}$ 7. $5\overline{)49}$ 8. $8\overline{)71}$

9. $3\overline{)62}$ 10. $5\overline{)69}$ 11. $4\overline{)46}$ 12. $5\overline{)82}$

13. $2\overline{)92}$ 14. $2\overline{)75}$ 15. $3\overline{)76}$ 16. $7\overline{)92}$

17. $7\overline{)53}$ 18. $8\overline{)22}$ 19. $2\overline{)67}$ 20. $6\overline{)71}$

Three Digits Divided by One Digit

1. $2\overline{)884}$ 2. $3\overline{)933}$ 3. $2\overline{)539}$ 4. $7\overline{)868}$

5. $1\overline{)725}$ 6. $6\overline{)187}$ 7. $2\overline{)467}$ 8. $3\overline{)399}$

9. $7\overline{)946}$ 10. $5\overline{)854}$ 11. $9\overline{)818}$ 12. $6\overline{)476}$

13. $8\overline{)418}$ 14. $6\overline{)282}$ 15. $3\overline{)572}$ 16. $4\overline{)766}$

17. $9\overline{)962}$ 18. $4\overline{)489}$ 19. $5\overline{)814}$ 20. $6\overline{)725}$

Three Digits Divided by One Digit (cont.)

1. $7 \overline{)295}$ 2. $6 \overline{)668}$ 3. $8 \overline{)641}$ 4. $7 \overline{)391}$

5. $9 \overline{)163}$ 6. $9 \overline{)839}$ 7. $4 \overline{)157}$ 8. $3 \overline{)159}$

9. $8 \overline{)398}$ 10. $4 \overline{)474}$ 11. $7 \overline{)658}$ 12. $3 \overline{)563}$

13. $3 \overline{)251}$ 14. $6 \overline{)553}$ 15. $1 \overline{)515}$ 16. $7 \overline{)323}$

17. $6 \overline{)234}$ 18. $2 \overline{)839}$ 19. $2 \overline{)436}$ 20. $9 \overline{)969}$

Three Digits Divided by One Digit (cont.)

1. 9) 331   2. 9) 229   3. 9) 231   4. 4) 317

5. 3) 326   6. 4) 514   7. 6) 398   8. 4) 699

9. 6) 661   10. 4) 739   11. 2) 711   12. 3) 577

13. 8) 622   14. 5) 238   15. 5) 175   16. 7) 483

17. 6) 798   18. 3) 653   19. 9) 839   20. 6) 468

Three Digits Divided by Two Digits

1. $47 \overline{)454}$ 2. $77 \overline{)456}$ 3. $85 \overline{)783}$ 4. $35 \overline{)263}$

5. $36 \overline{)736}$ 6. $19 \overline{)656}$ 7. $31 \overline{)561}$ 8. $82 \overline{)627}$

9. $77 \overline{)715}$ 10. $33 \overline{)533}$ 11. $78 \overline{)957}$ 12. $81 \overline{)525}$

13. $43 \overline{)855}$ 14. $63 \overline{)139}$ 15. $49 \overline{)223}$ 16. $89 \overline{)942}$

17. $41 \overline{)434}$ 18. $62 \overline{)384}$ 19. $73 \overline{)436}$ 20. $69 \overline{)374}$

Three Digits Divided by Two Digits (cont.)

1. 26) 235

2. 43) 519

3. 22) 137

4. 18) 895

5. 16) 921

6. 82) 881

7. 35) 209

8. 17) 921

9. 28) 777

10. 55) 801

11. 42) 841

12. 53) 207

13. 19) 221

14. 15) 822

15. 21) 625

16. 25) 927

17. 12) 225

18. 18) 355

19. 62) 994

20. 17) 631

Three Digits Divided by Two Digits (cont.)

1.　72$\overline{)672}$　　　2.　69$\overline{)531}$　　　3.　57$\overline{)242}$　　　4.　32$\overline{)834}$

5.　91$\overline{)787}$　　　6.　68$\overline{)921}$　　　7.　88$\overline{)318}$　　　8.　94$\overline{)599}$

9.　49$\overline{)895}$　　　10.　24$\overline{)656}$　　　11.　26$\overline{)684}$　　　12.　81$\overline{)956}$

13.　58$\overline{)658}$　　　14.　36$\overline{)578}$　　　15.　19$\overline{)246}$　　　16.　15$\overline{)678}$

17.　64$\overline{)667}$　　　18.　71$\overline{)241}$　　　19.　33$\overline{)358}$　　　20.　89$\overline{)441}$

Changing Improper Fractions to Mixed Numbers

Write each of these improper fractions as a mixed number. Simplify where possible.

1. $\dfrac{7}{4}$	2. $\dfrac{15}{7}$	3. $\dfrac{12}{5}$	4. $\dfrac{7}{5}$
5. $\dfrac{5}{3}$	6. $\dfrac{16}{9}$	7. $\dfrac{10}{3}$	8. $\dfrac{14}{13}$
9. $\dfrac{12}{11}$	10. $\dfrac{9}{2}$	11. $\dfrac{4}{3}$	12. $\dfrac{7}{2}$
13. $\dfrac{13}{8}$	14. $\dfrac{6}{5}$	15. $\dfrac{8}{3}$	16. $\dfrac{5}{4}$
17. $\dfrac{16}{5}$	18. $\dfrac{19}{10}$	19. $\dfrac{15}{12}$	20. $\dfrac{7}{6}$
21. $\dfrac{12}{9}$	22. $\dfrac{9}{6}$	23. $\dfrac{5}{2}$	24. $\dfrac{16}{12}$
25. $\dfrac{18}{11}$	26. $\dfrac{9}{5}$	27. $\dfrac{9}{8}$	28. $\dfrac{6}{4}$
29. $\dfrac{8}{7}$	30. $\dfrac{9}{7}$	31. $\dfrac{11}{5}$	32. $\dfrac{6}{5}$
33. $\dfrac{14}{9}$	34. $\dfrac{3}{2}$	35. $\dfrac{5}{4}$	36. $\dfrac{18}{13}$
37. $\dfrac{7}{6}$	38. $\dfrac{9}{8}$	39. $\dfrac{19}{8}$	40. $\dfrac{7}{2}$

Converting Mixed Numbers to Improper Fractions

Write each of the mixed numbers as an improper fraction.

1. $4\frac{4}{5}$ 2. $3\frac{1}{5}$ 3. $2\frac{5}{7}$ 4. $7\frac{1}{3}$ 5. $9\frac{1}{4}$

6. $1\frac{5}{7}$ 7. $9\frac{1}{2}$ 8. $9\frac{4}{5}$ 9. $2\frac{5}{8}$ 10. $9\frac{3}{5}$

11. $4\frac{6}{8}$ 12. $1\frac{6}{9}$ 13. $8\frac{3}{9}$ 14. $7\frac{5}{8}$ 15. $8\frac{3}{6}$

16. $5\frac{8}{9}$ 17. $2\frac{5}{6}$ 18. $4\frac{3}{5}$ 19. $3\frac{4}{6}$ 20. $1\frac{4}{5}$

21. $4\frac{2}{6}$ 22. $9\frac{8}{9}$ 23. $7\frac{1}{6}$ 24. $1\frac{1}{3}$ 25. $4\frac{2}{3}$

26. $5\frac{3}{6}$ 27. $8\frac{3}{7}$ 28. $6\frac{3}{9}$ 29. $3\frac{2}{4}$ 30. $6\frac{1}{8}$

31. $9\frac{1}{3}$ 32. $7\frac{1}{9}$ 33. $2\frac{3}{6}$ 34. $8\frac{1}{2}$ 35. $9\frac{6}{7}$

36. $1\frac{5}{8}$ 37. $6\frac{3}{4}$ 38. $5\frac{7}{8}$ 39. $8\frac{1}{9}$ 40. $6\frac{4}{5}$

Adding Fractions

Add the fractions and write your answer in simplest form where possible.

1. $1\frac{1}{2}$
    $+\ 1\frac{1}{2}$

2. $2\frac{1}{3}$
    $+\ 1\frac{1}{3}$

3. $5\frac{1}{6}$
    $+\ 2\frac{2}{6}$

4. $1\frac{1}{8}$
    $+\ \ \frac{3}{8}$

5. $6\frac{1}{9}$
    $+\ \ \frac{2}{9}$

6. $3\frac{2}{3}$
    $+\ 1\frac{1}{3}$

7. $5\frac{1}{4}$
    $+\ \ \frac{2}{4}$

8. $9\frac{1}{2}$
    $+\ 1\frac{1}{2}$

9. $2\frac{1}{6}$
    $+\ 1\frac{2}{6}$

10. $4\frac{2}{3}$
    $+\ 3\frac{1}{3}$

11. $2\frac{1}{8}$
    $+\ 1\frac{2}{8}$

12. $7\frac{1}{7}$
    $+\ 1\frac{3}{7}$

13. $2\frac{2}{8}$
    $+\ 3\frac{1}{8}$

14. $13\frac{1}{3}$
    $+\ 1\frac{2}{3}$

15. $22\frac{4}{5}$
    $+\ \ \frac{1}{5}$

16. $101\frac{1}{6}$
    $+33\frac{2}{6}$

Adding Fractions (cont.)

Add the fractions and write your answer in simplest form where possible.

1. $\begin{array}{r} \frac{2}{3} \\ + \frac{7}{8} \\ \hline \end{array}$ 2. $\begin{array}{r} \frac{7}{8} \\ + \frac{5}{7} \\ \hline \end{array}$ 3. $\begin{array}{r} \frac{1}{3} \\ + \frac{2}{6} \\ \hline \end{array}$ 4. $\begin{array}{r} \frac{4}{5} \\ + \frac{7}{8} \\ \hline \end{array}$

5. $\begin{array}{r} \frac{3}{5} \\ + \frac{3}{9} \\ \hline \end{array}$ 6. $\begin{array}{r} \frac{4}{5} \\ + \frac{3}{9} \\ \hline \end{array}$ 7. $\begin{array}{r} \frac{1}{6} \\ + \frac{4}{5} \\ \hline \end{array}$ 8. $\begin{array}{r} \frac{6}{7} \\ + \frac{2}{3} \\ \hline \end{array}$

9. $\begin{array}{r} \frac{7}{9} \\ + \frac{2}{8} \\ \hline \end{array}$ 10. $\begin{array}{r} \frac{1}{9} \\ + \frac{3}{5} \\ \hline \end{array}$ 11. $\begin{array}{r} \frac{4}{5} \\ + \frac{8}{9} \\ \hline \end{array}$ 12. $\begin{array}{r} \frac{7}{8} \\ + \frac{2}{5} \\ \hline \end{array}$

13. $\begin{array}{r} \frac{4}{6} \\ + \frac{4}{5} \\ \hline \end{array}$ 14. $\begin{array}{r} \frac{4}{7} \\ + \frac{1}{6} \\ \hline \end{array}$ 15. $\begin{array}{r} \frac{7}{9} \\ + \frac{2}{7} \\ \hline \end{array}$ 16. $\begin{array}{r} \frac{5}{9} \\ + \frac{6}{8} \\ \hline \end{array}$

Adding Fractions (cont.)

Add the fractions and write your answer in simplest form where possible.

1. $\dfrac{4}{7}$ 2. $\dfrac{7}{8}$ 3. $\dfrac{3}{8}$ 4. $\dfrac{4}{5}$

$+\dfrac{2}{4}$ $+\dfrac{2}{4}$ $+\dfrac{4}{9}$ $+\dfrac{2}{3}$

5. $\dfrac{2}{8}$ 6. $\dfrac{1}{2}$ 7. $\dfrac{3}{4}$ 8. $\dfrac{3}{7}$

$+\dfrac{3}{8}$ $+\dfrac{5}{7}$ $+\dfrac{1}{3}$ $+\dfrac{2}{8}$

9. $\dfrac{4}{5}$ 10. $\dfrac{3}{8}$ 11. $\dfrac{6}{7}$ 12. $\dfrac{2}{7}$

$+\dfrac{5}{9}$ $+\dfrac{2}{3}$ $+\dfrac{1}{2}$ $+\dfrac{6}{7}$

13. $\dfrac{1}{6}$ 14. $\dfrac{1}{6}$ 15. $\dfrac{5}{8}$ 16. $\dfrac{1}{5}$

$+\dfrac{2}{3}$ $+\dfrac{1}{5}$ $+\dfrac{5}{7}$ $+\dfrac{6}{7}$

Adding Fractions (cont.)

Add the fractions and write your answer in simplest form where possible.

1. $1\frac{5}{9}$
   $+\ 5\frac{2}{4}$

2. $3\frac{3}{4}$
   $+\ 9\frac{4}{8}$

3. $6\frac{2}{5}$
   $+\ 6\frac{1}{5}$

4. $3\frac{4}{6}$
   $+\ 4\frac{7}{9}$

5. $1\frac{3}{9}$
   $+\ 9\frac{6}{9}$

6. $9\frac{1}{9}$
   $+\ 1\frac{5}{8}$

7. $1\frac{8}{9}$
   $+\ 5\frac{6}{7}$

8. $2\frac{3}{7}$
   $+\ 7\frac{7}{9}$

9. $1\frac{1}{3}$
   $+\ 2\frac{7}{8}$

10. $6\frac{2}{6}$
    $+\ 1\frac{2}{4}$

11. $2\frac{3}{9}$
    $+\ 6\frac{2}{8}$

12. $5\frac{2}{6}$
    $+\ 4\frac{3}{7}$

13. $2\frac{4}{6}$
    $+\ 3\frac{5}{6}$

14. $8\frac{2}{9}$
    $+\ 8\frac{4}{6}$

15. $2\frac{5}{9}$
    $+\ 5\frac{3}{8}$

16. $6\frac{1}{5}$
    $+\ 9\frac{5}{6}$

Subtracting Fractions

Subtract the fractions and write your answer in simplest form where possible.

1. $\frac{4}{12}$
    $-\frac{3}{12}$

2. $\frac{7}{8}$
    $-\frac{2}{8}$

3. $\frac{13}{16}$
    $-\frac{7}{16}$

4. $\frac{3}{6}$
    $-\frac{1}{6}$

5. $\frac{5}{6}$
    $-\frac{1}{6}$

6. $\frac{2}{3}$
    $-\frac{2}{3}$

7. $\frac{9}{10}$
    $-\frac{1}{10}$

8. $\frac{5}{8}$
    $-\frac{1}{8}$

9. $\frac{3}{4}$
    $-\frac{1}{4}$

10. $\frac{2}{5}$
     $-\frac{1}{5}$

11. $\frac{10}{11}$
     $-\frac{2}{11}$

12. $\frac{9}{10}$
     $-\frac{3}{10}$

13. $\frac{9}{10}$
     $-\frac{8}{10}$

14. $\frac{11}{16}$
     $-\frac{7}{16}$

15. $\frac{7}{12}$
     $-\frac{3}{12}$

16. $\frac{13}{14}$
     $-\frac{12}{14}$

Subtracting Fractions (cont.)

Subtract the fractions and write your answer in simplest form where possible.

1.
$$\frac{4}{7}$$
$$-\frac{1}{2}$$

2.
$$\frac{6}{9}$$
$$-\frac{2}{5}$$

3.
$$\frac{4}{5}$$
$$-\frac{7}{9}$$

4.
$$\frac{7}{9}$$
$$-\frac{1}{3}$$

5.
$$\frac{3}{4}$$
$$-\frac{2}{9}$$

6.
$$\frac{5}{8}$$
$$-\frac{3}{7}$$

7.
$$\frac{5}{7}$$
$$-\frac{1}{3}$$

8.
$$\frac{2}{7}$$
$$-\frac{1}{5}$$

9.
$$\frac{1}{5}$$
$$-\frac{1}{8}$$

10.
$$\frac{5}{6}$$
$$-\frac{2}{6}$$

11.
$$\frac{2}{3}$$
$$-\frac{2}{4}$$

12.
$$\frac{5}{8}$$
$$-\frac{5}{9}$$

13.
$$\frac{5}{6}$$
$$-\frac{1}{6}$$

14.
$$\frac{7}{9}$$
$$-\frac{1}{3}$$

15.
$$\frac{8}{9}$$
$$-\frac{7}{8}$$

16.
$$\frac{5}{8}$$
$$-\frac{2}{6}$$

Multiplying Fractions

Multiply the fractions and write your answer in simplest form where possible.

1. $\dfrac{2}{4} \times \dfrac{2}{5}$

2. $\dfrac{4}{9} \times \dfrac{5}{6}$

3. $\dfrac{1}{6} \times \dfrac{3}{5}$

4. $\dfrac{4}{8} \times \dfrac{2}{3}$

5. $\dfrac{4}{7} \times \dfrac{4}{9}$

6. $\dfrac{8}{9} \times \dfrac{3}{4}$

7. $\dfrac{3}{8} \times \dfrac{6}{8}$

8. $\dfrac{1}{8} \times \dfrac{4}{9}$

9. $\dfrac{4}{8} \times \dfrac{4}{5}$

10. $\dfrac{3}{4} \times \dfrac{1}{2}$

11. $\dfrac{2}{3} \times \dfrac{7}{9}$

12. $\dfrac{7}{8} \times \dfrac{2}{6}$

13. $\dfrac{6}{9} \times \dfrac{5}{9}$

14. $\dfrac{1}{6} \times \dfrac{3}{6}$

15. $\dfrac{2}{5} \times \dfrac{3}{9}$

16. $\dfrac{4}{9} \times \dfrac{3}{4}$

17. $\dfrac{4}{7} \times \dfrac{3}{4}$

18. $\dfrac{1}{7} \times \dfrac{2}{5}$

19. $\dfrac{4}{5} \times \dfrac{1}{3}$

20. $\dfrac{1}{6} \times \dfrac{4}{9}$

21. $\dfrac{7}{9} \times \dfrac{4}{7}$

22. $\dfrac{1}{4} \times \dfrac{2}{6}$

23. $\dfrac{3}{6} \times \dfrac{3}{8}$

24. $\dfrac{2}{3} \times \dfrac{3}{4}$

Multiplying Fractions (cont.)

Multiply the fractions and write your answer in simplest form where possible.

1. $\dfrac{4}{7} \times \dfrac{6}{9}$

2. $\dfrac{4}{5} \times \dfrac{1}{2}$

3. $\dfrac{8}{9} \times \dfrac{1}{6}$

4. $\dfrac{1}{5} \times \dfrac{1}{4}$

5. $\dfrac{3}{9} \times \dfrac{5}{6}$

6. $\dfrac{3}{8} \times \dfrac{5}{9}$

7. $\dfrac{2}{5} \times \dfrac{5}{7}$

8. $\dfrac{7}{8} \times \dfrac{2}{8}$

9. $\dfrac{5}{6} \times \dfrac{7}{8}$

10. $\dfrac{2}{3} \times \dfrac{3}{9}$

11. $\dfrac{8}{9} \times \dfrac{7}{9}$

12. $\dfrac{4}{9} \times \dfrac{2}{9}$

13. $\dfrac{6}{9} \times \dfrac{1}{4}$

14. $\dfrac{4}{7} \times \dfrac{2}{6}$

15. $\dfrac{1}{3} \times \dfrac{3}{4}$

16. $\dfrac{4}{6} \times \dfrac{5}{9}$

17. $\dfrac{1}{2} \times \dfrac{2}{4}$

18. $\dfrac{3}{8} \times \dfrac{1}{6}$

19. $\dfrac{5}{7} \times \dfrac{3}{6}$

20. $\dfrac{5}{9} \times \dfrac{2}{5}$

21. $\dfrac{2}{3} \times \dfrac{4}{8}$

22. $\dfrac{7}{8} \times \dfrac{1}{3}$

23. $\dfrac{1}{2} \times \dfrac{2}{8}$

24. $\dfrac{3}{5} \times \dfrac{1}{9}$

Dividing Fractions

Divide the fractions and write your answer in simplest form where possible.

1. $\dfrac{1}{5} \div \dfrac{4}{8}$

2. $\dfrac{3}{9} \div \dfrac{1}{7}$

3. $\dfrac{2}{7} \div \dfrac{4}{5}$

4. $\dfrac{3}{5} \div \dfrac{7}{9}$

5. $\dfrac{5}{9} \div \dfrac{4}{6}$

6. $\dfrac{1}{7} \div \dfrac{4}{9}$

7. $\dfrac{3}{6} \div \dfrac{4}{5}$

8. $\dfrac{1}{8} \div \dfrac{2}{5}$

9. $\dfrac{4}{5} \div \dfrac{7}{8}$

10. $\dfrac{3}{8} \div \dfrac{7}{8}$

11. $\dfrac{2}{4} \div \dfrac{3}{5}$

12. $\dfrac{1}{8} \div \dfrac{6}{9}$

13. $\dfrac{1}{7} \div \dfrac{3}{7}$

14. $\dfrac{8}{9} \div \dfrac{4}{7}$

15. $\dfrac{1}{2} \div \dfrac{5}{6}$

16. $\dfrac{1}{5} \div \dfrac{4}{5}$

17. $\dfrac{3}{8} \div \dfrac{2}{6}$

18. $\dfrac{4}{6} \div \dfrac{1}{2}$

19. $\dfrac{2}{6} \div \dfrac{1}{5}$

20. $\dfrac{1}{4} \div \dfrac{5}{6}$

21. $\dfrac{9}{10} \div \dfrac{3}{5}$

22. $\dfrac{5}{9} \div \dfrac{2}{6}$

23. $\dfrac{4}{5} \div \dfrac{3}{7}$

24. $\dfrac{4}{9} \div \dfrac{2}{6}$

Dividing Fractions (cont.)

Divide the fractions and write your answer in simplest form where possible.

1. $\dfrac{3}{4} \div \dfrac{1}{8}$

2. $\dfrac{8}{9} \div \dfrac{2}{3}$

3. $\dfrac{2}{6} \div \dfrac{4}{7}$

4. $\dfrac{3}{4} \div \dfrac{4}{6}$

5. $\dfrac{5}{6} \div \dfrac{5}{9}$

6. $\dfrac{1}{2} \div \dfrac{1}{6}$

7. $\dfrac{6}{7} \div \dfrac{5}{6}$

8. $\dfrac{7}{8} \div \dfrac{2}{9}$

9. $\dfrac{7}{8} \div \dfrac{3}{4}$

10. $\dfrac{1}{8} \div \dfrac{5}{8}$

11. $\dfrac{4}{7} \div \dfrac{6}{9}$

12. $\dfrac{2}{6} \div \dfrac{1}{5}$

13. $\dfrac{5}{9} \div \dfrac{4}{7}$

14. $\dfrac{2}{9} \div \dfrac{2}{9}$

15. $\dfrac{4}{8} \div \dfrac{5}{6}$

16. $\dfrac{3}{9} \div \dfrac{3}{5}$

17. $\dfrac{6}{8} \div \dfrac{2}{3}$

18. $\dfrac{5}{6} \div \dfrac{2}{3}$

19. $\dfrac{1}{5} \div \dfrac{3}{8}$

20. $\dfrac{3}{4} \div \dfrac{7}{9}$

21. $\dfrac{6}{7} \div \dfrac{4}{7}$

22. $\dfrac{1}{8} \div \dfrac{2}{8}$

23. $\dfrac{2}{4} \div \dfrac{6}{9}$

24. $\dfrac{2}{9} \div \dfrac{7}{8}$

Dividing Fractions (cont.)

Divide the fractions and write your answer in simplest form where possible.

1. $\dfrac{1}{8} \div \dfrac{2}{3}$ 2. $\dfrac{5}{8} \div \dfrac{6}{8}$ 3. $\dfrac{8}{9} \div \dfrac{3}{9}$ 4. $\dfrac{1}{7} \div \dfrac{6}{9}$

5. $\dfrac{3}{8} \div \dfrac{2}{6}$ 6. $\dfrac{5}{6} \div \dfrac{4}{7}$ 7. $\dfrac{4}{5} \div \dfrac{4}{6}$ 8. $\dfrac{5}{9} \div \dfrac{4}{9}$

9. $\dfrac{1}{2} \div \dfrac{7}{9}$ 10. $\dfrac{4}{9} \div \dfrac{2}{3}$ 11. $\dfrac{3}{6} \div \dfrac{6}{8}$ 12. $\dfrac{3}{8} \div \dfrac{1}{3}$

13. $\dfrac{3}{4} \div \dfrac{1}{2}$ 14. $\dfrac{3}{4} \div \dfrac{1}{3}$ 15. $\dfrac{4}{9} \div \dfrac{3}{9}$ 16. $\dfrac{5}{8} \div \dfrac{1}{8}$

17. $\dfrac{8}{9} \div \dfrac{2}{4}$ 18. $\dfrac{7}{8} \div \dfrac{4}{8}$ 19. $\dfrac{1}{2} \div \dfrac{3}{4}$ 20. $\dfrac{4}{6} \div \dfrac{6}{7}$

21. $\dfrac{1}{8} \div \dfrac{3}{4}$ 22. $\dfrac{6}{9} \div \dfrac{2}{6}$ 23. $\dfrac{7}{8} \div \dfrac{4}{5}$ 24. $\dfrac{1}{4} \div \dfrac{1}{4}$

Greater Than and Less Than

Complete each problem to show greater than or less than. (Write > or < in the spaces.)

1. 14   49

2. 91   47

3. 34   72

4. 98   39

5. 86   22

6. 57   73

7. 27   38

8. 48   39

9. 98   78

10. 57   51

11. 46   65

12. 16   69

13. 43   33

14. 44   87

15. 61   41

16. 37   49

17. 46   31

18. 95   54

19. 36   54

20. 32   24

21. 42   86

22. 24   42

23. 74   83

24. 29   76

25. 33   66

26. 42   67

27. 34   46

28. 22   52

29. 62   22

30. 89   32

31. 69   64

32. 64   41

33. 22   82

McDonald's Math

The data in the box below is taken from dietary sheets provided by McDonald's restaurants. Read through the data box and use the information provided to figure out which side of each inequality has the greater number of calories. Place a < or > sign on the line to complete each problem.

Data

These figures reflect the number of calories in each item.

 hamburger—270

 cheeseburger—320

fish sandwich—360

 small French fries—210

 garden salad—80

 hot fudge sundae—290

 apple pie—260

 1% milk—100

 small cola—150

 chocolate shake—340

1. 2 hamburgers _____ 2 hot fudge sundaes

2. 1 fish sandwich _____ 4 garden salads

3. 5 small colas _____ 3 fish sandwiches

4. 3 chocolate shakes _____ 12 1% milks

5. 2 apple pies _____ 7 garden salads

6. 3 cheeseburgers _____ 5 small French fries

7. 2 garden salads + 3 cheeseburgers _____ 4 hamburgers

8. 4 fish sandwiches _____ 6 small French fries + 1 garden salad

9. 2 small colas + 1 chocolate shake _____ 2 apple pies + 3 1% milks

10. 2 hot fudge sundaes _____ 2 small French fries + 3 garden salads

11. 6 1% milks + 2 cheeseburgers _____ 4 small French fries + 1 shake

12. 2 apple pies + 2 fish sandwiches _____ 3 cheeseburgers + 3 small French fries

In the space below write two more inequalities using the data from the box above.

1. _____

2. _____

The Life of a Check

Use the information in the flow chart below to answer the questions at the bottom of the page.

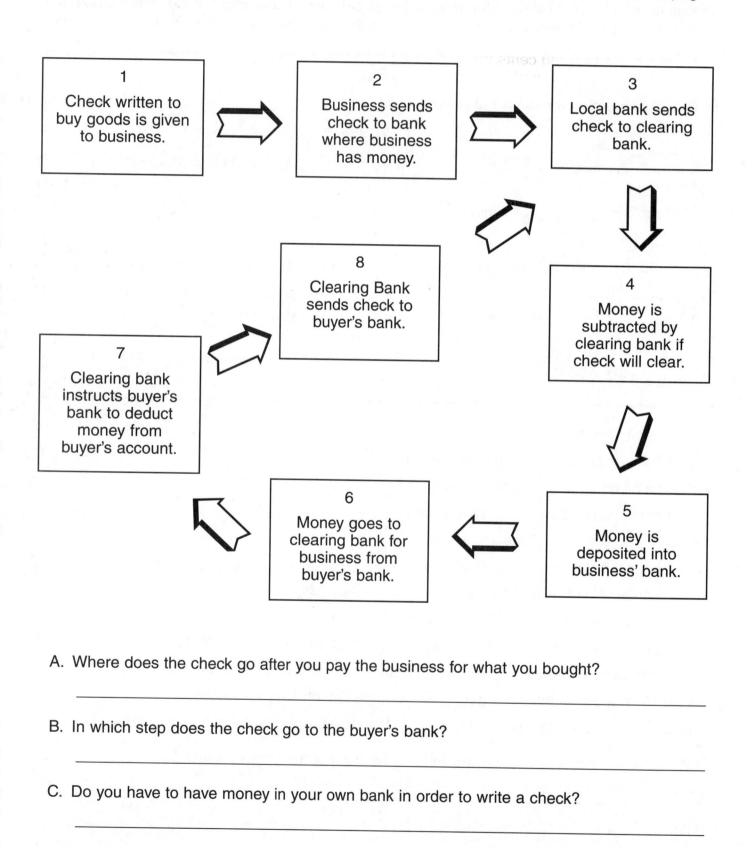

A. Where does the check go after you pay the business for what you bought?

_____

B. In which step does the check go to the buyer's bank?

_____

C. Do you have to have money in your own bank in order to write a check?

_____

Check It Out!

One way that you can purchase something if you do not have the cash in your pocket is to write a check. You will need to know how to write numbers out in words in order to be able to use checks properly. The exercises below will help you to do this.

A. Write in dollars and cents the value for each of the following amounts. For example, the amount, one dollar and thirty-five cents would be written $1.35.

   1. four dollars and twenty-seven cents _____

   2. nine dollars and sixty-two cents _____

   3. one dollar and ninety-nine cents_____

   4. eight dollars and twenty-two cents _____

   5. three dollars and sixteen cents_____

   6. sixteen dollars and sixty-six cents_____

B. Write in words the value for each of the following amounts. For example, $1.43 would be written one dollar and forty-three cents.

   1. $3.99 _____

   2. $9.33 _____

   3. $5.87 _____

   4. $2.22 _____

   5. $6.48 _____

   6. $8.72 _____

C. Using section **B** above, write how many dollars are represented in #1-6.

   1. _____

   2. _____

   3. _____

   4. _____

   5. _____

   6. _____

D. Using section **B** above, write how many cents are represented in #1-6.

   1. _____

   2. _____

   3. _____

   4. _____

   5. _____

   6. _____

Check It Out! (cont.)

A check tells your bank how much you want them to pay from your bank account into someone else's bank account. Study the check below to see how a check is written.

You must always have enough money in your checking account when you write a check. Paying by check gives you proof that you have paid a bill. Review the parts of a check and what is required on each line to make a check valid.

1. Your name, address, and phone number (usually pre-printed).

2. The name of the person or company you want to pay.

3. The date you are writing the check.

4. The amount in numbers.

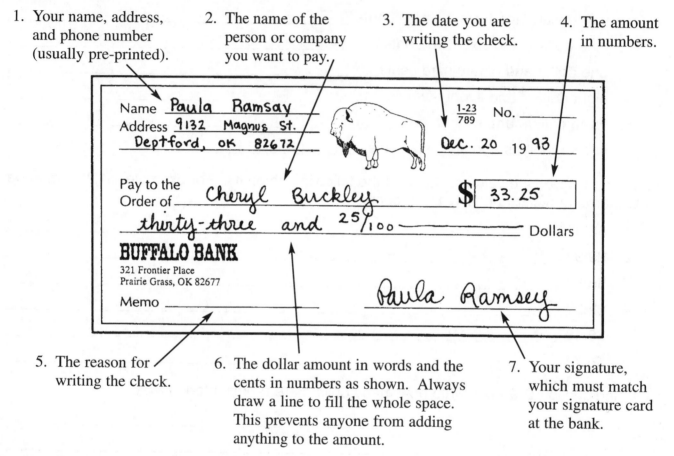

5. The reason for writing the check.

6. The dollar amount in words and the cents in numbers as shown. Always draw a line to fill the whole space. This prevents anyone from adding anything to the amount.

7. Your signature, which must match your signature card at the bank.

Activity: Practice filling out a check. You may write it to anyone you want for any amount you want. Refer to the sample above to guide you.

Writing Checks

A check tells your bank how much you want them to pay from your bank account to someone else. Fill in the blank checks to the person listed above each check.

To a relative:

Name _____ $\frac{1-23}{789}$ No. _____

Address _____

_____   _____ 19 _____

Pay to the
Order of _____ $ [   ]

_____ Dollars

BUFFALO BANK

321 Frontier Place
Prairie Grass, OK 82677

Memo _____   _____

To a famous television personality or movie star:

Name _____ $\frac{1-23}{789}$ No. _____

Address _____

_____   _____ 19 _____

Pay to the
Order of _____ $ [   ]

_____ Dollars

BUFFALO BANK

321 Frontier Place
Prairie Grass, OK 82677

Memo _____   _____

Writing Checks (cont.)

A check tells your bank how much you want them to pay from your bank account to someone else. Fill in the blank checks to the person listed above each check.

To a friend:

Name _____

Address _____

_____

$\frac{1-23}{789}$ No. _____

_____ 19 ____

Pay to the
Order of _____ $ [   ]

_____ Dollars

BUFFALO BANK

321 Frontier Place
Prairie Grass, OK 82677

Memo _____

To a friend:

Name _____

Address _____

_____

$\frac{1-23}{789}$ No. _____

_____ 19 ____

Pay to the
Order of _____ $ [   ]

_____ Dollars

BUFFALO BANK

321 Frontier Place
Prairie Grass, OK 82677

Memo _____

Penny Wise

Budgeting your money is a very important skill for everyone. If you receive an allowance, you should decide how and on what to spend your money. Will you spend part of it and save the rest? Are there upcoming events or activities for which you will need extra money?

When you become an adult, you will need to think very carefully about how to spend your money. Here is something you can do with an adult to help you understand more about keeping a budget. You are going to help with the grocery shopping today. You have $52.00 to spend, and you need to find out if you have enough money to purchase what is needed. You will need a pencil, a calculator, and a clipboard.

At Home: Make a list of six items that you need to get at the grocery store. Make these real items on your grocery list.

At the Store: Write the cost of each item next to it.

Item (List at home.)	Cost (Write this at the store.)
1. _____	_____
2. _____	_____
3. _____	_____
4. _____	_____
5. _____	_____
6. _____	_____

How much would you spend? _____   Can you get all of the items?

_____

What is the amount of money that you either need or have extra? _____

Extension: Imagine that you are going to make one of the recipes on page 152. First, check at home to see which ingredients you already have. (Be sure you have enough of each ingredient.) Make a list of the ingredients you need to buy. On a piece of paper, write down how much you think the ingredients will cost. Go to the store and check out the prices. How well did you estimate the cost? (With adult permission and help, you may wish to make one of the recipes.)

Penny Wise (cont.)

Applesauce

Ingredients:

- 4 large apples
- 1 tablespoon (15 mL) water
- 2 tablespoons (30 mL) sugar
- cinnamon (optional)

Utensils:

- 2-quart (2 L) saucepan with lid
- vegetable peeler
- table knife
- potato masher

Directions:

Peel apples and cut into fourths. Remove cores. Put apples into saucepan. Add water. Cover saucepan with lid. Cook over high heat until water begins to boil. Reduce heat to low. Simmer for 20 minutes until apples are soft. Remove from heat. Use potato masher to mash apples and sugar together. Eat applesauce hot or cold. Sprinkle cinnamon on top if desired.

Applesauce Drop Cookies

Ingredients:

- ½ cup (125 mL) butter, margarine, or softened shortening
- 1 cup (250 mL) sugar
- 1 egg
- 1 cup (250 mL) flour
- 1 tablespoon (15 mL) baking powder
- ½ teaspoon (2.5 mL) salt
- 1 teaspoon (5 mL) cinnamon
- ½ teaspoon (2.5 mL) cloves
- ½ teaspoon (2.5 mL) nutmeg
- 1 cup (250 mL) applesauce
- 1 cup (250 mL) raisins
- 1 ¾ cup (438 mL) quick rolled oats

Utensils:

- large bowl
- wire whisk
- mixing spoon or large spoon
- teaspoon
- baking sheet

Directions:

Mix butter and sugar until creamy. Beat in egg. Add all dry ingredients except rolled oats and raisins. Blend well. Stir in applesauce, raisins, and rolled oats. Drop by teaspoonsful onto greased baking sheet. Bake at 375°F (190°C) about 15 minutes or until lightly browned.

Pictographs

One type of graph that gives us information is called a *pictograph*. In a pictograph, pictures are used instead of numbers.

Read this pictograph to find out the number and types of instruments sold in April at Harmony Music Store.

April Instrument Sales at Harmony Music Store

pianos	
flutes	
guitars	
drums	
trumpets	

Key: 1 instrument = 5 instruments

1. How many of each of these instruments were sold?

   pianos _____ flutes _____ guitars _____ drums _____ trumpets _____

2. How many more guitars were sold than each of the following?

   pianos _____ flutes _____ drums _____ trumpets _____

3. Do you think the piano sales or the guitar sales brought in more money for Harmony Music Store? Explain the reason(s) for your choice.

   _____

   _____

   _____

   _____

   _____

Chocolate Consumers of the World

There are chocolate lovers all over the world! Listed below are some of the major chocolate-consuming countries of the world. Beside each country is the average number of pounds/kilograms (lbs/kg) of chocolate eaten per person each year. (Metric conversions, rounded to the nearest tenth, are listed for those using metric measurement.)

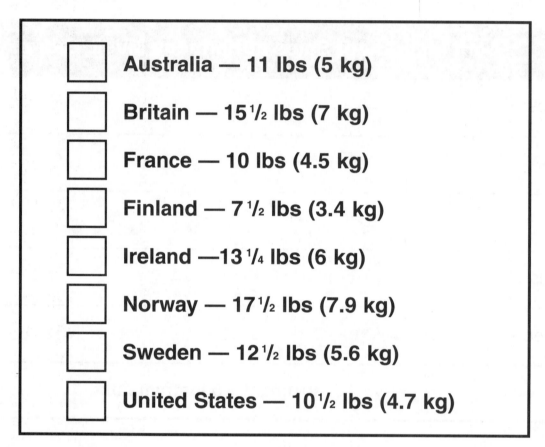

Australia — 11 lbs (5 kg)

Britain — 15 ½ lbs (7 kg)

France — 10 lbs (4.5 kg)

Finland — 7 ½ lbs (3.4 kg)

Ireland —13 ¼ lbs (6 kg)

Norway — 17 ½ lbs (7.9 kg)

Sweden — 12 ½ lbs (5.6 kg)

United States — 10 ½ lbs (4.7 kg)

Activity

A pictograph is a graph in which pictures or symbols represent information. The graph's key shows the value that each symbol or picture represents. The key on page 155 indicates that one chocolate candy symbol represents one pound of chocolate for each person in a year. Create a pictograph on the "Chocolate Consumers of the World" chart on page 155.

Directions

1. Arrange the countries in order from 1-8, with 1 representing the country that consumes the most chocolate and 8 representing the country with the least amount of chocolate consumed. Write the order in the boxes above. Copy the countries (in order) on the chart on page 155.

2. Cut out the correct number of candies from the bottom of page 155 to represent each country's chocolate consumption. (Use the key to determine how many chocolates to cut out.)

3. Complete the pictograph by gluing the correct number of chocolates next to each country. (Be sure to use half of a chocolate to represent ½ pound, one quarter of a chocolate to show ¼ of a pound, etc. Do the same for kilograms.)

Chocolate Consumers of the World (cont.)

Chocolate Consumption*

Country							

Key: * Each candy represents 1 pound (.45 kg) per person per year.

Circle Graphs

One type of graph that gives us information is called a *circle graph*. In a circle graph, you can show how things are divided into the parts of a whole.

Shown in this circle graph are the types and amounts of fruit sold at a produce stand in a week in July.

**Fruits Sold
at
O'Henry's
Fruit Stand**

| July 1 to July 7 |

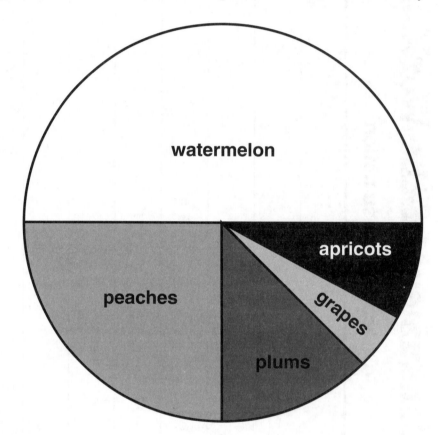

1. What fruit sold the most at O'Henry's Fruit Stand?_____

2. What fruit sold the least?_____

3. Rank the order of the fruits that were sold. Number 1 will be the fruit that sold the most and number 5 the least.

    1. _____   2. _____   3. _____

    4. _____   5. _____

4. Circle the correct fraction.

    Watermelon was $^1/_2$ $^1/_4$ $^1/_8$ of all the fruits sold.

    Peaches were $^1/_2$ $^1/_4$ $^1/_8$ of all the fruits sold.

    Plums were $^1/_2$ $^1/_4$ $^1/_8$ of all the fruits sold.

5. Which of the fruits represented on the circle graph is your favorite?

_____

Slices

In a *circle graph*, all the parts must add up to be a whole. Think of the parts as a pieces that add up to one whole pie.

Look at the circle graph below that shows what Chris did at home between 4 P.M. and 5 P.M. on November 5.

1. How many minutes did Chris spend on the following things?

   doing homework   _____

   eating a snack   _____

   changing clothes   _____

   playing a video game   _____

   walking the dog   _____

2. How did you figure out the number of minutes Chris did things?

   _____

   _____

   _____

Make a circle graph that shows what you did during one of your after school hours.

did homework   _____

played a video game   _____

walked the dog   _____

changed clothes   _____

ate a snack   _____

Write the title of your graph here.

Bar Graphs

One type of graph that gives us information is called a *bar graph*. A bar graph shows us many different types of things by the height or length of the bars.

Sam has to plan ahead to store food for the winter months. The graphs below show two ways Sam could organize his food. Use the graphs to answer the questions.

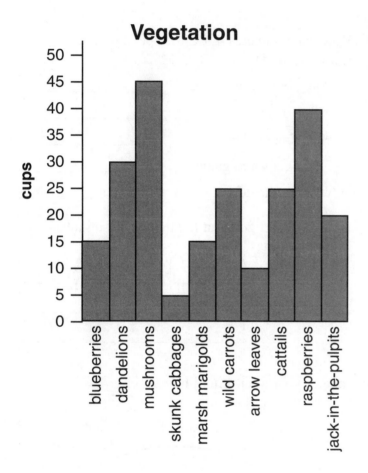

Vegetation

(**Hint:** 2 cups = 1 pint; 2 pints = 1 quart)

1. How many cups of cattails does Sam have? _____

2. How many cups of berries are there? _____

3. How many quarts of raspberries have been stored? _____

4. There are 10 cups of arrow leaves. How many more cups of dandelions than arrow leaves are there? _____

5. How many pints of jack-in-the-pulpits are there? _____

6. If Sam made bread and used one pint of cattails to make flour, how many cups would he have left? _____

7. Which plant has Sam stored the least amount of? _____

8. Which plant has Sam stored the greatest amount of? _____

9. If Sam ate half his store of wild carrots by January, how many cups would he have left for the spring months? _____

(**Hint:** 16 ounces = 1 pound)

1. How many pounds of squirrel are there? _____

2. How many ounces of rabbit meat does Sam have stored? _____

3. How many more pounds of venison than fish are there? _____

4. If Sam used 24 ounces of turtle to make soup, how many pounds would he have left? _____

5. How many pounds of meat does Sam have in all? _____

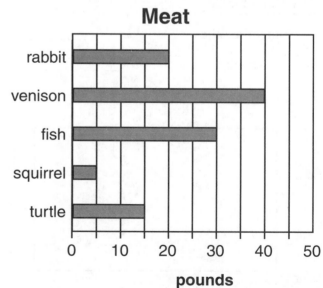

Meat

Using Distance Charts

Distance charts show you the distance between two places if you travel by road.

How Far to New York?

This distance chart shows the miles between 10 North American cities. Look at the chart carefully. Read it by locating the two cities and moving one finger across and one finger down until the two fingers come together to show the distance between cities. Practice. When you are comfortable using the chart, answer the questions below.

Ten-City Distance Chart	Albuquerque	Boston	Chicago	Denver	Indianapolis	Los Angeles	Miami	Montreal	New York City
Boston	2172		963	1949	906	2779	1504	318	206
Chicago	1281	963		996	181	2054	1329	828	802
Denver	417	1949	996		1058	1059	2037	1815	1771
Indianapolis	1266	906	181	1058		2073	1148	840	713
Los Angeles	807	2779	2054	1059	2073		2687	2873	2786
Miami	1938	1504	1329	2037	1148	2687		1654	1308
Montreal	2087	318	828	1815	840	2873	1654		378
New York City	1979	206	802	1771	713	2786	1397	378	
Seattle	1440	2976	2013	1307	2194	1131	3273	2685	2815

Find the distances between these cities.

1. Los Angeles and New York _____

2. Seattle and Albuquerque _____

3. Boston and New York City _____

4. Denver and Miami _____

5. New York City and Chicago _____

6. Montreal and Indianapolis _____

7. Chicago and Miami _____

8. Indianapolis and Denver _____

9. Montreal and Los Angeles _____

10. Seattle and Boston _____

11. Chicago and Boston _____

12. Denver and Albuquerque _____

Interpreting Charts

Students at Hudson Elementary School have been participating in a Read-a-Thon to raise money for their school library. Each student has tallied the number of books he or she has read and is now ready to collect the pledge money.

This chart represents the reading and pledges of 15 students involved in the Read-a-Thon. After reading the chart, answer the questions at the bottom of the page.

Hudson Elementary School Read-a-Thon: Room 3			
Student's Name	**Total Books Read**	**Pledge per Book**	**Money Collected**
Acevedo, Jennifer	31	10¢	$3.10
Adams, Joseph	5	10¢	$ .50
Barton, Michael	61	5¢	$3.05
Duran, Louis	17	15¢	$2.55
Edwards, Marylou	47	5¢	$2.35
Harrison, Trevor	11	25¢	$2.75
Lee, Rebecca	40	10¢	$4.00
Logan, Cassie	22	5¢	$1.10
Marshall, Barbara	9	50¢	$4.50
Peterson, David	102	5¢	$5.10
Ross, Kathryn	58	10¢	$5.80
Rublo, Anthony	83	5¢	$4.15
Shea, Sharon	39	10¢	$3.90
Tran, Alvin	14	10¢	$1.40
Yetter, Liz	75	5¢	$3.75
TOTAL	**614**	——	**$48.00**

1. Which student read the most books?_____

2. What was the highest amount of money collected by one student? _____

   Which student?_____

3. Who had the highest pledge of money per book? _____

4. Was the person who read the most books the same as the person who collected the most money? _____

5. Was the person who had the highest pledge of money per book the same as the person who collected the most money?_____

6. What was the total number of books read by these students? _____

7. How much money did these students earn for the library? _____

Would a Read-a-Thon be a good way to raise money at your school?_____

Using Chart Information

How much do you weigh? Your weight depends upon where you are. If you are in orbit around Earth, far away from Earth's gravitational pull, you would be weightless and would float. Mass is the amount of matter that makes up an object. The gravitational pull depends upon mass. Even a pencil has mass. Thus, it has a gravitational pull, but since it is far less than Earth's mass, it falls to the ground when you drop it.

If you were to visit planets and moons with more or less mass than Earth's, a scale would show you weighed a different amount than you do on Earth. Complete the chart to find out how much you would weigh on the planets in our solar system and on the Moon.

Planet	Surface Gravity	Your Weight on Earth	New Weight
Mercury	.38 x		
Venus	.90 x		
Earth	1.00 x		
Mars	.38 x		
Jupiter	2.64 x		
Saturn	1.13 x		
Uranus	.89 x		
Neptune	1.13 x		
Pluto	.06 x		
Earth's Moon	.17 x		

Using Chart Information (cont.)

Make a graph to show the results of the calculations from your data-capture sheet (page 161).

MY WEIGHT ON THE PLANETS AND THE MOON

Locating Points on a Graph

Jim earned a terrific prize for winning first place in the community talent show. The prize he won is spelled out in this graph.

Find the points on the graph that are identified below. Can you discover what Jim won? Each point you find will give you a letter of the hidden prize.

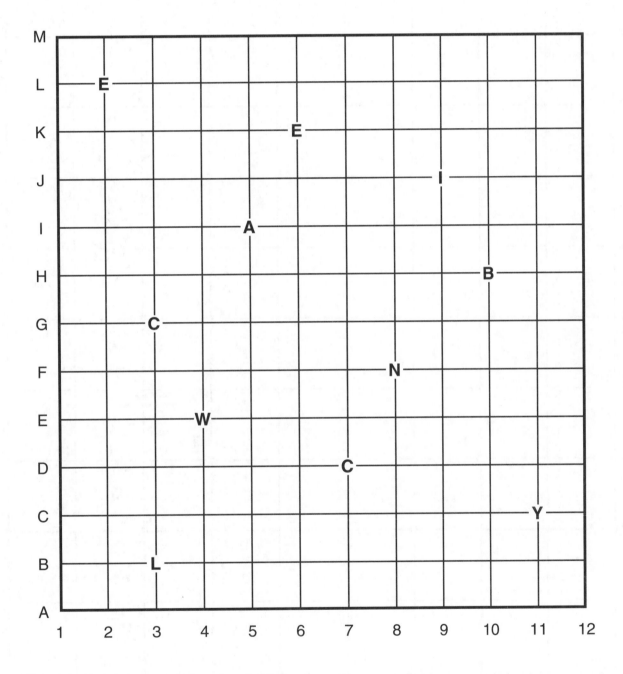

<u>   </u>   <u>   </u>   <u>   </u>   <u>   </u>   <u>   </u>   <u>   </u>   <u>   </u>   <u>   </u>   <u>   </u>   <u>   </u>

I,5   F,8   L,2   E,4   H,10   J,9   G,3   C,11   D,7   B,3   K,6

Finding Coordinates on a Graph

How Do You Make a Hot Dog Stand?

The answer to this riddle is written in a special code at the bottom of this page. Each pair of numbers stands for a point on the graph. Write the letter shown at the point near the intersection of each pair of numbers. Read numbers across and then up. The letters will spell out the answer to the riddle.

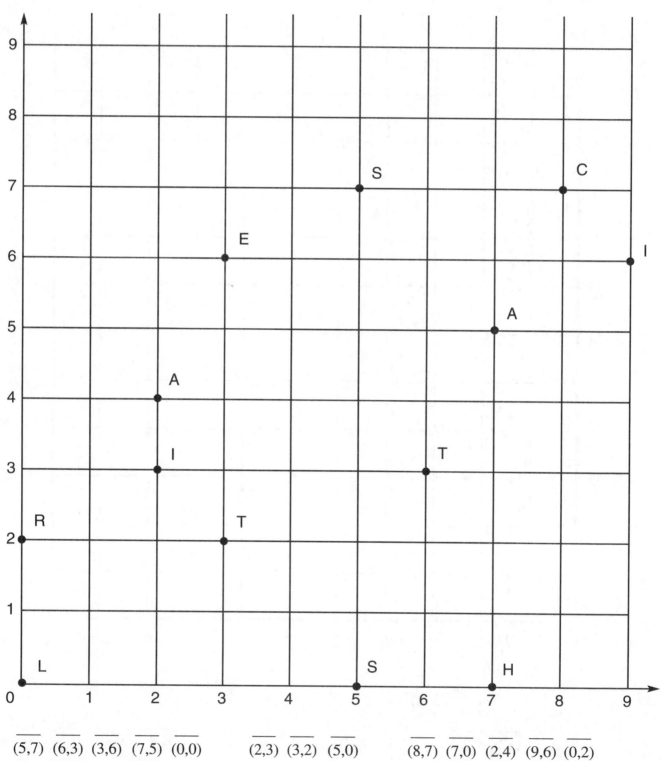

(5,7) (6,3) (3,6) (7,5) (0,0) (2,3) (3,2) (5,0) (8,7) (7,0) (2,4) (9,6) (0,2)

Simple Addition Word Problems

Read each word problem and then answer the questions.

1. Daniel bought 2 candy bars at 47 cents each. How much did he spend?	2. Laura had 92 cents. She wanted to buy a 35 cent juice and a 49 cent hog dog. How much did she spend? How much change does she receive?
3. Jim put his pennies into 2 small boxes. He put 1396 pennies into each box. How many pennies did he have?	4. The Wilson's drove their car 10,483 miles one year and 19,768 miles the next year. How far did they drive during the two years?
5. Robyn had 296 marbles in one box and 187 marbles in another box. How many marbles did she have?	6. In 1959, the population of Happyville was 28,746. During the next 20 years the population increased by 19,658. What was the population then?
7. Russell bought 4 bags of chips at 60 cents each, 2 sodas at 35 cents each and 2 cookies at 25 cents each. How much did he spend?	8. Tamra wanted to go bowling. She rented shoes for $10.00, paid for 2 games at $2.00 a game and bought one soda for $0.35. How much did she spend?
9. Kristen had 12 red socks, 27 green socks, 13 blue socks and 32 pink socks. How many socks did she have?	10. Paul has 75 rocks in his collection. His Uncle Joe has 139 and wants to give them to Paul. How many will he then have?

Addition and Subtraction Word Problems

Read the following problems. Circle the important facts you need to solve them. Use the space provided to find the solution to each problem.

1. There were 76 students in a school jog-a-thon. Twenty-six of them were in 3rd grade, 28 of them were in 4th grade, and 22 of them were in 5th grade.

   a. How many 4th- and 5th-grade students were in the jog-a-thon? _____

   b. Which grade had the most students in the jog-a-thon? _____

2. The jog-a-thon route covered 150 kilometers. There were 4 rest stops for the runners. Niki ran 52 kilometers and stopped at the second rest stop.

   a. How much further does Niki have to run to complete the route? _____

   b. Had she gone at least half the distance? _____

3. Melita's team wanted to collect a total of $325.00. They collected $208.75 from the jog-a-thon and $76.20 from a candy sale.

   a. How much money did they collect? _____

   b. Would they collect more money from 3 candy sales than from 1 jog-a-thon? _____

4. Twenty team members had lunch together at the third rest stop. They had traveled 70 kilometers. Thirteen team members drank milk with their lunch and the rest drank grape juice.

   a. How many team members drank grape juice? _____

   b. How many students did not drink grape juice? _____

5. Bill, Holly, and Katie collected contributions from their neighbors. Bill collected $13.78, Holly collected $16.85, and Katie collected $12.34.

   a. How much more did Holly collect than Bill? _____

   b. How much did Holly and Katie collect together? _____

6. To get ready, Carol bought new shoes for $36.00 and a new water bottle for $1.36. Her mom gave her $47.00 to spend.

   a. How much did she spend for the shoes and water bottle? _____

   b. How much more were the shoes than the water bottle? _____

Multiplication and Division Word Problems

Read each problem and then answer the questions.

The Bailey family runs a small market that not only sells but also grows fresh fruit and vegetables. They sell gardening tools, seeds, and plants. They help their customers with questions about picking which plants to grow and how to best care for them.

1. Two hundred fifteen watermelon seeds were planted in the ground. Five seeds were planted in each small hole. How many small holes were there?	2. The gardeners at Bailey's Market planted 48 onions in each of 12 rows. How many onions were planted?
3. A clerk sold Garrett a rake for $7.75 and a shovel for $13.77. He paid half and had his brother pay the other half. How much did each pay?	4. Tim bought 2,000 carrot seeds on Monday and 3,985 seeds on Tuesday. He needs to plant all of the seeds. He plants 7 seeds in each hole. How many holes will he have when he is done?
5. Randy planted 7 rows of corn and each row had 8 plants in it. He needed to wrap them into 4 bundles. How many bundles would he have?	6. Two customers each bought 25 potatoes for a pot luck supper. They made 10 pots of stew and used all of the potatoes. How many potatoes did they use in each stew?
7. Each seed packet cost $.79. Robyn bought 9 of them. How much did she spend?	8. Each seed packet has 135 seeds in it. Robyn will need to plant 15 seeds in a row. How many rows will she plant?
9. What will be the total cost of 2 bags of grapes at $2.00 each, 1 bag of potatoes at $1.99 each, and 4 baskets of strawberries at $3.46 each?	10. The workers need to move the display case that has the apples in it. There are 6 different kinds of apples. Each bin has 44 apples in it. How many apples are there in the display case?

Division Word Problems

Read each problem and then answer the questions.

1. You deliver 630 newspapers each week. You deliver the same amount each day. How many papers do you deliver each day?	2. You have a roll of film that will take 24 pictures. How many rolls would you need to take 108 pictures?
3. Patti has 396 gum balls and 12 friends to share them with. How many will each friend get?	4. You have collected 3,960 pennies in an old pickle jar. You have 22 friends that you want to give them to. How many would each friend receive?
5. Doug has 657 decals in his desk drawer. He wants to split them among his 9 friends. How many would each one receive?	6. Chris has 5,987 soccer cards. He wants to sell them in packages of 24. How many packages would he have? Would he have any left over. If so, how many?
7. Mike collects rocks. He has 627 in his collection. He wants to store them in 8 boxes. How many will he have in each box? How many will be left over?	8. Cathy was organizing her photographs and found that she had 156 vacation pictures. If she arranges eight pictures on a photo album page, how many pages will she need?
9. Susan's grandmother was making cookies for Susan's classroom. She made 90 cookies. There are 29 students in Susan's class and one teacher. How many cookies would each person get?	10. The pet store had 78 birds that they had to put in 13 cages. How many birds would be in each cage?

Splat!

Learn about the force of gravity.

Materials

- washable ink or thin paint

- eyedropper

- meter stick or yardstick

- large sheet of white paper (Butcher paper is best.)

- newspapers

- masking tape

- data-capture sheet (page 170), one per student

Procedure

1. Place newspapers down in the work area. Secure with masking tape.

2. In the center of the newspapers, tape a large sheet of white paper.

3. You will be dropping paint from different heights onto the paper. Release one drop of paint from each height. Practice with the eyedropper over the container of paint until you are able to release just one drop.

4. Drop paint from 4" (10 cm), 8" (20 cm), 12" (30 cm), 16" (40 cm), 20" (50 cm), 24" (60 cm), 28" (70 cm), 32" (80 cm), 36" (90 cm), and 40" (100 cm).

5. After each drop has landed, label it so that you know the height from which it was dropped.

6. Try to keep the splatters separated on the paper.

7. Answer the questions on your data-capture sheet (page 170).

The Big Why

Gravity forces the droplets to fall faster and faster the higher they are dropped. This create a larger and larger amount of energy upon impact. The energy causes the molecules of the droplets to scatter.

Splat! (cont.)

Data Capture Sheet

Compare your splats. Are they the same?

_____

_____

Did the splatters continue to break apart more explosively as you increased the height? Explain.

_____

_____

Was there a limit of how much splatter you were able to produce?

_____

_____

If so, where was the limit reached?

_____

_____

_____

What forces kept the paint together as it fell and also tried to resist the splat?

_____

_____

_____

As the paint was dropped from greater heights, what pattern did the resultant splats display?

_____

_____

Whirlybirds

Learn about gravity, air resistance, and whirlybirds.

Materials

- construction or index paper
- scissors
- small paperclips
- large paper clips
- index cards
- manila folder
- markers or crayons

Procedure

1. Cut along the dotted lines.

2. Fold along the dark lines.

3. Add one paper clip to the fuselage.

4. Fold one rotor back. Fold the other rotor forward.

5. Hold the whirlybird by the top of the rotors as high off the ground as you can reach.

6. Release the model. Observe how the whirlybird falls. Do several trials.

7. Use a marker or crayon to color one rotor. Drop the whirlybird and use the colored rotor as an aid in counting how many times the rotors turn before it lands.

8. Do several trials and keep a record of your results. Make a graph to compare your results.

The Twister

You can make a model that twirls faster by using a smaller design. Reduce the design illustrated and repeat the directions above.

Fuselage

Rotor   Rotor

Butterfly Balance

Learn about the center of gravity.

Materials

- heavy paper or card stock

- reproducible butterfly design (page 173)

- scissors

- pencil that has never been sharpened

- small ball of clay to use as a base

- two pennies

- rubber cement

- markers or crayons for decorating the butterfly

Procedure

1. Trace the butterfly pattern onto heavy paper. Cut out the design.
2. Decorate the butterfly.
3. Use the clay to form a sturdy base for the pencil. Be sure the pencil is perfectly straight.
4. Glue the pennies on the butterfly where indicated.
5. Balance the butterfly on the eraser of the pencil. The butterfly should balance on its "nose." It might take a little adjustment of the pennies to obtain a stable balance.

The Big Why

Artists use the center of gravity concept to create interesting effects. By manipulating where the weight is located (in this case by using coins), we change the point where the corner of gravity lies. This can cause the illusion of a balancing act that seems to defy gravity.

Butterfly Balance (cont.)

Use this pattern to make your balancing butterfly.

Facts About Motion

Refer to the information below as you complete the activities on pages 175-180.

Everything from the smallest atom to the largest sun is in motion! Movement is the mechanism that makes life possible. Newton's First Law deals with a fundamental principle that objects in motion will stay in motion, and objects at rest will stay at rest, unless a force acts upon them.

The First Law of Motion is a description of the property of *inertia*. Everybody has inertia. It is the lazy property. Inertia likes everything to stay the same. If a rock is lying on the ground and you want to move it, you will find that it is harder to start moving the rock than it is to keep it moving. That is because inertia says, "Leave me alone! I like what I am doing." On the other hand, if that same rock is traveling through space, it takes energy to get it to stop. Once again, the rock wants to be left alone to continue what it is doing.

The motion of an object is very easy to measure. When something is moving, we are interested in how much distance is covered in what period of time. For this reason, the units for motion are the units of distance divided by a unit of time. In the U.S. customary system of measurement, we most commonly use miles per hour. In the metric system, speed is measured in kilometers per hour or meters per second.

The word *speed* has been used on purpose throughout this activity. The concept of *velocity* is a very specific quantity that includes not only speed but also direction. It takes both speed and direction to describe velocity.

To understand motion, an important concept is the frame of reference. When we are measuring the speed of an object, we are always measuring in reference to ourselves or a particular spot on the surface of the earth. The ancients got into trouble with frame of reference when they thought that everything revolved around the earth. To them, the earth was the most important body in the heavens and, therefore, must be the stable, fixed point around which everything moved. This idea of reference point is key to Einstein's Theory of Relativity. In essence, Einstein said that we cannot know if we are standing still and the object is moving or the object is standing still and we are moving. It all depends on our point of view! All motion is relative.

Starting and Stopping

Learn about Newton's First Law.

Materials

- five blocks
- a wooden hammer or ruler
- data-capture sheet (page 176)
- safety glasses

Procedure

1. Stack the blocks on top of each other.

2. Put on your safety glasses. (**Note:** For safety purposes, be sure that other people are at a safe distance from moving blocks.) Slowly hit the bottom block away from the pile. Record the results on your data-capture sheet.

3. Set up the blocks again.

4. Strike the bottom again. This time hit it fast and hard. Record the results on your data capture sheet.

5. Set up the blocks again. Slowly strike the middle block. Record the results on your data-capture sheet.

6. Set up the blocks again. Strike the middle block hard and fast. Record the results on your data-capture sheet.

7. Review the results on your data-capture sheet. Then, read the information below. Does your experiment support the facts about inertia and Newton's First Law?

The Big Why

If something is at rest, it wants to stay that way, so it takes more force to move it. If something is moving, it wants to remain moving at the same speed and in the same direction, so it takes another force to stop it or change its direction. When you strike the blocks hard and fast, the inertia of the top blocks holds them in place. When you strike the blocks slowly, the force can be slowly applied to all the blocks, overcoming inertia and producing movement for all of the blocks.

Starting and Stopping (cont.)

Data-Capture Sheet

What happened when you hit the bottom block slowly?

_____

What happened when you hit the bottom block hard and fast?

_____

What happened when you hit the middle block slowly?

_____

What happened when you hit the middle block hard and fast?

_____

_____

_____

Using what you have observed in this experiment, explain why you think a magician can pull a tablecloth out from under a set of dishes and not break or disturb the table setting.

Newton's First Law of Motion states that an object at rest will remain at rest and an object in motion will remain in motion at constant velocity unless acted upon by another force. Inertia is the basis for this law. The word *inertia* comes from the Latin word *iners* which means "lazy" or "idle." In your own words, explain what inertia is.

_____

_____

_____

_____

_____

_____

_____

Racing Marbles

Learn about measuring speed.

Materials

- any book that is 1" (2.5 cm) or more thick

- plastic, 12" (30 cm) ruler that has a groove down the center

- a game marble

- smooth surface to work on (An uncarpeted floor is the best.)

- piece of chalk

- stopwatch

- calculator

- data-capture sheet (page 178), one per student

Procedure

1. Mark a starting point on the floor. From the starting point, measure and mark a distance of 20" (50 cm), 40" (100 cm), and 60" (150 cm)

2. Make an incline by placing one end of the ruler on the starting point and the other on a book. The incline will be directed toward the distance marks.

3. Place a marble at the top of the incline and let it accelerate down the ruler.

4. Begin timing when the marble crosses the starting point.

5. Time how long it takes until the marble crosses the 20" (50 cm) mark.

6. Repeat two more times.

7. Do a total of three trials for 20" (50 cm), three trials for 40" (100 cm), and three trials for 60" (150 cm).

8. Complete your data-capture sheet on page 178.

The Big Why

Speed is a measure of change—the change in distance over a particular time period.

Racing Marbles (cont.)

As you race your marbles, fill in the data below. Then calculate the average time for the three trials.

20 in. (50 cm)	Trial 1	Trial 2	Trial 3	Average
Time:				
40 in. (100 cm)	Trial 1	Trial 2	Trial 3	Average
Time:				
60 in. (150 cm)	Trial 1	Trial 2	Trial 3	Average
Time:				

Calculate Speed

Use the average time for each distance. Calculate the speed the marble was traveling as it covered the three distances. Record your answers below, using a calculator and the following equation:

speed = distance ÷ time

For 20" (50 cm) Speed = _____ inches (cm)/second

For 40" (100 cm) Speed = _____ inches (cm)/second

For 60" (150 cm) Speed = _____ inches (cm)/second

For Further Thought

Why are the speeds for the three distances different?

_____

Impact Craters

> ### Learn about force and acceleration.

Materials

- medium and large rocks

- sandy area or boxes filled with sand

- straight piece of cardboard for smoothing the sand

- ruler

- data-capture sheet (page 180)

Procedure

1. Pick an area of sand and smooth it with the cardboard.

2. The object is to drop the rocks from various heights and measure the craters made. Smooth the sand after each rock and record information on your data-capture sheet.

3. Throw the rocks straight down, one at a time, into the sand. Observe how the craters formed. Smooth the sand after each landing and record information on your data-capture sheet.

4. Throw the rocks down at an angle. Observe how the craters formed. Smooth the sand after each rock is thrown and record information on the back of your data-capture sheet.

The Big Why

When objects slow down or come to an abrupt stop, there must be a force applied to produce this change. When the change is abrupt, as in this experiment, the change in velocity produces a large amount of energy that is absorbed by the ground. This energy causes the dirt to move, hence an impact crater. Often there is enough energy to produce an explosion!

Impact Craters (cont.)

Data-Capture Sheet

Trial	Rock Size	How Dropped	Describe the Crater
1			
2			
3			
4			
5			
6			

Draw a picture of the crater made by dropping the largest rock straight down.

Draw a picture of the crater made by throwing a large rock into the sand at an angle.

What is different about each crater?

_____

_____

As the rocks came to a stop, they did not stop instantly. There was a period of deceleration or slowing down. What evidence is there of the forces involved in stopping an object?

_____

Making a Balloon Rocket

Materials

- long balloon
- thin string or yarn
- large straw with a short piece cut off
- tape
- measuring tape

Procedure

1. Place the string or yarn through the longer piece of straw. Attach the string or yarn to each side of the room.

2. Blow up the balloon. Do not let the air out. You may wish to use something to clamp the neck of the balloon closed.

3. Tape the longer piece of straw to the balloon, making sure not to let the air out of the balloon.

4. Place the shorter piece of straw into the neck of the balloon and tape it into place.

5. Stand at one end of the room and let the air out of the balloon. As the air rushes out, the balloon should travel along the string or yarn.

6. Launch your balloon rocket three times. Use the measuring tape to see how far your balloon rocket moves each time. Record your measurements on the back of this paper.

Blast Off!

Learn about trajectory.

Materials

- balloons of several shapes and sizes
- index cards or tagboard
- ruler
- markers
- colored pencils or crayons
- tape
- fishline

Procedure

1. Use an index card or tagboard to make a rocket like the one shown in the illustration.
2. Color the rocket pattern and roll it into a cylinder. Tape the cylinder together.
3. Blow up a balloon and hold it in the inflated condition as a partner gently tapes the rocket model to the top or side of the balloon.
4. Take the balloon rocket to the designated launch area preferrably outside the classroom.
5. Set the balloon rocket on the launching pad, lean away from the rocket, and release the balloon.

  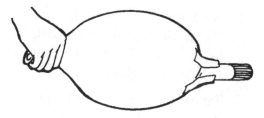

- How well did your rocket work?
- Try launching the rocket again with a different balloon. Try long balloons, twisties, very large spherical balloons, and any other sizes and shapes available.
- Try the slender design shown here. This design curls into a long, slender tube. It can be attached to the top or side of the balloon.
- With which balloon did this model work best?
- Design your own rocket version. Modify one of the two designs shown on this page or create an entirely new design.
- Try launching your design, using your favorite type of balloon.

- Test it on other balloon sizes.
- Compare your design with those launched by other class members.
- Why do you think that thin, cylindrical models often work best?

Blast Off! (cont.)

Guided Rockets

You can often get greater distance by guiding the launch.

1. Cut a 30-foot (9-meter) piece of fishline. Tie one end to the shaft of a pushpin and pin that end into a bulletin board about four feet (122 cm) off the floor or to a tree or pole outdoors.

2. Extend the string across the room or playground to the farthest distance possible. Keep the fishline out of the path of students and tape it against a wall until you are ready to launch.

3. Copy the design shown below onto an index card, manila folder, or similar thick paper. Color it with markers or crayons.

4. Tape the rocket design onto a straw in two places.

5. Thread the end of the fishline through the straw and hold it in place while a partner blows up a balloon and tapes it onto the rocket model.

6. Hold the string and model so that the straw sits easily on the fishline and the fishline is aimed slightly higher than where it is pinned.

7. Release the balloon and observe how well the rocket travels. Did it get to the end of the fishline?

   - Did the straw catch or run freely along the fishline? Did the balloon seem to run out of air before the rocket reached the end of the line?
   - Do several trials of your rocket. Use balloons of different styles and sizes. Hold the fishline at different angles to get the maximum amount of speed.
   - Create a model rocket of your own. Use a different style or type of rocket. Make your rocket longer or shorter, wider or narrower.
   - Try several different versions. Use different balloons and test each of your models.
   - Try mounting your rocket onto a double-length straw that you have hooked together.
   - Try making a cylinder to go around the straw.

Chutes Away

Learn about air resistance.

Materials

- fishline
- paper
- newspaper
- small trash bags
- construction paper
- large paper clips
- manila folder or tagboard
- plastic bottles
- boxes
- hole punch or pushpin
- masking tape
- scissors

The Basic Chute

1. Fold an 8½" x 11" (22 cm x 28 cm) piece of paper in fourths

2. Push out the side folded in so that all four folds face up.

3. Cover each corner on both sides with a piece of masking tape.

4. Use a hole punch or pushpin to make a hole at all four corners. Make the hole right through the tape.

5. Cut four pieces of fishline each about 16" (41 cm) long.

6. Tie one piece of fishline at each corner.

7. Tape three large paper clips together. Draw a small figure of a parachutist to tape onto the paper clips.

8. Tie all four ends of the fishline together at an even distance from the corners. Tie or tape them to the paper clip parachutist.

9. Hold your parachute as high as you can by the chute or canopy and drop it. Note how fast it falls and whether the canopy slows the fall.

10. Stand on a chair, stairs, or a stage (if available), and drop the chute from a higher level.

11. Try folding the entire chute and throwing it high into the air. Does it unfold in time or fall too soon?

Make Flying Saucers

Learn about the principles of flight.

Materials

- tagboard or manila folders
- paper fasteners (brads)
- large paper clips
- glue
- clear tape
- scissors
- math compass
- ruler

Procedure

1. Use a compass to make a circle with a radius of four inches (10 cm) on a piece of tagboard or a manila folder. This will make a circle with a diameter (distance across) of eight inches (20 cm).

2. Cut out the circle. This will be the base of the saucer.

3. Use the compass to make a second circle with a radius of three inches (8 cm). This will create a circle with a diameter of six inches (15 cm). Cut out this circle.

4. Use the compass to draw four more circles. Make each circle smaller than the one before it. Cut out each circle.

5. Arrange the circles in a concentric pattern as shown in the illustration below.

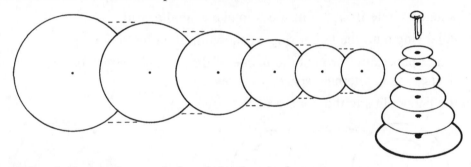

6. Glue each of the circles to the one below it in the stack.

7. Use a pushpin and the point of a compass to make a hole through the center of the stack so that a paper fastener (brads) can be pushed through the layers.

8. Fold the blades of the paper fastener down, and tape them onto the back of the largest circle.

9. Arrange six, large paper clips around the edges of the saucer as shown below, and tape them securely to the back of the largest circle.

10. Take the flying saucer outdoors and launch it with a swift, Frisbee-like snap of the wrist. Do several trials. Try different ways of throwing your saucer into the air. Observe how your saucer flies.

Make Flying Saucers (cont.)

The Ring Flyer

1. Set the compass for a four-inch (10 cm) radius to draw a circle eight inches (20 cm) in diameter. Cut out the circle.

2. Set the compass for a two-inch (5 cm) radius and draw a smaller circle with a four-inch (10 cm) diameter in the center of the larger circle you just cut out.

3. Cut the smaller circle out from the inside of the tagboard to make a ring as shown in the illustration.

4. Set the compass for a three-inch (8 cm) radius to draw a circle six inches (15 cm) in diameter. Cut out the circle.

5. Set the compass for a two-inch (5 cm) radius, and draw a smaller circle with a four-inch (10 cm) diameter in the center of the larger circle you just cut out.

6. Cut out the smaller circle from the inside to make a smaller ring.

7. Glue the smaller ring onto the larger ring as shown in the illustration.

8. Arrange six large paper clips around the inside of the ring. Arrange six large paper clips around the outside of the ring in alternate spaces as shown.

9. Tape down the paper clips to the bottom of the larger ring.

10. Launch the ring with a snap of the wrist like tossing a Frisbee or toss it into the air with a strong overhand throw. Do several trials. Observe how it flies. How does its flight differ from the flying saucer model (page 185)?

Unbalanced Saucers

Place six small paper clips between the large clips on your flying saucer. Tape them down on the bottom layer of the saucer. Throw this model into the air with a snap of the wrist. Does it fly better with the extra paper clips?

Rearrange the large paper clips and the small ones so that the weight on the saucer is unbalanced. You could have four or five paper clips of each size on one side of the saucer and only one or two clips on the other side.

Launch this model and observe what happens.

Make Flying Saucers (cont.)

Larger Saucers

1. Set your compass gauge at the five-inch (13 cm) mark to create a circle with a radius of five inches. Make a circle on a manila folder or tagboard. The circle will have a diameter across the center of 10 inches (25 cm).

2. Use tagboard, manila folders, or construction paper to make nine more circles, each progressively smaller than the one before.

3. Carefully arrange each circle in a concentric pattern with the smallest on top. Glue each circle to the one below it.

4. Use a pushpin to make a hole through the center of the stack and then make the hole large enough with the compass point until you can push a paper fastener through the stack.

5. Arrange six large paper clips evenly around the edges of the saucer. Arrange six small paper clips in between the large clips.

6. Securely tape the blades of the paper fastener (brads) and the paper clips to the back of the largest circle.

7. Launch your flying saucer with a snap of the wrist. Compare your results with the basic flying saucer and the ring flyer (pages 185 and 186).

Pyramid Saucer

Copy or cut out the pattern for a square pyramid illustrated below. Make the model pyramid from tagboard or a folder. Fold along the lines of the square to make the pyramid. Tape the edges of the pyramid and securely tape the pyramid onto the center of the flying saucer.

Launch your pyramid saucer. Do several trials. Compare your results with the results of other saucers and ring flyers.

Make Flying Saucers (cont.)

Domed Saucers

Use your best flying saucer or make a new one and mount a dome on the saucer as you did with the square pyramid. Use a plastic, Styrofoam, or paper cup, margarine or cup lids, bottle caps, or create a dome shape from a piece of tagboard or manila folder. The illustrations show several examples for you to try.

Launch each model. Do several trials. Compare your results. Which domed model works best?

Loaded Saucers

The illustrations here show several unusual models of flying saucers for you to try.

Use your own imagination and your experience in building flying saucers to create the best saucer you can make.

- Try different materials, such as paper plates, for the base.
- Try putting a load both underneath and above the saucer.
- Try changing the edge of the saucer to create a Frisbee-like curve along the edge.
- Try unbalanced saucers and saucers with shapes that aren't circular.
- Be imaginative!
- Test each model.
- Determine your best model.

Don't Give Me Any Static

Learn about static charges.

Materials

- salt
- pepper
- plastic comb
- piece of wool (or flannel) cloth
- small, clear dish
- data-capture sheet (page 190)

Procedure

1. Place a small amount of salt and a small amount of pepper in the glass dish.

2. Rub the comb vigorously with the wool cloth.

3. Move the comb slowly down over the salt and pepper mixture.

4. Move the comb even closer without touching the mixture. Finally, touch the comb to the mixture.

5. Record your observations on your data-capture sheet.

6. Test other items in the room to see what else is attracted by static forces.

The Big Why

By rubbing the plastic comb with the wool or flannel cloth, it is charged with electrons. Free-moving electrons from the material are transferred to the comb. The comb becomes negatively charged and acts similar to a magnet. The comb, however, does not have a north and south pole. The pepper rises first because it is lighter. If you come close enough, some of the salt will also jump to the comb.

The attraction is caused by the movement of electrons on the surface of the pepper. The negatively-charged comb forces the electrons on the pepper to move away from the comb. The pepper becomes charged by induction; that is, it now has a negative side (away from the comb) and a positive side (closest to the comb). Since opposite charges attract, the pepper is drawn to the comb. Another way to separate the salt and pepper is to put them both in a small amount of water. The salt will sink to the bottom (it is heavier), and the pepper will float.

Don't Give Me Any Static (cont.)

Data-Capture Sheet

Draw a picture of the top of the small clear dish after it was charged and then flipped over.

Where did the pepper stick?

_____

_____

Why did the pepper stick to the rubbed areas?

_____

_____

What charge did the plastic surface have?

_____

_____

Explain how this principle can be used in a photocopy machine.

_____

_____

Super Sound-Off

Learn about how sound is created.

Simple Sound Maker

Materials

- tagboard or manila folder
- index cards
- newspaper
- newsprint paper
- copy paper
- construction paper
- scissors
- ruler
- tape

Procedure

1. Use the ruler to measure a four-inch (10 cm) square on an index card, manila folder, or piece of tagboard.

2. Use the scissors to cut out the square.

3. Use the ruler to draw a diagonal line across the square, then fold along the diagonal, using the ruler or scissors to sharply crease the fold.

4. Use the ruler to measure a six-inch (15 cm) square on a piece of plain white paper. Cut out the square.

5. Draw one diagonal line across the square, dividing it in two.

6. Cut along the diagonal line. Set one piece aside for later use.

7. Lay the first square inside the two shorter sides of the triangle with the fold of the square between the two sides.

8. Fold up about one centimeter along the two shorter sides of the triangle, and tape the folds in place as shown in the illustration.

9. Fold the square again and place your thumb and forefinger along the untaped end of the folded figure.

10. Hold the figure above your head, and whip the model through the air as fast as you can. There should be a loud sound as the inner paper pops out of the folded square.

11. Practice holding and snapping the model in different positions. Try to make the loudest crack possible.

12. Try whipping the model sideways.

13. Try holding the model upside down.

Watch what happens to the paper as the sound is made. A wave of compressed air creates the sound as it is forced out by the inner paper.

Where do you have to hold your fingers to make the model crack?

Phone Fun

Learn how sound travels.

Basic Phone Model

Materials

- fishline
- small paper cups
- pushpins
- paper clips

Procedure

- Use a pushpin to make a hole in the bottom of each of two small paper cups.
- Cut a piece of nylon fishline about 20 feet (6 m) long.
- Feed one end of the fishline through the bottom of the cup and tie one small paper clip to the line.
- Pull the line and paper clip firmly against the inside bottom of the cup.
- Feed the other end of the fishline through the bottom of the second cup, tie another small paper clip to the line, and pull it firmly against the inside bottom of the cup.

- One partner should hold the cup over one ear while the other person talks into the cup.
- The line must be kept tight, or the phone will not work.

The Big Way

The speaker's voice vibrates molecules of air inside the cup. These vibrations are picked up by the bottom of the cup, which acts as a diaphragm. The line transfers the vibrations to the bottom of the second cup, which also acts as a diaphragm that vibrates the molecules of air in the second cup. These vibrations are then discerned by the ear of the listener.

Improving the phone always involves trying to make the message clearer and carrying it a longer distance. Here are some other ideas to experiment with.

- Try pinching the line while someone is talking. What happens? What happens if the line touches a chair, a wall, or another person?
- Will the phone work if the line gets a tangled knot in it?
- Will it work if the line is allowed to get loose? Why do you think the line must be tight?

The Best Bubble Maker

Learn about the properties of soap.

Materials

- string or thin twine
- insulated wire
- straws
- liquid handwashing dish detergent
- vegetable oil

Procedure

Use this formula to make a strong bubble solution:

- 20 ounces (600 mL) of liquid handwashing dish detergent (Dawn, Joy, etc.)
- 6 ounces (180 mL) of vegetable oil
- 2 gallons (7.6 L) of water

Stir the solution thoroughly in a tray or tub.

The Two-Handle Frame

Cut a piece of string or thin twine about 30 inches (76 cm) long. Thread the string through the two straws and tie the ends of the string together.

Using the two straws as handles, dip the frame into the bubble solution and see how large a bubble you can lift out of the solution.

Twist the frame to create two triangles. Can you lift two bubbles out of the solution with this frame?

Wire Frames

Twist thin, insulated wire into several of the shapes illustrated here.

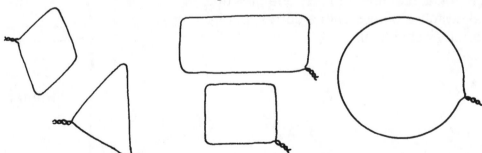

Try these shapes in your bubble formula. Observe how the bubbles form. Can you get any long bubbles using some of these frames? Thread wire through short pieces of cut straws to create the plane geometric figures illustrated here.

Facts About Chemical Reactions

Refer to the information below as you complete the activities on pages 195 and 196.

Chemicals react in many ways. They react and undergo chemical change to form new substances with new properties. Chemical changes are indicated when one of the following situations occurs:

the formation of a precipitate (e.g., solid falling out of solution)

a color change

a gain or loss of heat

Some of the ways that chemicals react are as follows:

- **Oxidation**

    In general, this is a reaction in which the element oxygen combines chemically with another substance.

- **Synthesis or Combination**

    In this chemical reaction, different substances (chemicals) are added together to form new substances (chemicals).

- **Decomposition**

    This is a chemical reaction in which a substance breaks down into its component parts.

- **Replacement**

    In this chemical reaction, at least one part of a chemical switches places with a corresponding part of another chemical.

Baking Soda

Vinegar

Add Oxygen

Learn about how chemicals react with oxygen.

Materials

- crayon
- apple
- piece of white paper
- water
- data-capture sheet (page 196)
- potato
- steel wool pad
- plastic knife
- paper cup

Procedure

1. Using the plastic knife, cut the potato in half. Note its appearance, and set it aside for later use.

2. Using the plastic knife, cut the apple in half. Note its appearance, and set it aside for later use.

3. Fill the paper cup two-thirds full of water.

4. Note the appearance of the piece of steel wool pad. Place a piece of it in the cup of water. Set it aside for about 20 minutes and again note its appearance.

5. Place the piece of wet steel wool on a sheet of white paper, and let it dry overnight.

6. Again note the appearance of the cut potato and the cut apple.

7. Let the cut potato and the cut apple sit overnight.

8. The next day, note the appearance of the cut potato, the cut apple, and the piece of steel wool.

9. Compare the information on your data-capture sheet. What do you think happened to each item when it was exposed to the oxygen in the air?

The Big Why

This activity reminds us that oxygen is present in the air. It demonstrates what happens when oxygen combines with various substances and what the resulting chemical reaction produces.

Add Oxygen (cont.)

Data-Capture Sheet

Item	Initial Appearance	Appearance at Second Observation	Appearance After Sitting Overnight
Cut Potato			
Cut Apple			
Steel Wool			

Grow a Crystal Garden

Learn about crystal formation.

Materials

- small bowl or plastic cup
- 3 tablespoon (45 mL) each of laundry bluing (usually found in grocery stores or drugstores), water, and ammonia
- 2 tablespoons (30 g) of salt (Regular table salt will work well.)
- dropper bottles of food coloring or colored ink
- sponge or charcoal (You may also want to try Styrofoam, a tennis ball, or a rough rock.)

Procedure

You can grow a lovely crystal garden at home. The crystals are delicate and look like white snowflakes. You can add food coloring before the crystals form, and they will be colored red, blue, green, yellow, or a combination of those colors where the drops overlap. This is a good activity to do outside since the ingredients include bluing and ammonia, which have a strong odor.

1. Mix the ingredients together in a bowl or measuring cup and stir to dissolve the salt.
2. Put the dry sponge or charcoal into a separate bowl. (This recipe is enough for three or four containers.)
3. Pour the liquid mixture over the sponge, charcoal, or other object.
4. Scatter several drops of food coloring over the solution.
5. Leave the dish in a well-ventilated room or outside.
6. The crystals take about 24 hours to form, less if it is a dry day. They will continue to grow until all the liquid has evaporated. They are delicate crystals which will break if bumped or touched.

Grow a Crystal Garden (cont.)

In the boxes below, make drawings of the crystals you see in your crystal garden.

Picture inside container just after pouring solution.

Time: _____

Date: _____

Picture inside container 15 minutes after pouring solution.

Time: _____

Date: _____

Grow a Crystal Garden (cont.)

In the boxes below, make drawings of the crystals you see in your crystal garden.

Picture inside container just after pouring solution.

Time: _____

Date: _____

Picture inside container after 24 hours of crystallizing.

Time: _____

Date: _____

Testing Towels

| Learn to test variables and make observations. |

Materials

- four different brands of paper towels
- facial tissue
- water
- clear plastic cups
- food coloring

Racing Water

1. Fill a clear plastic cup almost full of water. Place a few drops of food coloring in the water and stir.
2. Carefully tear four paper towels from four different brands of paper towel along the perforated line.
3. Roll each towel into a long, thin tube about equal in length to each other.
4. Mark the name of each towel on one end of the tube.
5. Write down the exact time. Place all four tubes in the cup at the same time.
6. Observe how the water climbs the paper towel tubes.
7. Keep track of which towel the water climbs fastest and which is second, third, and fourth.
8. Keep track of the elapsed time.

9. Do two more trials to confirm your results.
10. Make a chart illustrating the results of your trials.
11. Compare your results with other classmates.

The Squeeze Test

1. Arrange the four paper towel tubes as you did in the first activity. Make sure that only one piece of toweling is used from each brand and that they are about the same size, torn along the perforation as you would do in taking a paper towel for use. Make sure you have marked the brand name for each towel.

2. Wait until all four towels have absorbed water and are dripping onto the table.
3. Carefully remove one towel. Record the brand name.
4. Gently squeeze every drop from the toweling into the empty clear plastic cup.

Testing Towels (cont.)

The Squeeze Test *(cont.)*

5. Pour the squeezed water into a measuring cup to determine exactly how many milliliters (or cubic centimeters) of water it holds. (If your measurement cup doesn't indicate milliliters or cubic centimeters, you can use fractions of a fluid ounce on the cup or the millimeters measurement on a ruler to measure the height of the water.)

6. Squeeze the water out of each towel in turn and record the amount of water the paper towel held.

7. Make a chart indicating the amount of water absorbed by each towel.

Paper Towel Siphons

1. Choose any two of your paper towel brands.

2. Position two empty clear plastic cups near the cup of water.

3. Roll one towel from each brand into a long, thin tube. Bend the tubes slightly and put both of them into the cup of colored water. Write down the exact time.

4. As the water climbs up the paper towel, bend each tube so that it is leaning over one of the empty plastic cups.

5. Record the name of the towel leaning over each empty cup.

6. Leave the cups and paper towels undisturbed.

Observe what happens to the water which has climbed up the paper towel.

- Did the paper towels fill each cup as high as the water remaining in the first cup?

- Which paper towel carried water faster than the other?

- Do this activity again but place the full cup of water on a book or some elevated position with the empty cups at a lower level.

- How much water is carried out of the first cup?

Did either of the two empty cups fill more than the other?

- Do the same activity again with the empty cups situated on a raised area and the full cup at a lower level.

- Describe what happens to the water.

- Determine which paper towel holds the most water.

- Why might that indicate it is the best paper towel?

Testing Towels (cont.)

The Dry Test

This is one way to test the strength of a dry paper towel.

1. Use four pieces of masking tape to attach the four corners of one dry paper towel to an area between two desks.

2. Allow about two inches (5 cm) of each side of the towel to lie on the desk. The rest of the towel will be between the desks.

3. Keep count as you place pennies on the stretched-out paper towel.

4. Place as many pennies on the dry towel as you can until it breaks or tears apart. Retest only if the tape gives way.

5. Test each of the four paper towel brands in the same way.

6. Make a chart illustrating how many pennies each of the dry paper towels held.

   • Can you put more than 100 pennies on any towel?

7. Design another way of testing the strength of dry paper towels.

   • How much can you lift using each towel?

   • Do you get the same results using your test?

The Wet Test

Test the strength of a wet paper towel.

1. Dip one paper towel in water and gently squeeze out any dripping excess water.

2. Use four pieces of masking tape to attach the four corners of one wet paper towel to an area between two desks as you did in the dry test.

3. Place as many pennies on the wet towel as you can until it breaks or tears apart. Keep an accurate count.

4. Test each of your four paper towel brands in the same way.

5. Make a chart illustrating how many pennies each of your wet paper towels held.

6. Did you get more than 50 pennies on any wet towel? Did any of the paper towels do as well or better wet than dry?

7. Record the results of your wet paper towel test on a chart. Compare results with your classmates.

Testing Towels (cont.)

Double Layer Towels

Do two layers of towels actually work much better than one layer? Repeat the dry paper towel test that you used on the last page using two layers of each paper towel for the test.

Tape the first layer of towel and then the second layer. Record how many pennies the double layer holds for each brand. Do you get more than 150 pennies on any double towel layer? Which results surprise you? Why?

Test the strength of double layers of wet paper towels in the same way. Tape each layer separately and gradually place pennies on the stretched-out layers.

- Are any of the double layers particularly strong?
- Can you get more than 75 pennies on any wet double layer?
- Do any of the results surprise you?

The Stretch Test

How far will each paper towel stretch before it tears? Test one layer of each brand of dry paper towel in this manner:

1. Fold one paper towel the lengthwise into four layers.

2. Hold one end of the paper towel near the beginning of a ruler and pull gently on the other end until the paper towel tears apart.

3. Record how many centimeters each brand of paper towel stretched beyond its original length before breaking.

Test the stretching capacity of the four brands of paper towels when they are wet.

1. Soak each paper towel. Wring out the dripping, excess water.

2. Lay the wet towel along the length of the ruler and record how far it will stretch before tearing.

Design Your Own Tests

Paper towels are used for many different purposes, not just soaking up clean water.

Design some tests of your own to determine the best brand of towel.

Some of the tests might include the following:

- strength tests with soapy water
- ability to absorb cooking oil

- strength tests in holding different objects
- how many towels it takes to clean up a specific spill

The Earth

Learn about the earth's mantle.

Materials

• cornstarch   • water   • two plates

Procedure

1. Mix cornstarch and water until it is like a thick syrup.

2. Pour "magma" into one of your hands. Push the cornstarch together between your hands. Roll it quickly as if you were making a mudball. (This is like magma under pressure.)

3. Release the pressure and try to pass the cornstarch ball to your other hand. Keep it over your plate! (This is like magma without pressure.)

4. Draw the "magma" here.

With Pressure   Without Pressure

5. On the back of this paper, describe what happened when the cornstarch was under pressure and when it was not. What did you learn?

The Big Why

The earth's mantle is made of melted rock, or magma. When magma is under pressure below the earth's crust, it has one kind of property. When the magma (lava) escapes through a volcano and is no longer under pressure, it has a different property.

Shifting Crust

Materials

- three pieces of fresh whole wheat bread

- strawberry jam

- smooth peanut butter

- 2 tablespoons (30 g) of melted plain chocolate bar

- plastic spreading knife

- waxed paper and napkin or paper towel

- copy of The Movement of the Earth's Crust (page 207)

- data-capture sheet (page 208).

Procedure

1. Be sure to wash your hands before doing this activity.

2. Melt the chocolate bars in a microwave or over boiling water on a hot plate.

3. Divide students into groups and distribute the materials needed.

4. Spread the waxed paper in the middle of your work area and put the three slices of bread on the paper.

5. Have students work together to make a sandwich as follows:

   Spread a thin layer of chocolate on a slice of bread and spread peanut butter over it.

   Spread a thin layer of chocolate on a second slice of bread and spread jam over it.

6. Each of the materials represents:

   - *Chocolate*—igneous rock which was melted and forced between layers of rock

   - *Peanut butter*—metamorphic rock, made by rock changed through the pressure of grinding

   - *Jam*—sedimentary layer, with seeds being sedimentary rocks deposited in the ocean

   - *Bread*—more sedimentary layers

7. Put your bread together into a sandwich. (See diagram on page 206.)

Shifting Crust (cont.)

8. Draw on the data-capture sheets the three types of faults using your peanut butter and jelly sandwiches as a model.

9. Move your sandwich slices to represent the faults and to watch the results.

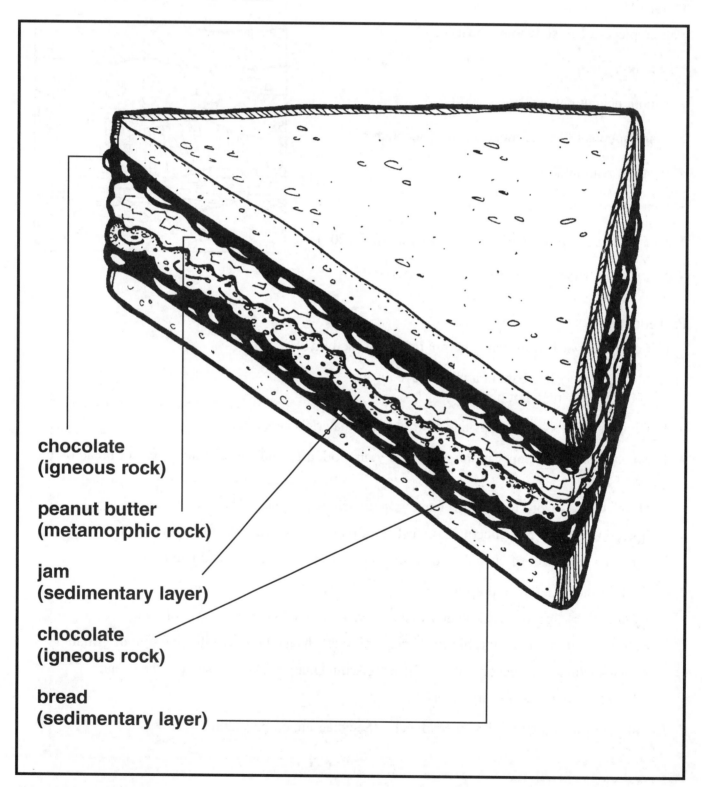

**chocolate
(igneous rock)**

**peanut butter
(metamorphic rock)**

**jam
(sedimentary layer)**

**chocolate
(igneous rock)**

**bread
(sedimentary layer)**

Shifting Crust (cont.)

The Movement of the Earth's Crust

The movement of the earth's crust is called *faulting*. This movement of the crust causes earthquakes. The three main types of faults are normal faulting, reverse faulting, and strike-slip faulting. All three are shown below.

Normal Faulting: Two blocks of the earth's crust move apart from each other. One block may also drop below the other.

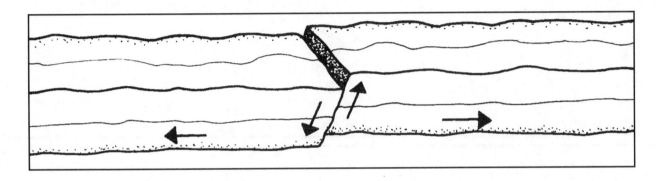

Reverse Faulting: Two blocks push together, and one is pushed under the other. This is called *subduction*.

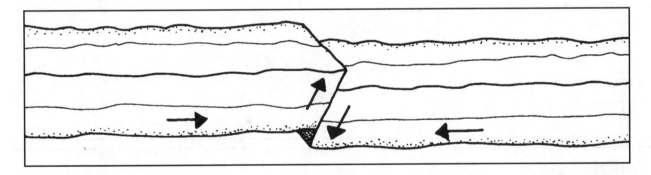

Strike-slip Faulting: The two blocks slide past each other, but neither moves up or down.

Shifting Crust (cont.)

Data-Capture Sheet

Draw and label each of the three types of faults using your peanut butter and jelly sandwich as a model.

Cold Tracks

Learn about glaciers.

Materials

- pint milk carton
- rocks
- water
- freezer
- sand
- dirt mound

Procedure

1. Fill a pint milk carton one-fourth full with sand and rocks. Fill the rest with water. Shake it, tape it closed, and freeze it.

2. Outside, make a dirt mound.

3. Peel off the carton and place the ice block on top of the dirt mount. Draw a BEFORE picture.

4. Watch what happens. Draw an AFTER picture.

5. On the back of this paper, describe what happened. Did your glacier dig a valley? Is that what you thought would happen? What did you learn?

The Big Why

A force that changes the earth's surface is moving ice, called a glacier. A glacier moves slowly, but it is so strong that it can dig out the ground as it moves. Glaciers can even dig out valleys and make lakes. A glacier carries large rocks, depositing them as it melts.

Invasion of the Mold

Learn about growing a simple plant.

Materials

- two pieces of white bread

- cup of sand

- paper plates

- magnifying glass

- large needle

- jelly or jam (any flavor)

- sealable plastic bag

- data-capture sheet (page 211)

Procedure

1. Day 1

   Place one slice of bread on a paper plate, sprinkle it with water. Place it in a plastic bag and seal it tightly. Set it in a warm place and observe it for a few days.

2. Day 4

   Step 1: Remove the bread from the plastic bag. Using a needle, carefully remove some spores from the mold. On a clean paper plate, sprinkle some sand and carefully put some spores on it. Seal the bag and put it in a warm place for 3-4 days. Watch what happens.

   Step 2: Put some spores on another piece of bread. Do not moisten the bread. Put the bread in a sealed plastic bag and set it aside for 3-4 days.

3. Add some jelly to the plate with the sand and spores on it. Reseal and set it in a warm place for 3-4 more days.

4. Record your findings on your data-capture sheet when all steps have been completed.

The Big Why

A simple plant mold is one that does not produce a seed. They must live off another plant or animal to get their food.

Invasion of the Mold (cont.)

Data-Capture Sheet

Draw a picture of what grew on each medium.

Moistened Bread	**Dry Bread**
Sand	**Sand with Jelly**

In your own words explain what your findings are. _____

_____

_____

_____

_____

Moldy Old Cheese

Learn more about growing simple plants.

Materials

- small piece of Muenster cheese
- small piece of Brie or Camembert cheese
- small piece of Roquefort or blue cheese
- 1 oz. (90 g) of cream cheese
- knife
- large-eyed needle
- straight pin

- waxed paper
- measuring spoons
- shallow dish
- pencil with an eraser
- magnifying glass
- data-capture sheets (pages 213 and 214)

Procedure

1. Cut three pieces of Muenster cheese.

2. Using a knife, scrape some mold off the Brie or the Camembert cheese.

3. Slide the mold onto a piece of Muenster cheese.

4. Wrap the cheese in waxed paper for some protection against airborne organisms.

5. Mix $\frac{1}{2}$ teaspoon (2.5 g) of Brie cheese mold with $\frac{1}{2}$ teaspoon (2.5 mL) of water.

6. Spread mixture over the second Muenster cube and a piece of cream cheese.

7. Let the water from the mixture evaporate, and wrap with waxed paper.

8. Construct an inoculation needle by sticking the large-eyed needle into the eraser of your pencil.

9. Punch some holes in the third cube of Muenster cheese and in some cream cheese.

10. Scrape some blue cheese from the Roquefort and put it into the holes you made.

11. Wrap the Muenster and cream cheese in waxed paper.

12. Using your straight pin, punch holes into the paper on all sides of the remaining pieces of cheese.

13. It will need to be set in a safe place for 17 days. Keep at room temperature! Be sure to place the cheese/materials where no one will eat them.

14. Observe and record information on your data-capture sheet.

The Big Why

A cheese manufacturer moved his/her factory. The cheese did not ripen properly in the new location. A worker took some cheese that was made in the old location and rubbed it on the walls. The new cheese ripened properly after that. How did this happen?

Mold cultures must be transferred from one kind of cheese to another. Mold is a type of fungus that forms a fuzzy coating on the surface of damp, or decaying substances.

Moldy Old Cheese (cont.)

Data-Capture Sheet

Draw and describe what your cheese looks like.

	Cube 1	Cube 2	Cube 3
Day 3			
Day 6			
Day 9			

Moldy Old Cheese (cont.)

Data-Capture Sheet *(cont.)*

Draw and describe what your cheese looks like.

	Cube 1	Cube 2	Cube 3
Day 12			
Day 14			
Day 17			

The Sun's Energy

Learn about how plants grow.

Materials

- two plants (Use the same kind and size of plants.)
- water

Procedure

1. Label one plant "More Light." Keep it in a sunny window.

2. Label one plant "Less Light." Keep it in an enclosed area except for putting it in a sunny window two hours each day.

3. Water both plants the same.

4. Check the plants every day for two weeks.

5. Use the chart below to record your observations. Complete a section at the end of each week.

More Light	**Less Light**
End of Week 1	End of Week 1
End of Week 2	End of Week 2

6. Do the results reflect what you thought would happen?

7. What did you learn?

The Big Why

The sun gives the leaves of a plant the energy they need to make food.

Get To the Root of It!

Learn about the function of plant roots.

Materials

- paper towel
- plastic sandwich bag
- several kinds of seeds

Procedure

1. Fold a paper towel into four parts.

2. Place the folded towel flat inside a sandwich bag.

3. Put the seeds on top of the paper towel inside the bag.

4. Wet the towel.

5. Close the bag.

6. Put your bag on a countertop and wait for results.

7. Observe what happens to the seeds. In the box, draw a picture of what you see at the end of the experiment.

8. Do the results reflect what you thought would happen? _____

9. What did you learn? _____

_____

The Big Why

Roots are formed from the growing seedling. The roots find and take in the water and minerals that a plant needs to live and grow. They also hold the plant in place.

Growing, Growing, Grown

Learn about plant growth.

Materials

- seeds (Bean or radish seeds grow quickly.)
- potting soil
- paper cups (or a planter)
- ruler

Procedure

1. Put potting soil in the paper cups.

2. Plant two or three seeds. If you are using packaged seeds, follow the directions on the package. Otherwise, place the seeds about an inch (2.5 cm) below the top of the soil.

3. Water the seeds, making sure not to overwater them. Put them in a place where they can get some sunlight for at least part of the day.

4. Continue to water the seeds as needed.

5. Observe the plants as they grow. Use the space below to keep a record of the observations you make every two or three days. Begin by recording the date and writing down exactly what you see. Then use your ruler to take measurements as your plants grow. Draw a sketch to show what your plants look like.

Record of Observations	**Record of Observations**
Date:	Date:
Record of Observations	**Record of Observations**
Date:	Date:

Flowers

Learn about the parts of a flower.

Materials

- a flower
- craft knife
- magnifying glass
- transparent tape
- plastic wrap
- copy of the Flower Identification Sheet (page 219)
- data-capture sheet (page 220)

Procedure

1. Put your flower on your data-capture sheet and examine it.

2. Compare your flower to the diagram on your Flower Identification Sheet (page 219). Can you find similar parts? You may need your magnifying glass to help you.

3. Carefully take your flower apart. Extra care is needed when using a craft knife.

4. Use transparent tape to attach your flower parts to your data-capture sheet (page 220).

5. Label the parts of your flower and cover your data-capture sheet with plastic wrap.

6. Research why each part of a flower is important to a plant.

Flowers (cont.)

Flower Identification Sheet

Parts of a Flower

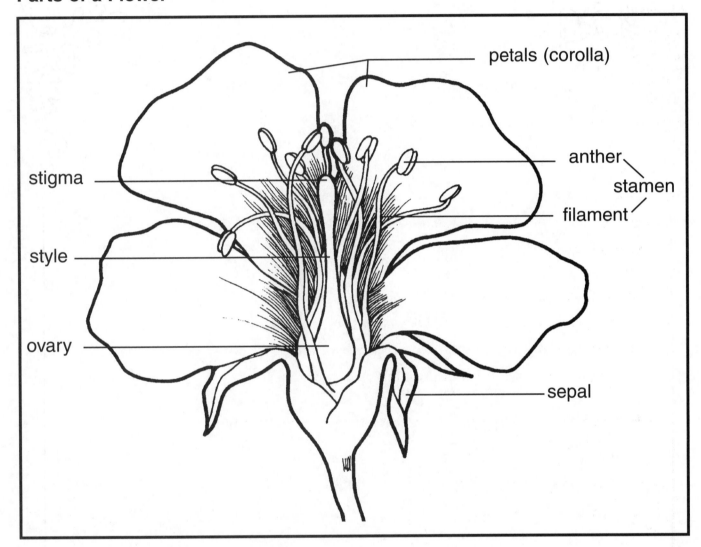

petals (corolla)

anther

stamen

filament

stigma

style

ovary

sepal

Flowers (cont.)

Data Capture Sheet

Use transparent tape to attach your flower inside this frame.

Stems

Learn about the function of stems.

Materials

- celery stalk
- glass
- dark food coloring

Procedure

1. Put a stalk of celery in a glass of colored water. Leave it in the glass for one day.

2. Observe what happens. Draw pictures in the BEFORE and AFTER boxes to show the results.

BEFORE

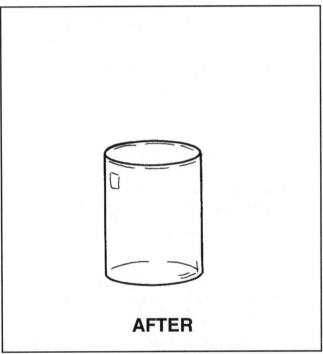

AFTER

3. Write why you think this happened. _____

_____

_____

_____

_____

The Big Why

Stems carry water and minerals from the roots to the leaves. They carry the materials in the leaves to all parts of the plant. Stems also hold the leaves and flowers up in the air so they can get light.

How Does Your Garden Grow?

Learn about the growth of seeds.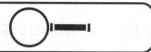

Materials

- jar with top
- paper towels
- data-capture sheet (page 223)
- seeds (e.g., bean, pea, lentil, flower, vegetable)
- water

Procedure

1. Choose ten different kinds of seeds. Record the seeds you chose on your data-capture sheet.

2. Soak your seeds in water overnight.

3. Prepare the jar. Cut two paper towels to the height of the jar. Cut the length so that the top of the paper fits just to the rim of the jar top.

4. Wet the inside of the jar. Line the jar with the paper towels. The dampness inside the jar should help the paper towels to stick to the jar.

5. Put 1" (2.5 cm) of water into the jar.

6. Carefully tuck each seed between the toweling near the top of the jar and screw on the lid.

7. Watch the seeds daily. Add a little water if necessary. Be sure to keep the toweling moist.

8. Draw a picture of your seedlings every 2-3 days on your data-capture sheet.

9. Do some research about angiosperms and gymnosperms. Examine your seeds to determine if they are angiosperms or gymnosperms.

10. Record the differences on your data-capture sheet.

1.

2.

3.

4. & 5.

6.

How Does Your Garden Grow? (cont.)

Data-Capture Sheet

Draw and label your seeds.

Measure and record the length of the seed tails.

Record the progress of your seeds.

Which seeds sprouted first? _____

Which sprouted next? _____

Which sprouted last? _____

What does this experiment tell you about angiosperms and gymnosperms?

_____

It's Not Easy Being Green

Learn about what makes some plants green.

Materials

- two green plants
- petroleum jelly
- data-capture sheet (page 225)

Procedure

1. Place the two plants next to each other in the sun.

2. Carefully rub the petroleum jelly on all the leaves of one of the green plants. Be sure to coat both the tops and bottoms of the leaves.

3. Observe your plants every other day for two weeks.

4. Record the results of your plants' progress on your data-capture sheet.

The Big Why

Why are some plants green? Chloroplasts are responsible for the green color in plants, but not all plants contain chloroplasts. Plants which are not green do not have chloroplasts. Only green plants produce their own food. Chloroplasts contain the substance chlorophyll, which is green. Chlorophyll plays an important part in the food-making process (photosynthesis) of a plant. *Photo* means light, and *synthesis* means to combine simple elements into a more complex one. Simply said, photosynthesis is the plant using light to make its own food. During photosynthesis, light from the sun is captured by the chloroplasts as light energy. The light energy combines with the water and carbon dioxide found in the cell and reacts to make glucose and oxygen.

$$\text{water} + \text{carbon dioxide} \xrightarrow{\text{light energy}} \text{glucose (sugar)} + \text{oxygen}$$

It's Not Easy Being Green (cont.)

Data-Capture Sheet

Draw a picture every other day of your plants and comment about what happened to your plants at the end of your experience.

Day 1

Day 3

Day 5

_____
_____
_____
_____
_____

_____
_____
_____
_____
_____

_____
_____
_____
_____
_____

Day 7

Day 9

Day 11

_____
_____
_____
_____
_____

_____
_____
_____
_____
_____

_____
_____
_____
_____
_____

What happened? _____

_____

_____

_____

_____

Cardinal Points

There are four directions that are of prime importance when we learn our way around the world in which we live. These directions are north, south, east, and west, and they are sometimes referred to as the four cardinal points. Cardinal points are shown on maps by the use of a compass rose.

There are several ways to make a compass rose.

North and south indicators are often longer than east and west indicators.

Fill in the direction words that are missing.

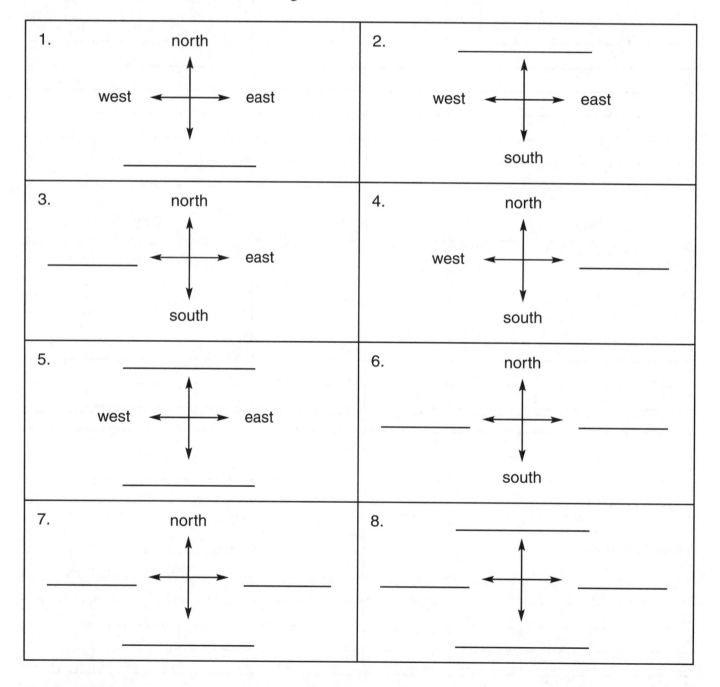

Through the Squares

Can you find your way through the squares by following the directions? Color your path as you go.
Write your name in the square where you finish.

1. Start above the square marked start here.

2. Go south 5 squares.

3. Go east 2 squares.

4. Go north 3 squares.

5. Go east 4 squares.

6. Go south 2 squares.

7. Go west 3 squares.

8. Go south 3 squares.

9. Go west 4 squares.

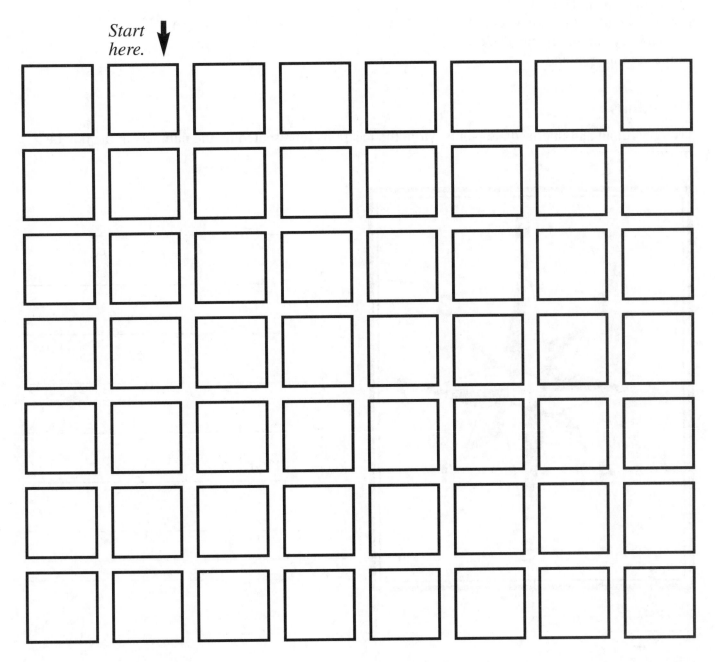

Start here.

Intermediate Points

You are familiar with the four cardinal points used to indicate the primary directions. There are times when directions cannot be given using simply north, south, east, or west. You need to be able to show points that come between the four primary directions.

Intermediate points give a map maker just such a tool. Study the compass rose on the right. As you can see, the new direction words are made by combining the names of the cardinal points.

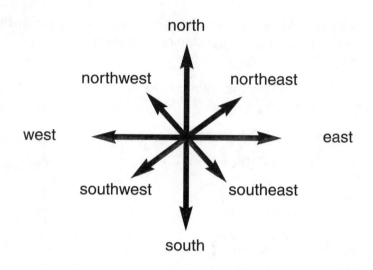

Directions

Using cardinal and intermediate points, write the locations represented by the numbers in the box on the left.

1. _____

2. _____

3. _____

4. _____

5. _____

6. _north_____

7. _____

8. _____

Scale

Map makers can make things on a map larger or smaller than they really are. They can do this by using a map scale. A map scale shows us a way to measure distance. We are told by the scale what kind of measurement equals what kind of distance.

Look at this scale. One inch represents one mile. A road five miles long can be shown on the map as five inches. A road 10 miles long can be shown as 10 inches.

Look at this scale. One centimeter stands for 1 kilometer. A road five kilometers long can be shown on the map as five centimeters. A road 10 kilometers long can be shown as 10 centimeters.

Directions

Use the scales on this page to complete the activities below.

1. Point A is _____ miles from Point F.

   _____ kilometers from Point E.

   _____ kilometers from Point C.

2. Point B is _____ kilometers from Point A.

   _____ kilometers from Point G.

   _____ kilometers from Point E.

3. Point H is _____ miles from Point D.

   _____ miles from Point A.

   _____ miles from Point F.

How Far?

Directions

Use this map scale and metric ruler to answer the distance questions on this page.

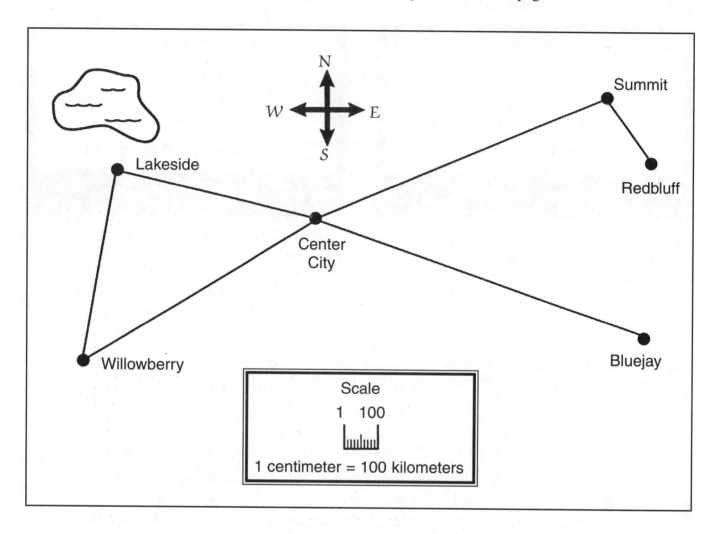

1. Center City is _____ kilometers from Bluejay.

2. Summit is _____ kilometers from Redbluff.

3. Willowberry is _____ kilometers from Lakeside.

4. Bluejay is _____ kilometers from Lakeside.

5. Summit is _____ kilometers from Center City.

6. Center City is _____ kilometers from Lakeside.

7. Willowberry is _____ kilometers from Summit.

8. Center City is _____ kilometers from Willowberry.

How to Measure

When you measure distances using a map scale, you can measure several different ways. The easiest and most accurate way is to use a standard-measure or metric-measure ruler.

You can also use a piece of string, paper, the joints of your fingers, a pencil or pen, or other things that could help you mark size.

Once you have chosen your measurement, place it along the imaginary or real line between the distances you want to measure.

Directions

Find the distance in miles between the following places:

1. Rivertown and the airport _____

2. Mountaintown and the forest_____

3. Rivertown and Laketown_____

4. Mountaintown and Pleasantown _____

5. Laketown and Mountaintown _____

6. Rivertown and the forest _____

I've Got the Key!

Map makers draw the symbols that are in a map key. The map key explains what each symbol represents.

Directions

Look at this map and the map key. Use them to answer **true** or **false** for the statements below. If a statement is false, write the correct answer on the back of this paper.

Map Key

mountains

lake

major highway

local road

railroad

town

forest

1. _____ A railroad track runs southwest to northeast.

2. _____ Mountains cover the northern section of the map.

3. _____ A lake and a forest are in the southeast.

4. _____ All towns can be reached by the major highway.

5. _____ There are towns along the railroad track.

6. _____ There is a large forest east of the lake and west of the railroad.

7. _____ The southernmost town is next to the major highway.

232

Using Grids

A grid is an arrangement of blocks that are made by vertical and horizontal lines intersecting on a page. Numbers and letters are used on the grid to help you name the blocks. You can find something on a grid by putting a finger of your right hand on a number and a finger of your left hand on a letter. Then, slide your fingers together until they meet. When grid points are identified, the letter is written before the number.

Grid A

	1	2	3	4
A	white	yellow	orange	gold
B	pink	green	tan	red
C	blue	purple	brown	silver
D	black	ivory	gray	lavender

Grid B

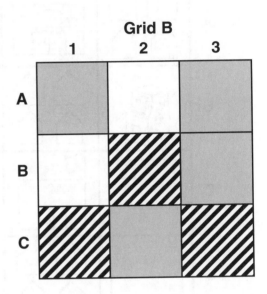

Directions

1. Use grid A to name each of the following colors:

A1 _____   D3 _____   B4 _____   D2 _____

C4 _____   A2 _____   D1 _____   C2 _____

B3 _____   A4 _____   C3 _____   B1 _____

D4 _____   B2 _____   A3 _____   C1 _____

2. Use grid B to answer these questions.

Which blocks are shaded?   _____

Which blocks are striped?   _____

Which blocks are unmarked?   _____

Where in This City?

Directions

Use the grid on the city map to find the places listed at the bottom of the page. Write the letter before the number for each place you find.

	1	2	3	4	5	6
A		Park Restaurant				City Zoo
B	Arcade		Green Park		Post Office	
C	The Mall Shops	High School		Town Hall		Grocery Store
D	The Mall Shops		Police Station	Fire Station	City Bank	
E		Medical Center	Sammy's Diner		Elementary School	Ball Field
F	Wilson's Factory		Machinery			

1. Medical Center _____

2. Machinery Warehouse _____

3. The Mall Shops _____, _____, and _____

4. Elementary School _____

5. Sammy's Diner _____

6. Green Park _____, _____, _____, and _____

7. Wilson's Factory _____, _____

8. City Zoo _____ and _____

9. City Bank _____

10. Town Hall _____

11. Ball Field _____

12. Arcade _____

13. Fire Station _____

14. Post Office _____

15. Grocery Store _____

16. High School _____

Your Map, Your Key

Directions

Create your own map on this page. Add map key symbols. Draw a compass rose on your map, too.

Map Key

The Equator and Hemispheres

The earth is divided into two parts by an imaginary line called the equator. The part of the earth that is north of the equator is called the Northern Hemisphere. The part of the earth that is south of the equator is called the Southern Hemisphere.

The equator is like an imaginary line that divides the sphere of the earth into two half spheres, or hemispheres.

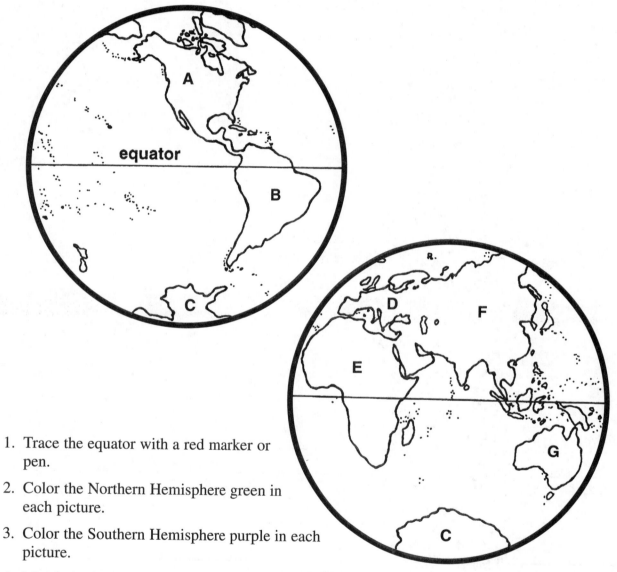

1. Trace the equator with a red marker or pen.

2. Color the Northern Hemisphere green in each picture.

3. Color the Southern Hemisphere purple in each picture.

4. Match the letters below to their locations on the maps above. Write the names of the continents next to their matching letters.

A. _____   E. _____

B. _____   F. _____

C. _____   G. _____

D. _____

Where Is It?

Use the hemisphere maps on this page to help you locate the correct hemispheres for the places listed below.

Hemisphere Location Chart		
Place	Hemisphere (Northern or Southern)	Hemisphere (Eastern or Western)
1. South Africa		
2. Norway		
3. Venezuela		
4. Canada		
5. Japan		
6. Mexico		
7. China		
8. Egypt		
9. United States		
10. Argentina		
11. Poland		
12. Greenland		
13. India		
14. Chile		
15. Madagascar		
16. Australia		

Latitude and Longitude

You can find places in the world by knowing how to read latitude and longitude lines. **Latitude** and **longitude** lines (also called **meridian** lines) are imaginary lines that divide the earth. You have already learned one of these lines—the equator. The equator is the main line of latitude. The **prime meridian** is the main line of longitude.

Latitude

Latitude lines run from west to east. They measure distances north and south of the equator.

The equator cuts the world into north and south latitude. The equator is marked 0 degrees. The latitude lines north of the equator are marked N (degrees north) and the latitude lines south of the equator are marked S (degrees south).

Longitude

Longitude lines run from north to south, pole to pole. They measure distances west and east of the prime meridian.

The prime meridian cuts the world into west and east longitudes. The longitude lines west of the prime meridian are marked W (degrees west) and the longitude lines east of the prime meridian are marked E (degrees east)

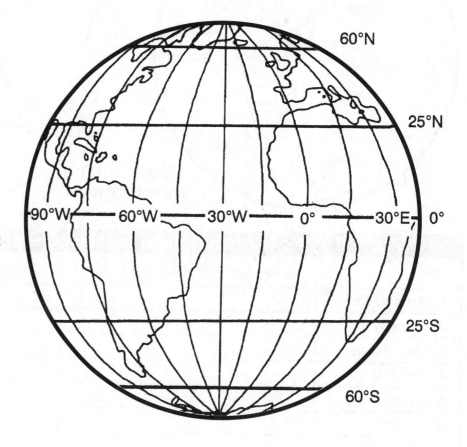

1. Which lines run from west to east?_____

2. Which lines run from north to south? _____

3. The equator is a line of (latitude or longitude)_____.

4. The prime meridian is a line of (latitude or longitude) _____.

Test Your Map Skills

Use the map on this page for the activity on pages 242 and 243.

United States

⭑ National Capital
Seattle • City
— International Boundary
— State Boundary
TX State Name

400 Miles
400 km

Test Your Map Skills (cont.)

Use a globe and the map on page 241 to answer the following questions.

1. Which mainland state is the farthest south?

_____

2. Which state is the largest?

_____

3. Which state is the smallest?

_____

4. Which states border Iowa?

_____

5. Which states are directly north of the Oklahoma border?

_____

6. Which states have shorelines on the Gulf of Mexico?

_____

7. Which state is made up of eight islands?

_____

8. Which state is farther west—Colorado or Idaho?

_____

9. What state is directly south of Wisconsin?

_____

10. Which state is farther north—New York or Virginia?

_____

Test Your Map Skills (cont.)

11. Which states border California?

    _____

12. Which states begin with the letter M?

    _____

13. Which states have shorelines on the Atlantic Ocean?

    _____

14. Which states have shorelines on the Pacific Ocean?

    _____

15. Which states have shorelines on the Great Lakes?

    _____

16. Which state reaches farthest west?

    _____

17. Which state is the farthest north?

    _____

18. Which states border on Mexico?

    _____

19. Which states border on Canada?

    _____

20. Which island has the largest United States city on it?

    _____

Geography Genius

How well do you know your world geography? As you play Geography Genius you will learn more about land formations, bodies of water, and places around the world.

Preparation

Cut out the rules below and the individual cards (pages 245–258).

(**Note:** For durability, you may wish to copy the game cards, rules, and answer key onto card stock, laminate all pieces, and store them in a box. If several groups are to play at the same time, make enough copies of the rules and the answer key so that each group has its own rule box and answer key.)

Rules for Geography Genius

This game is for three or four players and one judge.

1. The judge shuffles the cards and spreads them face down on the table.

2. The player to the judge's left goes first.

3. The first player takes a card, reads aloud the card number and question, and answers the question.

4. The judge checks the answer with the answer key.

5. Players earn points by keeping cards for questions they have answered correctly. When a player answers a question incorrectly, the card is shuffled back into the card pile to be used again.

6. When the game time is over or when all cards have been used, players count their cards. The player with the most cards is the winner.

1.

A man-made channel filled with water and used for boat transportation or for irrigation is called a _____.

2.

A deep, narrow gorge with high, steep sides that has been cut by running water is called a _____.

3.

A word meaning elevation or height above sea level is _____.

4.

The entire area that is drained by a large river is called a _____ _____.

5.

What word refers to a bay, cove, or other recess along the coast?

6.

What do we call the part of a river where it empties into a large body of water?

7.

An area of land that gets very little rainfall and has little plant life is called a _____.

8.

When a river empties into a larger body of water, it forms a triangle-shaped area of mud, sand, and silt known as a _____.

9.

When we measure the degree of hotness or coldness of an environment, we are measuring the _____.

10.

Moisture that falls from the clouds as sleet, rain, snow, or hail is known as _____.

11.

A small river that flows into a larger one is called a _____.

12.

A stream or other body of water where a river begins is called the river's _____.

13.

What landform is completely surrounded by water?

14.

What landform is surrounded by water on three sides?

15.

The periodic rise and fall of the water level of the ocean is called the _____.

16.

The rise and fall of the tide is caused by the gravitational pull of the _____.

17.

The point on a mountain above which there is snow all year round is called the _____ _____.

18.

What word is defined as a narrow passageway of water that connects two large bodies of water?

19.

What do we call the highest point of a hill or a mountain?

20.

A _____ is a large stream of water of natural origin which drains an area of land and empties into another body of water.

21.

Low, spongy ground that is too wet for farming but has abundant plant and animal life is called a _____.

22.

The point on a mountain above which no trees will grow because of the cold temperature is called the _____ _____.

23.

The average level of the ocean's surface as measured along the shoreline is known as _____ _____.

24.

A flat, elevated region of land is known as tableland or a _____.

25.

Useful materials that are found in nature such as water, minerals, and trees are called _____ _____.

26.

A small, still body of water that is smaller than a lake is called a _____.

27.

The vast area of natural grassland in the middle part of the United States is called the _____.

28.

The part of a river or stream where the water flows swiftly over rocks is called the _____.

29.

A cone-shaped mountain formed by eruption of molten rock, cinders and steam is called a _____.

30.

What is the general term for all growing plants?

31.

A _____ is a bank beside a stream or river created to prevent flooding.

32.

Imaginary lines that are used to help locate places and objects are called lines of _____ and _____.

33.

What is the imaginary line that divides the Northern Hemisphere from the Southern Hemisphere?

34.

A very large ocean inlet such as the one that separates Florida from Mexico is called a _____.

35.

The wearing away of soil and rock by wind and water is called _____.

36.

When someone recycles newspapers, cans, and plastic containers, he or she is helping to save natural resources by practicing _____.

37.

A book of maps is called an _____.

38.

The portion of a continent that is submerged beneath the ocean is called the _____ _____.

39.

The bowl-shaped depression at the top of a volcano is called a _____.

40.

The line where the earth and sky seem to meet is called the _____.

41.

A hill or a ridge of sand that is piled up by the wind is called a _____.

42.

A narrow piece of land that joins two larger areas of land is called an _____.

43.

The largest bodies of land on the earth are called _____.

44.

Name the largest continent.

45.

Name the smallest continent.

46.

On which continent is Canada located?

47.

What do we mean when we say the "contiguous" 48 states? Name the two U.S. states that are not "contiguous."

48.

What do we call a person who follows a career of mapmaking?

49.

Name the "grand" natural site in the western U.S. where the Colorado River flows.

50.

This large lake in the western U.S. has no outlet, loses water only through evaporation, and is called the _____ _____ _____.

51.

On which of the Hawaiian Islands is the capital city of Honolulu located?

52.

Name the largest island in the Hawaiian Islands group.

53.

Name the longest river in the U.S.

54.

Name the Great Lakes.

55.

The lowest place in the U.S. is in California. Name this valley.

56.

What American desert is located in Southern California?

57.

The deepest lake in the U.S. is almost 2,000 feet deep. It is in Oregon. Name this lake.

58.

The place in the world which receives the most rain is in the U.S. state of _____.

59.

On the east the U.S. is bordered by an ocean. On the west the U.S. is bordered by an ocean. Name these oceans.

60.

New York City, the largest city in the U.S., is located at the mouth of what river?

61.

The world's second largest country is located in North America. Name this country.

62.

The world's second largest lake is in North America. Name this lake.

63.

The second largest lake in the world is Lake Superior. What two countries border on this lake?

64.

What famous waterfall is located on the river that connects Lake Erie and Lake Ontario?

65.

If one travels across the Great Lakes from west to east, on which lake will one begin the trip?

66.

All of the 48 contiguous states border at least two other states except for one. Name this state that borders only one other U.S. state.

67.

The U.S. is divided into 50 states. Canada is divided into two territories and ten _____.

68.

What large U.S. river flows east and empties into the Mississippi River at St. Louis, Missouri?

69.

Name the seaway that connects the Great Lakes with the Atlantic Ocean.

70.

The city of Chicago is located on the shore of what body of water?

71.

What major U.S. river flows west and empties into the Mississippi River at Cairo, Illinois?

72.

The Rocky Mountain ridge that separates rivers that flow west to the Pacific and rivers that flow east to the Atlantic is called the _____ _____.

73.

Which Great Lake is the smallest in length and width?

74.

The best-known swamp in the U.S. is a national park in Florida. Name this swamp.

75.

Which U.S. state has a coastline on both the Atlantic Ocean and the Gulf of Mexico?

76.

Which mountain chain in the United States has the highest mountains— the Rocky Mountains or the Appalachian Mountains?

77.

Name the river that separates Texas from Mexico.

78.

What large body of water is bordered by Texas, Louisiana, Mississippi, Alabama, and Florida?

79.

What large island is located approximately 200 miles from Miami, Florida?

80.

Which of these California cities is closest to the Mexican border: Los Angeles, San Francisco, or San Diego?

81.

The Yucatan is a land area of Mexico. Is the Yucatan a mountain, a desert, or a peninsula?

82.

Baja California is a long, narrow peninsula that is part of Mexico. What U.S. state borders this peninsula on its north?

83.

If you were visiting the states of Sonora and Chihuahua, you would be in what country?

84.

The people of Mexico and other countries of Central America speak what language?

85.

What is the capital of Mexico?

86.

If you fly due south from New York City and you land in Brazil, on what continent will you be standing?

87.

The second longest river of the world is in South America. Name this river.

88.

Which country of South America has the largest area?

89.

Which country of South America is the second largest in area?

90.

Name the very high mountain range that runs 4,000 miles down the west coast of South America.

91.

What animal found in South America's Andes Mountains has been tamed to carry both people and materials?

92.

The world's largest waterfall is Angel Falls. Name the country and continent where you would go to see this famous waterfall.

93.

The world's highest city is 9,343 feet above sea level and is the capital of Ecuador in South America. Name this capital city.

94.

The driest place in the world is the Atacama Desert in a long, narrow South American country that borders Argentina. Name this country.

95.

If you left South America and sailed east along the equator, you would come to what continent?

96.

The longest river in the world is the _____ River on the continent of _____.

97.

The highest mountain in Africa is in Tanzania. Name this mountain.

98.

The largest city in Africa is the capital of Egypt. Name this capital city.

99.

Name the large body of water that borders Africa on the north.

100.

Egypt has coastline on what two seas?

101.

Africa is bordered by the _____ Ocean on the west and by the _____ Ocean on the east.

102.

The world's largest desert covers much of Northern Africa. Name this desert.

103.

Name the southernmost country of Africa.

104.

The country of South Africa is well-known for mining what valuable gems?

105.

If you were visiting the African savannah, would you be in a jungle or grassland?

106.

Name the largest country of Africa.

107.

Liberia, a country on the west coast of Africa has a capital city that is named for a U.S. President. Name this city.

108.

Name the long, narrow sea that separates Africa from the Middle East country of Saudi Arabia.

109.

Name the canal that is a passageway between the Mediterranean Sea and the Red Sea.

110.

Name the waterway through which ships pass from the Mediterranean Sea into the Atlantic Ocean.

111.

The Strait of Gibraltar separates the African country of _____ and the European country of _____.

112.

You are traveling by boat from Greece westward to Turkey. What small sea are you crossing?

113.

Which two countries of Europe are separated by the English Channel?

114.

What boot-shaped country of Europe is a peninsula that sticks out into the Mediterranean Sea?

115.

The Iberian Peninsula is surrounded by ocean on three sides. What two European countries make up this peninsula?

116.

In the Norwegian Sea, about halfway between Norway and Greenland, is the island nation of _____.

117.

The two most well-known cities of Europe are _____, the capital of England, and _____, the capital of France.

118.

Iceland, a large island in the North Atlantic Ocean is a part of what continent?

119.

Name the four countries that make up the area known as Scandinavia.

120.

Name the four countries that make up the area known as Great Britain.

121.

What mountains separate Europe from Asia?

122.

What ocean lies to the south of Asia?

123.

The largest country in Asia is also the largest country in the world. Name this country.

124.

Name the second largest country of Asia.

125.

What large desert lies in northern China and southern Mongolia?

126.

Name the large sea that borders Turkey on its north.

127.

The world's highest mountain is in Asia. Name this mountain.

128.

The world's largest city in terms of population is _____, located in the small island nation of _____.

129.

What large gulf separates Saudi Arabia from Iran?

130.

Name the large country of southern Asia that is bordered on the east by the Bay of Bengal and on the west by the Arabian Sea.

131.

Mount Everest, the world's highest mountain, is in what Asian mountain chain?

132.

Name the capital of India.

133.

Name the capital of Russia.

134.

Name the capital of China.

135.

Name the capital of Japan.

136.

What is Japan's largest island?

137.

The Asian country of _____ has more people than any other country in the world.

138.

What name is often used to refer to Europe and Asia together?

139.

The Caspian Sea is bordered on three sides by Russia. What Asian country borders the Caspian Sea on the south?

140.

The Philippines is a country made up of a group of islands lying southeast of China. Name the capital of this island country.

Answer Key for "Geography Genius"

1. canal
2. canyon
3. altitude
4. river system
5. inlet
6. mouth
7. desert
8. delta
9. temperature
10. precipitation
11. tributary
12. source
13. island
14. peninsula
15. tide
16. moon
17. snow line
18. strait
19. summit or peak
20. river
21. swamp
22. tree line
23. sea level
24. mesa or plateau
25. natural resources
26. pond
27. prairie
28. rapids
29. volcano
30. flora or vegetation
31. levee or dike
32. latitude; longitude
33. equator
34. gulf
35. erosion

36. conservation
37. atlas
38. continental shelf
39. crater
40. horizon
41. dune
42. isthmus
43. continents
44. Asia
45. Australia
46. North America
47. states that touch each other; Alaska, Hawaii
48. cartographer
49. Grand Canyon
50. Great Salt Lake
51. Oahu
52. Hawaii
53. Mississippi River
54. Huron; Ontario; Michigan; Erie; Superior
55. Death Valley
56. Mojave Desert
57. Crater Lake
58. Hawaii
59. Atlantic; Pacific
60. Hudson River
61. Canada
62. Lake Superior
63. Canada; United States
64. Niagara Falls
65. Lake Superior
66. Maine
67. provinces
68. Missouri River
69. St. Lawrence Seaway
70. Lake Michigan

Answer Key for "Geography Genius" (cont.)

71. Ohio River
72. Continental Divide
73. Lake Ontario
74. Everglades
75. Florida
76. Rocky Mountains
77. Rio Grande
78. Gulf of Mexico
79. Cuba
80. San Diego
81. peninsula
82. California
83. Mexico
84. Spanish
85. Mexico City
86. South America
87. Amazon River
88. Brazil
89. Argentina
90. Andes Mountains
91. llama
92. Venezuela, South America
93. Quito
94. Chile
95. Africa
96. Nile; Africa
97. Mount Kilimanjaro
98. Cairo
99. Mediterranean Sea
100. Mediterranean Sea; Red Sea
101. Atlantic; Indian
102. Sahara Desert
103. South Africa
104. diamonds
105. grassland

106. Sudan
107. Monrovia (named for James Monroe)
108. Red Sea
109. Suez Canal
110. Strait of Gibraltar
111. Morocco; Spain
112. Aegean Sea
113. France; England
114. Italy
115. Portugal and Spain
116. Iceland
117. London; Paris
118. Europe
119. Norway; Sweden; Finland; Denmark
120. England; Scotland; Northern Ireland; Wales
121. Ural Mountains
122. Indian Ocean
123. Russia
124. China
125. Gobi Desert
126. Black Sea
127. Mount Everest
128. Tokyo; Japan
129. Persian Gulf
130. India
131. Himalayan Mountains
132. New Delhi
133. Moscow
134. Beijing (formerly Peking)
135. Tokyo
136. Honshu
137. China
138. Eurasia
139. Iran
140. Manila

Impact

The first meetings between the Europeans and the natives of the "new world" resulted in change that profoundly affected both peoples. Some changes benefited the Europeans, but many changes had a negative impact on the Native Americans. Find out more about these changes by reading the paragraph below. Unscramble the groups of letters to make words that will complete each sentence. If you need help, use the Word Bank at the bottom of the page.

Some Europeans became (*eltwayh*) _____ from all the gold,

silver, and fur that they obtained from the (*aitvNe*) _____ Americans.

The European diet changed as new foods such as corn, (*ocaoc*) _____,

and (*mosetato*) _____ were introduced.

The Native Americans, however, did not fare well. Contagious (*seidases*) _____

were passed on to them by the explorers. (*plamSlxo*) _____ killed

close to (*enysvet-vfie*) _____ percent of the Native Americans who

once inhabited both North and South (*rAicmea*) _____. Many

others died when they were forced to (*bolar*) _____ in mines and on farms.

Their lives were changed forever as they acquired European (*solot*) _____,

weapons, and cooking (*slenutis*) _____; began to breed horses,

cows, and (*heicksnc*) _____; and grew wheat and rice.

Word Bank

diseases	Smallpox	utensils	tomatoes
tools	chickens	wealthy	America
Native	labor	cocoa	seventy-five

A Colonial Word Search

Test your knowledge of daily life in the 13 colonies. Use these clues to find the 20 words in the word search.

1. the only sport in which women could participate
2. metal from which some plates and cups were made
3. the only utensil used for eating
4. common method of punishment for criminals
5. type of home built by early Dutch settlers
6. plant used in making candles
7. girls embroidered these
8. they sold wares and spread news
9. cloth spun from the flax plant
10. dish made from wood or stale bread

11. children ages six to eight attended these
12. plant grown for its blue dye
13. windows were made by soaking cloth in this oil
14. a basic ingredient of soap
15. game in which metal rings were tossed at an iron stake
16. one page of letters fastened to a wooden frame
17. waist-length jacket worn by men
18. fried cornmeal bread
19. type of house with sloping roof
20. day of worship

o	a	l	p	p	l	i	n	s	e	e	d	m	n	i
s	t	o	s	e	y	c	u	t	a	p	i	h	d	n
f	x	h	r	w	e	e	s	i	m	p	e	u	u	d
o	o	t	e	t	v	s	t	o	c	k	s	o	g	i
e	m	a	l	e	a	k	e	u	b	o	c	f	o	g
y	a	b	d	r	e	a	d	q	h	o	g	e	u	o
r	t	b	d	b	a	t	d	o	u	b	l	e	t	w
r	r	a	e	x	u	i	h	e	u	n	e	n	i	l
e	e	s	p	o	o	n	v	l	c	r	b	b	n	j
b	n	d	e	b	e	g	d	c	m	o	o	d	a	a
y	c	z	r	t	p	f	m	y	j	h	q	z	x	o
a	h	e	f	l	j	o	h	n	n	y	c	a	k	e
b	e	g	d	a	m	e	s	c	h	o	o	l	u	k
r	r	h	t	s	a	m	p	l	e	r	s	n	r	l

Where Did It Happen?

For this activity you will need a United States and a European map with clearly marked latitude and longitude lines.

Draw a line to match each place with its grid point. Then write the matching points and answers to the questions at the bottom of the page.

London	47°N 71°W
West Point	36°N 80°W
Yorktown	41°N 74°W
Paris	37°N 76°W
Boston	35°N 82°W
Savannah	49°N 2°E
Cowpens	43°N 74°W
Guilford Courthouse	42°N 71°W
Quebec	32°N 81°W
Saratoga	51°N 0°(Prime Meridian)

1. Treaty that officially ended the Revolutionary War was signed here.

   Place _____   Grid Point_____

2. Cornwallis surrendered to Washington here.

   Place _____   Grid Point_____

3. In this place, Richard Montgomery and Benedict Arnold lost to the British.

   Place _____   Grid Point_____

4. This major Southern port was held by the British.

   Place _____   Grid Point_____

5. Victory here convinced France that the Americans could win in a war against the British.

   Place _____   Grid Point_____

6. Soon after this battle, Cornwallis decided to leave North Carolina.

   Place _____   Grid Point_____

7. This is where the taxes for the North American colonists were decided.

   Place _____   Grid Point_____

8. Patriots dressed as Indians and dumped tea into this city's harbor.

   Place _____   Grid Point_____

9. Benedict Arnold asked George Washington to give him command of this defensive post.

   Place _____   Grid Point_____

10. The riflemen of the Southern Army won a battle in this cattle-grazing area.

    Place _____   Grid Point_____

Frontier Words

Frontier living generated many new words that were commonly used by the pioneers. Figure out these words by reading the clues first. Then find the coordinates on the grid below.

Write the letter that is in that space on the proper lines. (To find the coordinates, go across the first number of spaces. From there, count up the second number of spaces.)

4	l	d	s	i	g	e	m	c	p	s	u	g	l	a	t
3	f	e	a	n	r	o	i	u	i	h	e	u	o	n	d
2	p	o	h	e	m	a	s	f	c	y	m	t	p	r	s
1	c	a	e	y	l	t	g	r	o	n	d	o	a	f	s
0	1	2	3	4	5	6	7	8	9	10	11	12	13	14	15

1. ___ ___ ___ ___ ___   a prairie sod house
   3,4 13,3 2,4 11,1 10,2

2. ___ ___ ___ ___ ___ ___ ___ ___ ___ ___ ___   also known as johnnycake
   8,4 9,1 5,3 4,3 15,3 2,2 2,4 5,4 6,4 14,2 7,2

3. ___ ___ ___ ___ ___ - ___ ___ ___ ___ ___ ___   they rushed to California to find gold
   8,2 12,1 8,1 15,4 4,1   4,3 7,3 10,1 3,1 5,3 10,4

4. ___ ___ ___ ___ ___   dried buffalo manure used for fires
   8,4 3,2 9,3 13,2 3,4

5. ___ ___ ___ ___ ___ ___ ___ ___   settlers of the western frontier
   4,2 7,4 4,4 7,1 5,3 2,1 14,3 6,1 7,2

6. ___ ___ ___ ___   disease now known as malaria
   6,2 12,4 8,3 11,3

7. ___ ___ ___ ___ ___ ___ ___ ___   thieves who stole cattle
   5,3 11,4 15,2 6,1 13,4 2,3 8,1 15,1

8. prairie ___ ___ ___ ___ ___ ___ ___ ___   nickname for covered wagon
           7,2 1,1 10,3 2,2 9,1 14,3 3,1 5,3

Identify the Locations

For this activity you will need a United States map with clearly marked latitude and longitude lines.

In the two columns below, you will find places and grid points that will identify the locations of those places on a map. Draw a line to match each place with its grid point. Then write the pairs as answers to the questions at the bottom of the page.

Ohio River	39°N	78°W
Chattanooga	39°N	83°W
Vicksburg	40°N	77°W
Kansas	37°N	77°W
Andersonville	38°N	100°W
Harpers Ferry	32°N	84°W
Richmond	32°N	81°W
Savannah	33°N	80°W
Gettysburg	32°N	91°W
Fort Sumter	35°N	85°W

1. Once crossed, slaves knew they were nearly free.

    Place _____   Grid Point_____

2. The Civil War began here.

    Place _____   Grid Point_____

3. This city served as the capital of the Confederacy.

    Place _____   Grid Point_____

4. John Brown tried to start a slave rebellion in this place.

    Place _____   Grid Point_____

5. This was the key city that guarded the Mississippi River.

    Place _____   Grid Point_____

6. An overcrowded prison was located in this Confederate camp.

    Place _____   Grid Point_____

7. This was an important battle in the Tennessee campaign.

    Place _____   Grid Point_____

8. This July battle was the turning point of the war.

    Place _____   Grid Point_____

9. The first case of popular sovereignty was tested in this place.

    Place _____   Grid Point_____

10. Sherman's march through Georgia ended in this place.

    Place _____   Grid Point_____

Time Zones and Daylight Savings

Use the information below to complete the activity on page 267.

Why is it that at the time many New Yorkers are enjoying a lunchtime meal, most Californians are eating their breakfast? Why is the United States, as well as the entire globe, divided up into various sections of time?

The divisions of time that surround the earth, known as time zones, clarified some of the problems that once plagued the modernizing world. For hundreds of years each town in the United States decided what the time would be. When the sun was directly overhead, casting no shadows, it was noon. Radios and televisions had not been invented, and telephones were not available yet. Travel was slow by horse and buggy, so it really was not much of a problem that each town was in charge of its own time. In fact, it worked quite well until the railroad was built. Can you imagine how hard it was to print train schedules of arrivals and departures when each town had a different time? This confusing problem was finally resolved in 1883 when the railroad helped devise the system of standard time. Standard time means that everyone in a certain region shares the same established time. Since time zones span great distances, it is no longer necessarily true that the sun will be directly above you at noon. Today, people set their clocks and watches according to the standard time instead of by the sun.

With the new "standard time," the United States was divided into four zones going from east to west—eastern standard time, central standard time, mountain time, and Pacific standard time. Later, when Alaska and Hawaii became part of our country, we added Yukon standard time, Alaska standard time, Bering standard time and Hawaii-Aleutian standard time to the group of time zones in the United States.

In 1884 a conference with countries from all over the globe joined together to develop a system of 24 time zones around the earth. Each segment or zone is 15 longitude degrees apart from the next. It takes the earth one hour to rotate these 15 degrees. Some time zone lines are not perfectly straight because it is often more convenient to follow state or town boundaries. There is an imaginary line in the Pacific Ocean at 180 degrees longitude where all the time zones begin and end. This international dateline is where each new day first begins.

When World War I broke out, a new custom was started in keeping time. During war time resources were scarce. In order to save the coal supplies (which were burned to make electricity), it was decided to move the clocks ahead one hour. This way, there would be more light at the end of the day, and people would not need to turn on their lights as early in the evening. Even after the war ended, daylight savings time continued because people enjoyed having more daylight during the summer months. For a while it was confusing since all the states did not practice daylight savings time. Today, almost every state in our country turns its clocks ahead one hour the first Sunday in April. On the first Sunday in November the clocks are turned back one hour. "Spring ahead—fall back" may be an easier way to remember which way to move the hands on your clocks.

So the next time you sit down to eat your lunch, think about what other meals students may be eating in time zones other than your own. Now that's food for thought!

Time Zone Riddle

Directions: Circle the correct answers to each of the statements. Enter that letter in the "Your Choice" box. Once you have all 14 answers, rearrange the letters to discover the answer to the riddle at the end of the puzzle. See the example below. Do not use the answer in the example to solve the puzzle!

	True	False	Your Choice
Example: The automobile industry invented our system of time.	K	S	*S*

	True	False	Your Choice
1. Each state must vote to determine whether they are to follow daylight savings time.	M	E	
2. Some of the irregular divisions exist on the map to avoid towns being split into two time zones.	N	P	
3. The continental U.S. has 4 time zones.	D	M	
4. Turn your clock back one hour in the fall when daylight savings is finished for the year.	A	C	
5. Daylight savings time was started during World War II to save fuel.	B	C	
6. There are 20 time zones in the world.	N	U	
7. After World War I ended, daylight savings time continued because people liked having the extra daylight.	I	T	
8. In 1884, representatives gathered to develop a standard system of time.	L	W	
9. It takes the earth one hour to rotate 15 degrees of longitude.	N	S	
10. If you never adjust your clocks to daylight savings time, you will be on time for about eight months of the year.	F	R	
11. When the sun is directly overhead, it must be 12:00 noon in all areas of the time zone.	L	D	
12. We turn our clocks ahead one hour in the spring.	H	D	
13. The U.S. government devised the first standardized system of time.	S	N	
14. The grand international dateline is where each new day begins.	E	N	

Unscramble all of the letters that you have collected in the "Your Choice" column and solve the following riddle. Do not include the example letter in the riddle answer.

What are two things a cowboy cannot eat for breakfast?

____ ____ ____ ____ ____   ____ ____ ____ ____ ____ ____ ____

Famous Faces of WWI

Match the names of the following people with their involvement in World War I. You may use a variety of resource materials to help you.

A. He wrote the words to a famous World War I song.

_____ Archduke Francis Ferdinand

B. His assassination initiated the beginning of World War I.

_____ Woodrow Wilson

C. He wore a black moustache, stood straight and rigid, and had been the bold leader of Germany since 1890.

_____ General Ferdinand Foch

D. He urged the passing of the League of Nations and wrote the famous Fourteen Points.

_____ Captain Eddie Rickenbacker

_____ Lt. Colonel Wise

E. He was chosen to be the commander in chief of the American Expeditionary Force.

F. He was the commander in chief of the French Army.

_____ George M. Cohan

G. He was named the Supreme Allied Commander.

_____ Hans Otto Bischoff

H. He was the commander of the British Fifth Army.

_____ Kaiser Wilhelm

I. He directed the German defense at Belleau Wood.

_____ General John "Black Jack" Pershing

J. His battalion had stopped the Germans at their closest point to Paris.

_____ General Sir Hubert Gough

K. He was America's leading ace of World War I.

_____ General Henri Pétain

Events of the Great War

Listed below are events that occurred during World War I. Create a time line and place each event on the line.

- President Wilson revealed his "Fourteen Points."
- First Armistice Day
- Belgium was invaded by Germany.

- United States declared war on Germany.
- Germans first used chlorine gas.
- British first used army tanks.

June 28, 1914   Archduke Francis Ferdinand was assassinated.

August 3, 1914   _____.

October 30, 1914   Turkey joined the Central Powers.

April 22, 1915   _____.

May 7, 1915   German submarine sank the *Lusitania*.

September 15, 1916   _____.

December 5, 1916   The Allies finally stopped the Germans in the Battle of Verdun.

April 6, 1917   _____.

November 7, 1917   The Bolsheviks took over Russia.

January 8, 1918   _____.

September 26, 1918   Allies began their last attack on the Western Front.

November 11, 1918   _____.

Extension:

On Armistice Day, the German army surrendered to the Allies. Armistice today is now called Veterans Day, and it is a time set aside to honor war veterans. Research this day and contact your local veterans groups for more information.

Time Line of World Events, 1933-1945

Use your knowledge of World War II and research skills to match the event with the correct date.

Event

_____ 1. General Montgomery leads the Allies to a victory over the Axis troops in North Africa.

_____ 2. The Germans take over Austria.

_____ 3. Adolf Hitler becomes the leader of Germany.

_____ 4. Japanese planes bomb the United States naval base at Pearl Harbor.

_____ 5. The Japanese attack China.

_____ 6. Germany surrenders (V-E Day) and Japan surrenders (V-J Day).

_____ 7. Japan takes over the Philippines.

_____ 8. Poland is invaded by German and Soviet troops.

_____ 9. The Allies send invasion forces to Normandy, France.

_____ 10. Franklin D. Roosevelt is re-elected as president of the United States for a third term.

Date

A. 1940

B. 1933

C. 1945

D. 1941

E. 1944

F. 1937

G. 1938

H. 1939

I. 1942

J. 1943

Now, use the dates and events that you matched above to construct a time line for World War II.

Time Line of World Events, 1933–1945

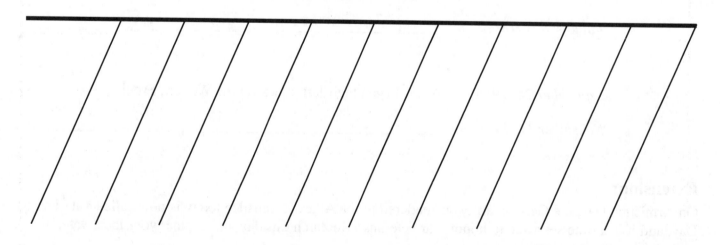

In the Know

This brief study guide lists, defines, and explains six documents that played an important role in the history of the Constitution. After you have studied, test your knowledge with a partner. One partner reads the name of each document aloud, while the other partner describes the term in as much detail as possible. Then trade roles. You can also play a matching or concentration game after cutting the cards apart.

Document	Explanation
Declaration of Independence	One of the most famous documents in the world, it officially declared the American colonies free and independent from British rule. It was signed into effect on July 4, 1776.
Articles of Confederation	During the Revolution, the thirteen states wrote a set of governing rules. This document unified them in their fight against the British. Each state had only one vote and the rules could not be changed unless every state agreed.
Virginia Plan	This document did away with the "one state—one vote" rule and suggested two houses of Congress. Edmund Randolph's plan further called for three branches of government—the Executive, the Legislative, and the Judicial.
Great Compromise	An alternate plan of electing officials was designed by a specially appointed committee. In this plan, Congress would have two houses. One house (Representatives) would be based on population and in the other house (Senate) each state was considered equal with two votes each.
Constitution	This is the basic set of laws for our nation. It contains rules for writing and passing the laws which affect every citizen. A group of 55 delegates wrote these provisions during a four-month period in 1787.
Bill of Rights	These first 10 amendments to the Constitution list those things the government cannot take away from its citizens. They protect the individual from the power of the government.

Which Came First?

Work with a partner. Read the following pairs and determine which came first. Circle the appropriate answer for each set of choices.

1.	the Continental Congress	or	the Constitutional Convention
2.	the War of 1813	or	the Revolutionary War
3.	James Madison	or	Ben Franklin
4.	ratification by Rhode Island	or	ratification by New Hampshire
5.	Constitution	or	Articles of Confederation
6.	Whisky Rebellion	or	Shay's Rebellion
7.	Federalists	or	Republican Party
8.	Louisiana Purchase	or	Treaty of Ghent
9.	Great Compromise	or	Virginia Plan
10.	Capitol in Washington, D.C.	or	Capitol in Philadelphia
11.	Bill of Rights	or	Constitution
12.	ratification by New York	or	ratification by North Carolina
13.	Preamble	or	Virginia Plan
14.	U.S. freedom from England	or	U.S. becomes a nation
15.	the Federalist Papers	or	Bill of Rights
16.	Declaration of Independence	or	Constitutional Convention
17.	"Star-Spangled Banner"	or	"Yankee Doodle"
18.	Sedition Act	or	Embargo Act

Citizenship Test

People who apply to become United States citizens must answer 10 or 15 randomly selected questions about American history and government. Below are a few from the list of 100 possible questions. Could you pass the test?

1. What do the stripes on the American flag represent? _____
_____
_____

2. What country did we fight during the Revolutionary War? _____

3. What are the three branches of our government? _____
_____

4. Who becomes president should the president and vice president die?_____

5. What did the Emancipation Proclamation do? _____
_____

6. Who has the power to declare war? _____

7. What kind of government does the United States have? _____

8. What are the first 10 amendments to the Constitution called?_____

9. Name one right guaranteed by the first amendment. _____

10. Who was the first president of the United States? _____

11. How many U.S. Supreme Court justices are there? _____

12. Who helped the Pilgrims in the New World? _____

13. Which countries were our enemies during World War II? _____

14. Who is the Chief Justice of the U.S. Supreme Court? _____

15. How many amendments are there to the Constitution? _____

16. How many states are there today?_____

17. What are the colors of the American flag and what does each symbolize? _____
_____
_____

18. What are the duties of Congress? _____
_____
_____

What Do You Know?

Fill in the answers to the clues by using the word parts in the box. The number of groups of letters from the box to be used in each answer is shown in parentheses. The first answer has been done for you. (**Note:** The letter groups in the box are listed so that each group must be used once.)

A	A	AD	AR	BRU	CAR	COLN	CON
DE	DY	FE	GIN	VER	HO	DAMS	WASH
ING	I	IA	KA	LAN	LAS	LIN	LU
LU	MAD	NO	NON	NIX	O	Y	ON
ROO	SE	SON	TED	TER	GRESS	VELT	VIR
MOUNT	TON						

1. Theodore Roosevelt's nickname (2) ___Teddy___

2. The face on the quarter (3) _____

3. Franklin Roosevelt's middle name (3) _____

4. The father of the Constitution (3) _____

5. A month for celebrating presidents (4) _____

6. President whose father was also a president (2) _____

7. The capital of Hawaii (4) _____

8. A president and a peanut farmer (2) _____

9. The sixteenth president (2) _____

10. The first president to resign from office (2) _____

11. An original colony (3) _____

12. The home of George Washington (2 words) (3) _____

13. The state closest to Russia (3) _____

14. A face on Mount Rushmore (3) _____

15. The Senate and House of Representatives (2) _____

American Social Studies Trivia

1. What does *"e pluribus unum"* mean? _____

2. How long is a senator's term of office? _____

3. Which president is shown on the five-dollar bill? _____

4. Where is the Alamo? _____

5. During what years was the Civil War fought? _____

6. Who wrote "The Pledge of Allegiance"? _____

7. The president is chief of which branch of government? _____

8. Which president's former occupation was acting? _____

9. On the flag, what does red signify? _____

10. Who became president after Dwight D. Eisenhower? _____

11. Who invented the cotton gin? _____

12. Which was the last state to join the Union? _____

13. On the Statue of Liberty, is Miss Liberty carrying the torch in her left or her right hand? _____

14. Which English explorer sailed along the West Coast in 1579? _____

_____

15. What is the official song of the president of the United States? _____

_____

Famous Women

Match these women to their major accomplishments. Put the letter of the accomplishment before the corresponding name.

_____ 1. Harriet Tubman

_____ 2. Harriet Beecher Stowe

_____ 3. Grandma Moses

_____ 4. Juliette Gordon Low

_____ 5. Shirley Chisholm

_____ 6. Pearl S. Buck

_____ 7. Mary McLeod Bethune

_____ 8. Clara Barton

_____ 9. Louisa May Alcott

_____ 10. Susan B. Anthony

_____ 11. Jane Addams

_____ 12. Amelia Earhart

_____ 13. Helen Hayes

_____ 14. Helen Keller

_____ 15. Victoria C. Woodhull

A. social worker and humanitarian

B. primitive painter

C. novelist and reformer

D. stage and screen actress

E. author of *The Good Earth*

F. aviator

G. author of *Little Women*

H. educator who worked to improve educational opportunities for blacks

I. significant "conductor" of the Underground Railroad

J. first woman to run for president of the U.S.

K. first African American woman in the U.S. Congress

L. founded the Girl Scouts of America

M. founded the American Red Cross

N. overcame physical handicaps; helped thousands of handicapped people lead fuller lives

O. reformer and leader in the American women's suffrage movement

Presidents' First Names

Listed below are some last names of former presidents. Write each president's first name on the blank.

1. _____ Adams

2. _____ Eisenhower

3. _____ Reagan

4. _____ Jefferson

5. _____ Nixon

6. _____ Lincoln

7. _____ Carter

8. _____ Hoover

9. _____ Roosevelt

10. _____ Washington

11. _____ Coolidge

12. _____ Cleveland

13. _____ Grant

14. _____ Taylor

15. _____ Harrison

16. _____ Truman

17. _____ Buchanan

18. _____ Polk

19. _____ Garfield

20. _____ Johnson

Which President?

1. Which president was nicknamed "Honest Abe"? _____

2. Which president was called the "Father of the Constitution"?

_____

3. Which president and his wife were the first to occupy the White House in Washington, D.C.? _____

4. Which future president was the author of the *Declaration of Independence*?
_____

5. Which president was the only one to serve two nonconsecutive terms of office? _____

6. Which president was nicknamed "Old Rough and Ready"?

_____

7. Which president was assassinated in Ford's Theater? _____

8. Which two presidents are buried in Arlington National Cemetery?

_____

9. Which president served more than two terms? _____

10. Which president was in office when the White House was set on fire?

_____

11. Which president was the grandson of another president?

_____

12. Which president was the shortest? _____

13. Which president never married? _____

14. Which president was the first to talk to a man on the moon?

_____

15. Which seven presidents were/are left-handed? _____

_____

_____

Answer Key

Page 9

photography, Mo-Qu
dinosaurs, Cu-Ex
Hawaii, Gy-Ju
chocolate, A-Cu
rattlesnakes, Qu-Ty
lightning, Ju-Mo
wildflowers, We-Z
computers, A-Cu
Beatles, The, A-Cu
volcanoes, Ty-We
space shuttle, Qu-Ty
gorillas, Ex-Gy

Page 10

1. fact
2. opinion
3. opinion
4. fact
5. fact
6. opinion
7. opinion
8. fact
9. fact
10. opinion

Page 17

Nouns:
1. summer time year
2. weather children swimming
3. schools people time vacation
4. days hours sunlight
5. pool beach lake
6. teacher Mr. Dawson Metropolitan Museum of Art New York City July
7. care concern visitors
8. friends Tim Carol Statue of Liberty Ellis Island
9. scent flowers Central Park lunch
10. hamburgers grill backyard

Person:
   Ms. Lizt
   Dr. Forest

Place:
   France
   city
   building
   Texas

Thing:
   clouds
   shoelaces
   bicycles
   sounds
   glasses
   table

Idea:
   happiness
   science
   loyalty
   fairness
   love
   pain

Page 18

1. action
2. action
3. linking
4. linking
5. linking
6. action
7. linking
8. action
9. action
10. action
11. action
12. linking
13. linking
14. linking

Page 20

A.1. beautiful
2. slowly
3. thinly
4. very
B.1. pretty
2. big
3. green
4. happy
5. thin

6. round
7. wet
8. excellent
9. broken
10. smelly
C.1. slowly
2. quickly
3. quickly
4. down
5. joyfully
6. sloppily
7. closely
8. loudly
9. badly
10. wildly

Page 23

1. All birds have feathers, wings, and beaks.
2. My sister is sleepy, grumpy, and clueless.
3. I would have done my homework, but I was abducted by aliens, was left in Siberia, and had to wait for the Marines to rescue me.
4. I ordered a pizza with cheese, pickles, and sliced cherries.
5. Please go to the store and get flypaper, chopsticks, and kumquats.
6. I went to the door with rollers in my hair, a mud mask on my face, and wearing my bathrobe.
7. My dog has brown spots, a short tail, and fuzzy feet.
8. My little brother can't go anywhere without his blanket, his stuffed duck, and his rabbit's foot key chain.
9. When I go to college, I am taking a stereo, a microwave, and a treadmill.
10. For her birthday, Mindy wants some edible flowers, sparkly socks, and a pony.

Answer Key (cont.)

1. My rabbit has long, floppy ears.
2. A large, heavy sparrow could weigh 200 pounds.
3. My teacher has a green, pointy nose.
4. My dad used to have curly, frizzy hair.
5. A friendly, playful giraffe ate all my spaghetti.

Page 24

A.

1. My parents bought their first home on January 13, 1976.
2. My mon was born on March 31, 1948.
3. We went to Disneyland on Tuesday, August 18, and it was really crowded!
4. My brother's birthday is November 17, 1973.
5. On Saturday, April 19, we are flying to my grandma's house.
6. I get my tonsils out on Monday, September 16, and then I can eat lots of ice cream.
7. Our puppies were born on February 14, 1997.
8. It rained cats and dogs on January 18, 1995.

C.

1. Yesterday, I met a girl from Canberra, Australia.
2. A hurricane went on shore at Acapulco, Mexico.
3. I've never been to Seattle, Washington.
4. It can get very cold in Buffalo, New York.
5. Yesterday I received e-mail from Bordeaux, France.
6. Many movie stars live in La Canada-Flintridge, California.
7. Alexandria, Virginia, is an interesting historic town.

8. You can take a great train ride in Durango, Colorado.
9. Have you been on the roller coasters in St. Louis, Missouri?
10. The mountains are really high in Vail, Colorado.

Page 25

1. H
2. Halloween, Hanukkah

Page 26

1. Amanda Panda
2. Jeffrey R. Hardy
3. Carlos Custard Appleseed
4. Gilbert McGillicutty
5. Leslie Q. Presley

Page 27

1. I love my purple bicycle!
2. I saved enough money to buy it last year.
3. Would you like to try it?
4. My brother has a blue bicycle.
5. One time he crashed into me, and I fell off my bike.
6. Have you ever fallen off your bike?
7. Did you skin your knee?
8. I was so mad at my brother!
9. He told me he was sorry.
10. I'm so glad that my bike did not break. Or: I'm so glad that my bike did not break!
11. Watch out for the glass in the road!
12. Don't ride your bike in the street! Or Don't ride your bike in the street.
13. Can you park a bike right here?
14. I have to go inside now.
15. Will I see you tomorrow?

Page 28

1. The first day of school is exciting.
2. Freddy Wilson's frog Peepers hopped into Mrs. Woolsey's purse.
3. As I walked outside, I smelled smoke.
4. In the play, Robin Hood was played by Lieutenant Bronksy.
5. The fourth Thursday in November is Thanksgiving.
6. I like Halloween best when it is on a Saturday.
7. Aunt Susan went to Yellowstone National Park.
8. Connie lives on Maple Street in Bismark, North Dakota.
9. Brazil, Argentina, and Peru are in South America.
10. The Mediterranean Sea and the Atlantic Ocean touch Spain.
11. The letter was signed, "Love always, Esther."
12. Davis Medical Center opened in January last year.
13. One of the religions practiced by many African people is Islam.
14. Italians and Germans belong to the Caucasian race.
15. Last Tuesday Ruben walked his dog Spotty down Tulip Street to Central Park.

Page 32

B.

1 bait a hook

3 clean a fish

5 eat a fish

2 catch a fish

4 cook a fish

C.

4 mail the letter

2 put the letter in an envelope

1 write a letter

5 wait for an answer

3 seal the letter

Answer Key (cont.)

D.

3 write a book report

2 click on word processing

4 turn on the printer

1 turn on the computer

5 print book the report

E.

4 slap your arm

2 see a mosquito

3 feel a bite

1 hear a buzz

5 scratch a bump

F.

3 buy popcorn

5 leave the theater

1 stand in line

2 buy a ticket

4 watch a movie

G.

2 find an old Halloween mask

1 clean up your room

4 sneak up on your brother

3 put it on

5 jump out at him

H.

3 snap on the leash

5 guide your dog back home

1 get the leash

2 whistle for your dog

4 walk your dog

Page 37

A.

1. c	4. b
2. d	5. a
3. e	

B.

1. His accomplishments were as follows: He was a painter, a publisher, a writer, an inventor, a scientist, a diplomat, a statesman, and an inspiration to others.

2. He decided to devote himself to the study of science.

3. He proved that lightning was electricity and that things could be positively or negatively charged with electricity.

4. He did not patent his inventions. He wanted to share them freely with the world.

5. Answers will vary.

Page 38

A.

1. c	4. a
2. d	5. b
3. e	

B.

1. The name of the poem was "The Defense of Fort McHenry."

2. The bombardment of Fort McHenry was taking place.

3. It became the official national anthem on March 3, 1931.

4. President Herbert Hoover signed the bill.

5. Answers will vary.

Page 39

A.

1. b	4. e
2. c	5. a
3. d	

B.

1. A system of dashes and dots is used.

2. Samuel Morse developed this code.

3. No, is not used a telephone to send messages with Morse code.

4. Morse code is most commonly used in emergency situations.

5. Answers will vary.

Page 40

A.

1. b	4. d
2. c	5. a
3. e	

B.

1. You can find them at Stanley Park in Vancouver, B.C., and at Thunderbird Park in Victoria, British Columbia.

2. Totem poles have been used by Native Americans as a way to record history.

3. Animals, birds, fish, plants, or other natural objects that would represent a Native American tribe are carved on totem poles.

4. The family's symbol is at the top of the pole.

5. Answers will vary.

Page 41

A.

1. c	4. a
2. d	5. b
3. e	

B.

1. The Frisbie company began in the late 1800s.

2. They threw them to each other.

3. It was marketed as the Pluto Platter.

4. The sales of the Frisbee took off in the 1960s.

5. Answers will vary.

Page 42

A.

1. d	4. c
2. e	5. a
3. b	

B.

1. They were looking for a product to eliminate moisture from electrical circuitry and to prevent corrosion on airplanes.

2. Norman Larsen, president and head chemist at the Rocket Chemical Company, invented it.
3. It was a water displacement (WD) formula developed on his fortieth try.
4. The Friendship VII was covered with it.
5. Answers will vary.

Page 43
A.
1. c   4. e
2. b   5. a
3. d
B.
1. John Lennon started the group.
2. The name of the first group was "the Quarrymen."
3. Ringo Starr replaced Pete Best.
4. The Ed Sullivan show made them famous in America.
5. Answers will vary.

Page 44
A.
1. c   4. a
2. d   5. b
3. e
B.
1. Butchart Gardens is located in Victoria, British Columbia.
2. You can find Japanese gardens, a rose garden and a sunken garden.
3. People go and count how many flowers and buds they see.
4. Children are given an hour off of school to help count.
5. Answers will vary.

Page 45
A.
1. c   4. b
2. d   5. a
3. e

B.
1. Spider-Man is Peter Parker, the freelance photographer.
2. He got his special powers by being bitten by a spider that had been exposed to huge amounts of radiation.
3. He made a red and blue uniform for himself to wear when he was Spider-Man.
4. His uncle was killed by a burglar and as a result Spider-Man decided to devote his life to fighting crime.
5. Answers will vary.

Page 46
A.
1. b   4. c
2. e   5. a
3. d
B.
1. The first Olympics were in 776 B.C.
2. They have changed over the years.
3. The first Olympic Games were held in Greece.
4. No, the winter and summer games are held 2 years apart.
5. Answers will vary.

Page 47
A.
1. e   4. b
2. d   5. a
3. c
B.
1. Barbie made her debut in 1959.
2. Ruth Handler invented Barbie.
3. She invented Barbie for her daughter who preferred to play with dolls designed for teens.
4. Ruth Handler went on to be president of Mattel, Inc.
5. Answers will vary.

Page 48
A.
1. d   4. c
2. a   5. b
3. e
B.
1. It was the fastest selling toy for 6 months.
2. The craze did not last very long.
3. The Hula-Hoop was based on wooden hoop used by Australian youths.
4. Richard Knerr, a partner in the Wham-O toy manufacturing company, invented it.
5. Answers will vary.

Page 49
A.
1. d   4. b
2. e   5. c
3. a   6. f
B.
1. In the mid 1980s fur trade was thriving.
2. The sea otter was prized for its pelt and demand was high.
3. It is illegal to hunt sea otters today.
4. The sea otters off the coast of California are increasing.
5. Answers will vary.

Page 50
A.
1. b   4. f
2. e   5. d
3. c   6. a
B.
1. No one knows the identity of the real Spider Woman.
2. No one knows if she was born with special powers or acquired them later.
3. She concentrates intensely to create a web and does not need any separate devices.

Answer Key (cont.)

4. She can sense danger as well as an ordinary person and no better than one.
5. A criminal can only break loose from a web that is weaker and far away from Spider-Woman.
6. Answers will vary.

Page 51
A.
1. b   4. a
2. d   5. c
3. e

B.
1. Walter Elias Disney was born on December 5, 1901.
2. Walt's wife, Lillian, thought his original name, Mortimer the Mouse was too stuffy. She made it up.
3. Walt went into business with his brother, Roy.
4. Mickey Mouse's first movie was *Steamboat Willie*.
5. Answers will vary.

Page 52
A.
1. c   4. e
2. d   5. a
3. f   6. b

B.
1. Construction began for a major trans-Amazon highway.
2. Huge areas of the Amazon rain forest were cut down and burned.
3. Each family would be given a 240-acre piece of land, housing, and a small salary for a few months.
4. Schools, health facilities and other services would be available for these families.
5. The plan was a failure. Life in the rain forest was too difficult.
6. Answers will vary.

Page 53
A.
1. f   4. d
2. b   5. c
3. e   6. a

B.
1. Robin Hood was a legendary English hero.
2. A group of outlaws rescues him.
3. His faithful followers were Maid Marian, Friar Tuck, and Little John.
4. He treats them with contempt.
5. He treats them with respect.
6. Answers will vary.

Page 54
A.
1. a   4. d
2. e   5. b
3. c

B.
1. Kristi was born in Hayward, California, in 1971.
2. She was 6 years old.
3. She decided to concentrate on her singles career.
4. She won the gold medal.
5. Answers will vary.

Page 55
A.
1. c   4. e
2. d   5. b
3. a

B.
1. The zeppelins were 40 times bigger than blimps.
2. The largest and most luxurious zeppelin ever built was the Hindenburg.
3. The Hindenburg was going to America in 1937.
4. When it landed there was a loud thump, and the tail section burst into flames.
5. Answers will vary.

Page 56
A.
1. a   4. b
2. e   5. c
3. d

B.
1. The first book was *Are You there God? It's Me, Margaret*.
2. She was an A student and did as she was told.
3. She liked to read Nancy Drew mysteries, biographies, and horse stories.
4. She met and married John W. Blume and took his last name.
5. Answers will vary.

Page 57
A.
1. b   4. c
2. d   5. a
3. e

B.
1. She helped to hunt for food.
2. She met him in a shooting match.
3. She could shoot a dime that was in her husband's hand or a cigarette that was in his mouth. She also could shoot a playing card thrown in the air 90 feet away from her.
4. Her nickname was "Little Sure Shot."
5. Answers will vary.

Page 58
A.
1. b   4. a
2. d   5. c
3. e

B.
1. The statue symbolizes welcome and a promise of freedom for immigrants to the Untied States.

Answer Key (cont.)

2. The statue was given to the United States by the people of France in 1884.
3. Frédéric Bartholdi designed and sculpted it.
4. Bartholdi named the statue Liberty Enlightening the World.
5. The seven spikes stand for the seven seas, the seven continents, and the seven liberties.

Page 59
A.
1. c
2. d
3. b
4. e
5. a

B.
1. He became a writer when his brother bet that he couldn't compose a verse.
2. During WWI he wrote his first children's book and a play to entertain the troops.
3. He wrote *Winnie-the-Pooh* in 1926.
4. Walt Disney Company made it into a movie.
5. Answers will vary.

Page 60
A.
1. b
2. d
3. e
4. c
5. a
6. f

B.
1. Ancient people used the stars to guide their way and lives.
2. We call them constellations.
3. The constellations written about were the Big Dipper, the Bear, the Wagon, the Plow, Seven Rishis, and Cassiopeia.

4. Many of the stars names were based on ancient stories and myths.
5. She claimed that she was more beautiful than the lovely sea nymphs.

Page 61
A.
1. e
2. c
3. d
4. a
5. b

B.
1. Hercules' father was Zeus.
2. When he was a baby he killed two serpents who were about to attack him.
3. Hercules learned wrestling, archery and fencing. (you only need two)
4. He was banished from Thebe because of his bad temper.
5. He had to serve King Eurystheus for 12 years and accomplish many difficult tasks.
6. Individual answers.

Page 62
A.
1. c
2. e
3. d
4. b
5. a

B.
1. He was a pilot for the US Navy.
2. The name of the space flight was Gemini 8.
3. After docking, the two spacecrafts went into a violent roll. They were able to deal with it and save the mission.
4. He retired in 1971 and became an aerospace engineering professor.
5. Answers will vary.

Page 63
A.
1. b
2. d
3. e
4. f
5. a
6. c

B.
1. He was born in Baltimore.
2. As a child he got into trouble and went to a Catholic boy's school where he played baseball.
3. He played as a pitcher, an outfielder, and a left-handed pitcher.
4. In 1920 he broke the 1884 record of 24 home runs in one season by hitting 54.
5. Yankee Stadium was also called "the house that Ruth built."
6. Answers will vary.

Page 64
A.
1. e
2. b
3. f
4. d
5. c
6. a

B.
1. When Elvis was eight, he won his first talent contest.
2. He recorded his first song as a present for his mother.
3. He was drafted into the army.
4. He started doing live tours.
5. He made over 40 albums in his lifetime.
6. Answers will vary.

Page 65
A.
1. c
2. b
3. d
4. a
5. e

B.
1. Baseball was his favorite sport.
2. He could not play in college at first because his grades and his playing were not good enough.

Answer Key (cont.)

3. He started as a pitcher for the Los Angeles Dodgers minor-league team.
4. He was not a great player, however, his coach felt that he had potential and convinced him to keep working on his pitch.
5. Answers will vary.

Page 67

A.

1. b   4. f
2. d   5. c
3. e   6. a

B.

1. Merlin, the magician, raised Arthur.
2. He easily pulled it from the stone and became king of Britain.
3. He was a fair and wise ruler.
4. This table was round and could seat 1,600 knights without anyone knight having a better seat than another. Arthur felt that this would keep his knights from arguing.
5. When Arthur returned home from conquering most of western Europe, he had to fight and kill his nephew, Mordred. He was injured badly and later died.
6. Answers will vary.

Page 69

1. Beethoven was born in Bonn, Germany, in 1770.
2. He began to study music when he was four years old.
3. His father wanted him to be a musician.
4. Beethoven went on his first concert tour when he was 11 years old.
5. Beethoven was 17 years old when Mozart heard him play.
6. He went to Vienna, Austria.

7. Beethoven studied with Haydn, another great musician and composer.
8. Beethoven wrote about 300 pieces of music.
9. His compositions included sonatas, symphonies, concertos, and operas.
10. Beethoven gradually lost his hearing after an illness.

Page 70

1. Austria
2. Bonn
3. composer
4. composition
5. concerto
6. Germany
7. harmony
8. Haydn
9. melody
10. Mozart
11. musician
12. notation
13. opera
14. orchestra
15. piano
16. sonata
17. symphony
18. tempo
19. Vienna
20. violin

Page 71

Page 73

Chapters 1-4

1. Sara has low self-esteem, and she feels like nothing in her life is right.
2. Charlie is Sara's retarded 10-year-old brother.
3. Their mother died and their father works in a different state, so their aunt moved in to look after them.
4. Sara compares her life to a kaleidoscope because it seems that it has been turned around. Now the pieces are no longer the same; everything has changed and continues to change from moment to moment.
5. She feels she has no time to herself or space of her own because she has Charlie to entertain all day and Wanda sharing her room all night.

Page 74

Chapters 5-9

1. Charlie loves to look at and listen to the watch because the ticking sound and rhythm make him feel secure.
2. Charlie squeezes Sara's hand, and he stares at the swans.
3. Most of the time the swans live on a lake at the university.
4. Sara says she does not like Frank because he ignores Charlie and because he calls Wanda by a pet name. She may be jealous of the affection Frank and Wanda have for each other.

Chapters 10-14

1. Sara goes back to the lake because she thinks that Charlie will go there to see the swans.

2. She does not know what to do. She does know that something is really wrong because she has the same feeling in her neck that she always gets when something bad happens.

3. Aunt Willie promised the children's mother that she would take good care of Charlie and not let anything happen to him.

4. Aunt Willie feels that if she had sewn on Charlie's button as he wanted instead of watching television, Charlie would not have run away.

5. Sara begins to doubt herself and her feelings of revenge toward Joe Melby when he explains that he did not steal Charlie's watch and offers to help her find Charlie.

Page 75

Chapters 15-18

Mary tells Sara that Aunt Willie confronted Joe about stealing the watch and learned the truth—that he had found it and returned it to Charlie.

Sara is embarrassed to face Joe after accusing him of stealing and finding out she was wrong.

Joe tells of a guru who had the same problem of trying to find the right words to say.

Charlie becomes very stressed when he realizes his wristwatch has stopped. He gets upset.

Joe makes it easy for Sara to apologize. He does not make her feel bad for falsely accusing him, he helps Sara find Charlie, and he encourages her to keep trying when she is about to give up.

Chapters 19-20

1. Sara twists Charlie's bedroom slipper as she listens and looks for Charlie.

2. Charlie feels secure when his same routine is followed regularly and there are not surprises.

3. Joe lets Charlie wear his own wristwatch so that Charlie will feel secure.

4. Once Sara understands that she was wrong about Joe, she also realizes that perhaps she could be wrong about others, including her father.

5. Sara realizes there are more important things in life than looks. She begins to feel better about herself and her life. She feels she understands people better. She knows that a boy finds her attractive enough and likes her enough to ask her to a party.

Page 76

Matching

1. d
2. b
3. e
4. a
5. c

True or False

1. false
2. true
3. true
4. false
5. true

Short Answer

1. Sara constantly complains about how she looks.

2. Aunt Willie cares for the children because their mother died and their father works in a different state.

3. Charlie suffered two high fevers in a row that left him retarded and unable to speak.

4. Sara thinks Wanda is prettier, is jealous that Wanda has a boyfriend, and resents sharing a room with Wanda. Sara feels conflicted over her love for her brother and her feelings of being responsible for him. Sara thinks that Aunt Willie keeps her from having any fun, even though she is glad her aunt is there to take care of them. Sara loves her father and misses him. He is withdrawn, and she does not know how to reach him. Consequently, she thinks the worst of him.

5. Sara was so convinced she was right that she went out of her way to make Joe feel bad. Then she found out she was wrong about Joe.

Page 77

Chapters 1-3

1. On one of his late afternoon strolls, Marty spotted the dog by the Shiloh schoolhouse. Shiloh followed shyly along until Marty whistled. That is when Shiloh exploded with affection. He followed Marty all the way home.

2. The three children are Marty, 11; Dara Lynn, 7; Becky, 3.

3. The story takes place in Friendly, West Virginia. It is summertime.

4. Judd kicks Shiloh. Later, he doesn't feed him dinner. Marty is upset by Judd's actions.

5. Marty wants to save money by collecting aluminum cans.

Page 78

Chapters 4-7

1. Marty promises Shiloh that Judd Travers will never kick him again.

2. Marty keeps Dara Lynn off the hill by telling her it is snake-infested.

Answer Key (cont.)

3. We learn that Judd was beaten by his father. Marty feels sorry for him.
4. At Mr. Wallace's store, Marty spends the 53 cents he earns collecting cans. He asks Mr. Wallace for old food so that he may feed Shiloh.
5. Some of the lies Marty tells include telling Dara Lynn the hill has snakes, telling his dad he is looking for ground hogs on the hill, telling his mom he wants to save food for after dinner, telling Judd he has not see his dog, and telling Mrs. Howard that his mom has had a headache.

Chapters 8-11

1. Marty plans to save Shiloh by holding up a sign by the side of the road. The sign would say something like "Free World's Best Dog."
2. Shiloh gets hurt when Baker's German shepherd leaps into his pen and attacks.
3. At Doc Murphy's, Shiloh is stitched up. The doctor finds out Shiloh is Judd's dog. Marty and his dad go home, unsure of Shiloh's survival.
4. Marty feels relieved after he tells David Howard about Shiloh. David is mesmerized and has a hard time letting Marty tell the story!
5 . The Prestons and Judd agree that Shiloh will be returned once his wounds are healed.

Page 79

Chapters 12-15

1. Marty knows that the authorities will not have time for an animal abuse case. He also knows that he has no proof that Judd is mistreating his dogs.

2. Some of Marty's chores include cutting weeds, mowing grass, hoeing corn, picking beans, cutting wood, and digging holes. (Accept supported statements.)
3. Judd leaves out the name Shiloh. Marty insists Judd include the name in case he tries to give him another dog.
4. Judd says the contract is no good because they had no witness.
5. When Marty completes his work, Judd gives him a dog collar. It is a sign of their camaraderie, their newly found understanding of one another.

Page 80

Matching

1. e
2. a
3. j
4. h
5. c
6. g
7. b
8. d
9. f
10. i

True or False

1. false
2. true
3. false
4. true
5. false

Sequence

3, 5, 2, 4, 1

Short Answer

1. Some towns in Tyler County include Friendly, Parkersburg, and Middlebourne.
2. Marty will not go to heaven if Shiloh is not allowed in.
3. Shiloh responds to a whistle.

Page 81

1. 15
2. 9
3. 17
4. 13
5. 5
6. 8
7. 14
8. 7
9. 16
10. 10
11. 13
12. 6
13. 6
14. 5
15. 8
16. 4
17. 11
18. 10
19. 7
20. 12
21. 7
22. 18
23. 6
24. 8
25. 12
26. 13
27. 14
28. 11
29. 7
30. 10
31. 15
32. 4
33. 9
34. 14
35. 1
36. 14
37. 9
38. 17
39. 10
40. 13
41. 10
42. 9
43. 12
44. 9

Answer Key (cont.)

45. 3
46. 6
47. 8
48. 13
49. 16
50. 11

Page 82

51. 8
52. 11
53. 14
54. 7
55. 4
56. 2
57. 15
58. 6
59. 2
60. 8
61. 12
62. 9
63. 3
64. 12
65. 16
66. 5
67. 9
68. 11
69. 5
70. 9
71. 7
72. 10
73. 4
74. 14
75. 11
76. 5
77. 12
78. 9
79. 10
80. 5
81. 0
82. 7
83. 15
84. 10
85. 3
86. 2
87. 9

88. 8
89. 6
90. 11
91. 13
92. 8
93. 3
94. 10
95. 7
96. 8
97. 6
98. 10
99. 2
100. 12

Page 83

1. 6
2. 12
3. 5
4. 13
5. 10
6. 11
7. 17
8. 19
9. 15
10. 16
11. 14
12. 19
13. 10
14. 12
15. 20
16. 16

Page 84

1. 26
2. 6
3. 18
4. 15
5. 9
6. 17
7. 15
8. 22
9. 18
10. 23
11. 20
12. 16 20

Page 85

1. 52
2. 49
3. 52
4. 38
5. 33
6. 35
7. 42
8. 46
9. 50
10. 38
11. 46
12. 31
13. 37
14. 40
15. 22
16. 27

Page 86

1. 19
2. 20
3. 17
4. 49
5. 60
6. 53
7. 30
8. 75
9. 78
10. 87
11. 45
12. 61
13. 58
14. 22
15. 63
16. 19
17. 35
18. 87
19. 87
20. 50
21. 57
22. 42
23. 97
24. 56
25. 98

Answer Key (cont.)

Page 87
1. 121
2. 154
3. 131
4. 94
5. 81
6. 89
7. 44
8. 120
9. 91
10. 39
11. 124
12. 47
13. 125
14. 138
15. 107
16. 196
17. 111
18. 67
19. 54
20. 127
21. 120
22. 119
23. 160
24. 135
25. 73

Page 88
1. 169
2. 177
3. 191
4. 157
5. 132
6. 179
7. 111
8. 148
9. 188
10. 195
11. 193
12. 81
13. 218
14. 192
15. 187
16. 176

Pageq 89
1. 266
2. 300
3. 182
4. 265
5. 182
6. 196
7. 212
8. 128
9. 358
10. 303
11. 248
12. 91

Page 90
1. 898
2. 825
3. 1,072
4. 873
5. 988
6. 1,019
7. 1,336
8. 861
9. 389
10. 1,117
11. 1,090
12. 621
13. 843
14. 1,402
15. 1,012
16. 1,670
17. 823
18. 1,822
19. 967
20. 938
21. 1,248
22. 925
23. 623
24. 947
25. 1,314

Page 91
1. 2,035
2. 1,879
3. 2,160
4. 1963
5. 1,431
6. 1,762
7. 1,260
8. 2,275
9. 1,661
10. 1,744
11. 1,994
12. 1,622
13. 1,700
14. 1,832
15. 2,013
16. 1,023

Page 92
1. 1,404
2. 2,675
3. 1,096
4. 1,824
5. 3,184
6. 1,825
7. 1,671
8. 2,210
9. 3,056
10. 2,359
11. 2,678
12. 2,361

Page 93
1. 17,339
2. 14,490
3. 15,499
4. 5,737
5. 13,216
6. 10,335
7. 6,869
8. 16,045
9. 4,685
10. 14,358
11. 10,519
12. 7,336
13. 8,610
14. 8,323
15. 12,244
16. 7,787

Answer Key (cont.)

17. 7,753
18. 8,040
19. 9,097
20. 12,031
21. 8,415
22. 10,786
23. 16,877
24. 7,129
25. 5,166

Page 94

1. 19,555
2. 14,017
3. 9,155
4. 15,563
5. 16,152
6. 17,552
7. 15,169
8. 15,388
9. 15,817
10. 12,793
11. 14,186
12. 24,204
13. 24,649
14. 17,700
15. 25,076
16. 13,821

Page 95

1. 27,788
2. 27,827
3. 24,036
4. 25,815
5. 12,814
6. 29,265
7. 25,490
8. 23,657
9. 28,244
10. 12,801
11. 25,132
12. 18,138

Page 96

1. 76
2. 11
3. 120

4. 9
5. 15
6. 4,670
7. 39
8. 17
9. 181
10. 1,778
11. 140
12. 19
13. 180
14. 1,843
15. 18
16. 16
17. 158
18. 101
19. 3,449
20. 110

Page 97

1. 9
2. 8
3. 8
4. 6
5. 5
6. 8
7. 5
8. 6
9. 8
10. 5
11. 7
12. 5
13. 0
14. 4
15. 4
16. 3
17. 6
18. 6
19. 7
20. 9
21. 5
22. 9
23. 4
24. 3
25. 6
26. 6

27. 6
28. 5
29. 7
30. 4
31. 9
32. 2
33. 9
34. 9
35. 1
36. 7
37. 3
38. 9
39. 7
40. 4
41. 9
42. 0
43. 3
44. 7
45. 3
46. 6
47. 5
48. 8
49. 9
50. 4

Page 98

51. 7
52. 8
53. 4
54. 4
55. 1
56. 2
57. 7
58. 3
59. 1
60. 6
61. 5
62. 2
63. 1
64. 8
65. 7
66. 0
67. 4
68. 7
69. 3

Answer Key (cont.)

70. 1
71. 1
72. 1
73. 0
74. 8
75. 2
76. 2
77. 4
78. 5
79. 8
80. 1
81. 0
82. 3
83. 8
84. 3
85. 2
86. 9
87. 6
88. 1
89. 2
90. 3
91. 5
92. 2
93. 0
94. 1
95. 2
96. 0
97. 1
98. 2
99. 0
100. 7

Page 99
1. 35
2. 14
3. 34
4. 44
5. 41
6. 75
7. 13
8. 81
9. 91
10. 85
11. 88
12. 46

13. 94
14. 50
15. 53
16. 70
17. 41
18. 21
19. 67
20. 53
21. 32
22. 79
23. 8
24. 90
25. 25

Page 100
1. 360
2. 625
3. 219
4. 349
5. 581
6. 823
7. 533
8. 247
9. 534
10. 340
11. 118
12. 381
13. 457
14. 262
15. 930
16. 764
17. 339
18. 879
19. 533
20. 595
21. 678
22. 357
23. 657
24. 826
25. 553

Page 101
1. 845
2. 159
3. 257

4. 821
5. 888
6. 201
7. 233
8. 759
9. 406
10. 461
11. 532
12. 555
13. 167
14. 223
15. 708
16. 585
17. 887
18. 233
19. 840
20. 816
21. 146
22. 748
23. 250
24. 708
25. 443

Page 102
1. 4,213
2. 3,311
3. 2,322
4. 4,227
5. 4,173
6. 2,860
7. 4,251
8. 9,332
9. 1,612
10. 1,831
11. 5,162
12. 2,131
13. 6,305
14. 9,050
15. 7,130
16. 9,233
17. 7,634
18. 3,630
19. 7,246
20. 8,242
21. 2,234

Answer Key (cont.)

22. 8,112
23. 7,570
24. 9,640
25. 1,171

Page 103

1. 9,331
2. 1,243
3. 9,117
4. 5,651
5. 8,312
6. 4,125
7. 2,451
8. 7,123
9. 9,841
10. 6,153
11. 4,041
12. 3,246
13. 1,533
14. 4,510
15. 5,330
16. 8,015
17. 6,311
18. 3,271
19. 7,174
20. 6,404
21. 4,153
22. 759
23. 1,647
24. 4,266
25. 6,633

Page 104

1. 62
2. 24
3. 330
4. 785
5. 7,146
6. 8,448
7. 75
8. 2,788
9. 9,605
10. 8,922
11. 125
12. 7,767

13. 8
14. 6,594
15. 1,148
16. 815
17. 40
18. 854
19. 29
20. 68

Page 105

1. 0
2. 169
3. 2
4. 532
5. 2
6. 1,833
7. 8,557
8. 5,783
9. 115
10. 5
11. 209
12. 5
13. 189
14. 3,204
15. 4,452
16. 524
17. 118
18. 3
19. 3,916
20. 6,758

Page 106

1. 36
2. 0
3. 21
4. 28
5. 72
6. 48
7. 35
8. 12
9. 0
10. 30
11. 8
12. 36
13. 14

14. 6
15. 8
16. 12
17. 0
18. 15
19. 5
20. 54
21. 7
22. 16
23. 21
24. 7
25. 30
26. 20
27. 42
28. 42
29. 54
30. 2
31. 25
32. 56
33. 14
34. 0
35. 3
36. 81
37. 9
38. 18
39. 24
40. 36
41. 0
42. 8
43. 27
44. 0
45. 9
46. 15
47. 6
48. 10
49. 63
50. 8

Page 107

51. 1
52. 56
53. 64
54. 48
55. 18
56. 0

Answer Key (cont.)

57. 6
58. 4
59. 4
60. 0
61. 0
62. 12
63. 28
64. 12
65. 40
66. 45
67. 63
68. 0
69. 0
70. 27
71. 3
72. 9
73. 18
74. 24
75. 24
76. 32
77. 24
78. 49
79. 45
80. 40
81. 0
82. 6
83. 0
84. 72
85. 0
86. 0
87. 4
88. 16
89. 20
90. 32
91. 0
92. 0
93. 18
94. 1
95. 35
96. 0
97. 16
98. 5
99. 0
100. 10

Page 108
1. 378
2. 792
3. 288
4. 90
5. 584
6. 405
7. 45
8. 616
9. 176
10. 231
11. 375
12. 552
13. 36
14. 304
15. 567
16. 225
17. 108
18. 36
19. 144
20. 70
21. 90
22. 490
23. 864
24. 150
25. 272

Page 109
1. 44
2. 273
3. 276
4. 295
5. 104
6. 51
7. 252
8. 291
9. 44
10. 284
11. 84
12. 78
13. 175
14. 255
15. 290
16. 388
17. 162

18. 33
19. 258
20. 96
21. 455
22. 266
23. 344
24. 192
25. 285

Page 110
1. 770
2. 1,771
3. 484
4. 3,074
5. 5,170
6. 3,216
7. 2,590
8. 8,008
9. 561
10. 3,869
11. 3,162
12. 8,118
13. 2,914
14. 1,116
15. 1,260
16. 7,722
17. 2,523
18. 2,432
19. 4,686
20. 1,092
21. 522
22. 3,416
23 713
24. 1,298
25. 7,275

Page 111
1. 1,568
2. 3,872
3. 2,664
4. 3,038
5. 576
6. 3,626
7. 4,158
8. 1,421

Answer Key (cont.)

9. 3854
10. 1,748
11. 3,752
12. 2,964
13. 2,788
14. 2,596
15. 2,304
16. 6,461
17. 5,621
18. 1,914
19. 2,233
20. 4,704
21. 2,945
22. 2,700
23. 4,118
24. 6,935
25. 4,264

Page 112

1. 3,080
2. 3,875
3. 1,260
4. 5,553
5. 5,391
6. 2,802
7. 1,284
8. 1,982
9. 930
10. 1,010
11. 3,846
12. 1,738
13. 1,816
14. 4,270
15. 864
16. 3,528
17. 602
18. 6,147
19. 2,648
20. 3,664
21. 4,788
22. 1,089
23. 6,699
24. 1,718
25. 2,370

Page 113

1. 1,981
2. 2,076
3. 7,384
4. 1,592
5. 2,384
6. 4,055
7. 1,848
8. 1,236
9. 1,074
10. 2,559
11. 5,456
12. 1,053
13. 1,272
14. 7,956
15. 3,716
16. 393
17. 2,422
18. 4,010
19. 597
20. 7,640
21. 1,728
22. 3,328
23. 2,184
24. 1,125
25. 3,405

Page 114

1. 2,547
2. 4,476
3. 985
4. 738
5. 896
6. 5,481
7. 4,374
8. 2,205
9. 6,376
10. 1,812
11. 1,028
12. 4,398
13. 4,254
14. 4,988
15. 261
16. 2,680
17. 228

18. 3255
19. 576
20. 4590
21. 498
22. 4004
23. 109
24. 5769
25. 4522

Page 115

1. 37,351
2. 47,124
3. 5,248
4. 24,012
5. 32,034
6. 11,856
7. 10,934
8. 29,634
9. 34,056
10. 38,184
11. 23,304
12. 58,044
13. 83,979
14. 52,785
15. 31,140
16. 25,704
17. 9,177
18. 4,995
19. 13,498
20. 15,950
21. 20,925
22. 13,545
23. 34,892
24. 25,428
25. 7,696

Page 116

1. 18,531
2. 4,131
3. 29,481
4. 51,810
5. 21,600
6. 4,408
7. 16,215
8. 80,132

Answer Key (cont.)

9. 76,930
10. 28,028
11. 53,361
12. 26,109
13. 34,336
14. 41,922
15. 15,916
16. 13,365
17. 32,580
18. 54,096
19. 49,329
20. 7,228
21. 10,336
22. 14,055
23. 25,637
24. 31,668
25. 20,460

Page 117
1. 45
2. 162
3. 368
4. 27
5. 2,208
6. 6
7. 270
8. 155
9. 60
10. 388
11. 6,992
12. 230
13. 170
14. 9
15. 3,713
16. 140
17. 88
18. 56
19. 114
20. 35

Page 118
1. 8,625
2. 2,548
3. 48,546
4. 56

5. 25
6. 1,100,337
7. 23,324
8. 86,044
9. 1,925
10. 43,798
11. 3,598,771
12. 12,643
13. 54
14. 7,209
15. 27
16. 2,924
17. 37,422
18. 12
19. 12
20. 45

Page 119
1. 5
2. 7
3. 8
4. 7
5. 5
6. 8
7. 6
8. 3
9. 5
10. 0
11. 4
12. 8
13. 5
14. 7
15. 4
16. 9
17. 0
18. 6
19. 7
20. 5
21. 2
22. 7
23. 9
24. 9
25. 2
26. 6
27. 8

28. 4
29. 0
30. 3
31. 9
32. 4
33. 4
34. 3
35. 9
36. 6
37. 9
38. 9
39. 5
40. 7

Page 120
41. 1
42. 4
43. 8
44. 1
45. 3
46. 3
47. 1
48. 6
49. 0
50. 2
51. 3
52. 9
53. 3
54. 5
55. 4
56. 0
57. 6
58. 0
59. 6
60. 2
61. 7
62. 9
63. 3
64. 4
65. 3
66. 0
67. 2
68. 6
69. 8
70. 1

Answer Key (cont.)

71. 0
72. 1
73. 8
74. 5
75. 6
76. 7
77. 2
78. 4
79. 8
80. 5
81. 3
82. 8
83. 2
84. 1
85. 1
86. 1
87. 0
88. 2
89. 7
90. 1

Page 121

1. 3 r1
2. 1 r2
3. 1 r1
4. 5
5. 2
6. 2 r2
7. 2
8. 1r1
9. 1 r3
10. 2 r1
11. 2 r1
12. 4
13. 1 r1
14. 6
15. 3
16. 1 r3
17. 1
18. 1 r3
19. 1
20. 9

Page 122

1. 4
2. 2 r2
3. 1
4. 4
5. 1 r2
6. 1 r3
7. 3 r1
8. 2
9. 1 r2
10. 1 r2
11. 7
12. 1 r3
13. 1 r3
14. 2 r1
15. 2 r1
16. 1 r1
17. 4
18. 6
19. 1 r1
20. 1 r2

Page 123

1. 19
2. 11 r1
3. 27
4. 9 r5
5. 10 r2
6. 21 r1
7. 6
8. 93
9. 5 r3
10. 27
11. 16 r3
12. 20 r2
13. 15 r4
14. 21
15. 9 r3
16. 22
17. 1 r4
18. 14 r2
19. 9 r1
20. 13 r2

Page 124

1. 5
2. 4 r3
3. 11 r6
4. 10 r7
5. 8 r4
6. 15 r1
7. 9 r4
8. 8 r7
9. 20 r2
10. 13 r4
11. 11 r 2
12. 16 r2
13. 46
14. 37 r1
15. 25 r1
16. 13 r1
17. 7 r4
18. 2 r6
19. 33 r1
20. 11 r5

Page 125

1. 442
2. 311
3. 269 r1
4. 124
5. 725
6. 31 r1
7. 233 r1
8. 133
9. 135 r1
10. 170 r4
11. 90 r8
12. 79 r2
13. 52 r2
14. 47
15. 190 r2
16. 191 r2
17. 106 r8
18. 122 r1
19. 162 r4
20. 120 r5

Answer Key (cont.)

Page 126

1. 42 r1
2. 111 r2
3. 80 r1
4. 55 r6
5. 18 r1
6. 93 r2
7. 39 r1
8. 53
9. 49 r6
10. 118 r2
11. 94
12. 187 r2
13. 83 r2
14. 92 r1
15. 515
16. 46 r1
17. 39
18. 419 r1
19. 218
20. 107 r6

Page 127

1. 36 r7
2. 25 r4
3. 25 r6
4. 79 r1
5. 108 r2
6. 128 r2
7. 66 r2
8. 174 r3
9. 110 r1
10. 184 r3
11. 355 r1
12. 192 r1
13. 77 r6
14. 47 r3
15. 35
16. 69
17. 133
18. 217 r2
19. 93 r2
20. 78

Page 128

1. 9 r31
2. 5 r71
3. 9 r18
4. 7 r18
5. 20 r16
6. 34 r10
7. 18 r3
8. 7 r53
9. 9 r22
10. 16 r5
11. 12 r21
12. 6 r39
13. 19 r38
14. 2 r13
15. 4 r27
16. 10 r52
17. 10 r24
18. 6 r12
19. 5 r71
20. 5 r29

Page 129

1. 9 r1
2. 12 r3
3. 6 r5
4. 49 r13
5. 57 r9
6. 10 r61
7. 5 r34
8. 54 r3
9. 27 r21
10. 14 r31
11. 20 r1
12. 3 r48
13. 11 r12
14. 54 r12
15. 29 r16
16. 37 r2
17. 18 r9
18. 19 r13
19. 16 r2
20. 37 r2

Page 130

1. 9 r24
2. 7 r48
3. 4 r14
4. 26 r2
5. 8 r59
6. 13 r37
7. 3 r54
8. 6 r35
9. 18 r13
10. 27 r8
11. 26 r8
12. 11 r65
13. 11 r20
14. 16 r2
15. 12 r18
16. 45 r3
17. 10 r27
18. 3 r28
19. 10 r28
20. 4 r85

Page 131

1. 1 3/4
2. 2 1/7
3. 2 2/5
4. 1 2/5
5. 1 2/3
6. 1 7/9
7. 3 1/3
8. 1 1/13
9. 1 1/11
10. 4 1/2
11. 1 1/3
12. 3 1/2
13. 1 5/8
14. 1 1/5
15. 2 2/3
16. 1 1/4
17. 3 1/5
18. 1 9/10
19. 1 1/4
20. 1 1/6
21. 1 1/3
22. 1 1/2

Answer Key (cont.)

23. 2 1/2
24. 1 1/3
25. 1 7/11
26. 1 4/5
27. 1 1/8
28. 1 1/2
29. 1 1/7
30. 1 2/7
31. 2 1/5
32. 1 1/5
33. 1 5/9
34. 1 1/2
35. 1 1/4
36. 1 5/13
37. 1 1/6
38. 1 1/8
39. 2 3/8
40. 3 1/2

Page 132

1. 24/5
2. 16/5
3. 19/7
4. 22/3
5. 37/4
6. 12/7
7. 19/2
8. 49/5
9. 21/8
10. 48/5
11. 38/8
12. 15/9
13. 75/9
14. 61/8
15. 51/6
16. 53/9
17. 17/6
18. 23/5
19. 22/6
20. 9/5
21. 26/6
22. 89/9
23. 43/6
24. 4/3
25. 14/3

26. 33/6
27. 59/7
28. 57/9
29. 14/4
30. 49/8
31. 28/3
32. 64/9
33. 15/6
34. 17/2
35. 69/7
36. 13/8
37. 27/4
38. 47/8
39. 73/9
40. 34/5

Page 133

1. 3
2. 3 2/3
3. 7 1/2
4. 1 1/2
5. 6 1/3
6. 5
7. 5 3/4
8. 11
9. 3 1/2
10. 8
11. 3 3/8
12. 8 4/7
13. 5 3/8
14. 15
15. 23
16. 134 1/2

Page 134

1. 1 13/24
2. 1 33/56
3. 2/3
4. 1 27/40
5. 14/15
6. 1 2/15
7. 29/30
8. 1 11/21
9. 1 1/36
10. 32/45

11. 1 31/45
12. 1 11/40
13. 1 7/15
14. 31/42
15. 1 4/63
16. 1 11/36

Page 135

1. 1 1/14
2. 1 3/8
3. 59/72
4. 1 7/15
5. 5/8
6. 1 3/14
7. 1 1/12
8. 19/28
9. 1 16/45
10. 1 1/24
11. 1 5/14
12. 1 1/7
13. 5/6
14. 11/30
15. 1 19/56
16. 1 2/35

Page 136

1. 7 1/18
2. 13 1/4
3. 12 3/5
4. 8 4/9
5. 11
6. 10 53/72
7. 7 47/63
8. 10 13/63
9. 4 5/24
10. 7 5/6
11. 8 7/12
12. 9 16/21
13. 6 1/2
14. 16 8/9
15. 7 67/72
16. 16 1/30

Page 137

1. 1/12
2. 5/8

Answer Key (cont.)

3. 3/8
4. 1/3
5. 2/3
6. 0
7. 4/5
8. 1/2
9. 1/2
10. 1/5
11. 8/11
12. 3/5
13. 1/10
14. 1/4
15. 1/3
16. 1/14

Page 138
1. 1/14
2. 4/15
3. 1/45
4. 4/9
5. 19/36
6. 11/56
7. 8/21
8. 3/35
9. 3/40
10. 1/2
11. 1/6
12. 5/72
13. 2/3
14. 4/9
15. 1/72
16. 7/24

Page 139
1. 1/5
2. 10/27
3. 1/10
4. 1/3
5. 16/63
6. 2/3
7. 9/32
8. 1/18
9. 2/5
10. 3/8
11. 14/27

12. 7/24
13. 10/27
14. 1/12
15. 2/15
16. 1/3
17. 3/7
18. 2/35
19. 4/15
20. 2/27
21. 4/9
22. 1/12
23. 3/16
24. 1/2

Page 140
1. 8/21
2. 2/5
3. 4/27
4. 1/20
5. 5/18
6. 5/24
7. 2/7
8. 7/32
9. 35/48
10. 2/9
11. 56/81
12. 8/81
13. 1/6
14. 4/21
15. 1/4
16. 10/27
17. 1/4
18. 1/16
19. 5/14
20. 2/9
21. 1/3
22. 7/24
23. 1/8
24. 1/15

Page 141
1. 2/5
2. 2 1/3
3. 5/14
4. 27/35

5. 5/6
6. 9/28
7. 5/8
8. 5/16
9. 32/35
10. 3/7
11. 5/6
12. 3/16
13. 1/3
14. 1 5/9
15. 3/5
16. 1/4
17. 1 1/8
18. 1 1/3
19. 1 2/3
20. 3/10
21. 1 1/2
22. 1 2/3
23. 1 13/15
24. 1 1/3

Page 142
1. 6
2. 1 1/3
3. 7/12
4. 1 1/8
5. 1 1/2
6. 3
7. 1 1/35
8. 3 15/16
9. 1 1/6
10. 1/5
11. 6/7
12. 1 2/3
13. 35/36
14. 1
15. 3/5
16. 5/9
17. 1 1/8
18. 1 1/4
19. 8/15
20. 27/28
21. 1 1/2
22. 1/2
23. 3/4
24. 16/63

Answer Key (cont.)

Page 143

1. 3/16
2. 5/6
3. 2 2/3
4. 3/14
5. 1 1/8
6. 1 11/24
7. 1 1/5
8. 1 1/4
9. 9/14
10. 2/3
11. 2/3
12. 1 1/8
13. 1 1/2
14. 2 1/4
15. 1 1/3
16. 5
17. 1 7/9
18. 1 3/4
19. 2/3
20. 7/9
21. 1/6
22. 2
23. 1 3/32
24. 1

Page 144

1. <
2. >
3. <
4. >
5. >
6. <
7. <
8. >
9. >
10. >
11. <
12. <
13. >
14. <
15. >
16. <
17. >
18. >

19. <
20. >
21. <
22. <
23. <
24. <
25. <
26. <
27. <
28. <
29. >
30. >
31. >
32. >
33. <

Page 145

1. <
2. >
3. <
4. <
5. <
6. <
7. >
8. >
9. <
10. <
11. >
12. <

Page 146

A. It goes to the bank where the business has money.
B. Step #8
C. Yes you do.

Page 147

A.
1. $4.27
2. $9.62
3. $1.99
4. $8.22
5. $3.16
6. $16.66

B.
1. Three dollars and ninety-nine cents

2. Nine dollars and thirty-three cents
3. Five dollars and eighty-seven cents
4. Two dollars and twenty-two cents
5. Six dollars and forty-eight cents
6. Eight dollars and seventy-two cents

C.
1. $3
2. $9
3. $5
4. $2
5. $6
6. $8

D.
1. 99¢
2. 33¢
3. 87¢
4. 22¢
5. 48¢
6. 72¢

Page 153

1. 5 pianos, 10 flutes, 30 guitars, 15 drums, 5 trumpets
2. 25, 20, 15, 25
3. Accept any reasonable explanation.

Page 156

1. watermelon
2. grapes
3. watermelon, peaches, plums, apricots, grapes
4. watermelon 1/2, peaches 1/4, plums 1/8

Page 157

1. homework, 30 minutes; snack, 5 minutes; clothes, 6 minutes; video game, 9 minutes; walking the dog, 10 minutes
2. Answers will vary. Check as a class exercise.

Answer Key (cont.)

Page 158
1. 25 cups
2. 55 cups
3. 10 quarts
4. 20 cups
5. 10 pints
6. 23 cups
7. skunk cabbage
8. mushrooms
9. 12 1/2 cups
1. 5 pounds
2. 320 ounces
3. 10 pounds
4. 13 1/2 pounds
5. 110 pounds

Page 159
1. 2786 miles
2. 1440 miles
3. 206 miles
4. 2037 miles
5. 802 miles
6. 840 miles
7. 1329 miles
8. 1058 miles
9. 2873 miles
10. 2976 miles
11 963 miles
12. 417 miles

Page 160
1. David Peterson
2. $5.80—Kathryn Ross
3. Barbara Marshall
4. no
5. no
6. 614
7. $48.00

Page 163
a new bicycle

Page 164
steal its chair

Page 165
1. $.94

2. $.84, $.08
3. 2792
4. 30,251
5. 483
6. 48,404
7. $3.60
8. $14.35
9. 84
10. 214

Page 166
1. a. 50   b. 4th grade
2. a. 98 km   b. no
3. a. $284.95   b.yes
4. a. 7   b.13
5. a. $3.07   b.$29.19
6. a.$37.36   b. $34.64

Page 167
1. 43
2. 576
3. $10.76 each
4. 855 holes
5. 14
6. 5
7. $7.11
8. 9
9. $19.83
10. 264

Page 168
1. 90
2. 5
3. 33
4. 180
5. 73
6. 249, 11 left over
7. 78, 3 left over
8. 20
9. 3
10. 6

Page 226
1. south
2. north
3. west
4. east

5. north (top) south (bottom)
6. east (left) west (right)
7. west (left), east (right), and south (bottom)
8. west (left), north (top), east (right), and south (bottom)

Page 227
Ending square is bottom left corner square.

Page 228
1. southeast
2. west
3. northeast
4. southwest
5. south
6. north
7. east
8. northwest

Page 229
1. point A: 5 miles—F, 9 kilometers—E, 4 kilometers—C
2. point B: 2 kilometers—A, 12 kilometers—G, 7 kilometers—E
3. 3 miles—D, 6 miles—A, 1 mile—F

Page 230
1. 900
2. 200
3. 500
4. 1400
5. 800
6. 500
7. 1500
8. 700

Page 231
1. 20 miles
2. 10 miles
3. 40 miles
4. 20 miles
5. 20 miles
6. 10 miles

Answer Key (cont.)

Page 232
1. true
2. false—western and southeastern
3. false—northeast
4. false—only one, the others are reached by local roads
5. false
6. false—west of lake, east of railroad
7. true

Page 233
example—silver
A1—white
D3—gray
B4—red
D2—ivory
C4—silver
A2—yellow
D1—black
C2—purple
B3—tan
A4—gold
C3—brown
B1—pink
D4—lavender
B2—green
A3—orange
C1—blue
shaded: A1, A3, B3, C2
striped: B2, C1, C3
unmarked: A2, B1

Page 234
1. E2
2. F3
3. C1, D1, E1
4. E5
5. E3
6. A3, A4, B3, B4
   F1, F2
   5, A6

12. B1
13. D4
14. B5
15. C6
16. C2

Page 236
4. A. North America
   B. South America
   C. Antarctica
   D. Europe
   E. Africa
   F. Asia
   G. Australia

Page 237
1. Southern, Eastern
2. Northern, Eastern
3. Northern, Western
4. Northern, Western
5. Northern, Eastern
6. Northern, Western
7. Northern, Eastern
8. Northern, Eastern
9. Northern, Western
10. Southern, Western
11. Northern, Eastern
12. Northern, Western
13. Northern, Eastern
14. Southern, Western
15. Southern, Eastern
16. Southern, Eastern

Page 238
1. latitude
2. longitude
3. latitude
4. longitude

Page 239
1. Grand Junction
2. Sterling
3. Denver
4. Lamar
5. Durango
6. Colorado Springs

7. Glenwood Springs
8. Campo
9. Craig
10. Kanorado

Page 240
3. Continents:
   North America
   South America
   Asia
   Australia
   Antarctica
   Europe
   Africa
   Oceans:
   Pacific
   Atlantic
   Arctic
   Indian

Page 242
1. Florida
2. Alaska
3. Rhode Island
4. Minnesota, Wisconsin, Illinois, Missouri, Nebraska, South Dakota
5. Kansas, Nebraska, South Dakota, North Dakota
6. Florida, Alabama, Missouri, Louisiana, Texas
7. Hawaii
8. Idaho
9. Illinois
10. New York

Page 243
11. Oregon, Nevada, Arizona
12. Minnesota, Mississippi, Missouri, Montana, Michigan, Maine, Maryland, Massachusetts
13. Maine, New Hampshire, Connecticut, Rhode Island, New York, New Jersey, Delaware, Maryland, Virginia, North Carolina, South Carolina, Georgia, Florida

Answer Key (cont.)

14. California, Oregon, Washington, Alaska, Hawaii
15. Minnesota, Wisconsin, Michigan, Illinois, Indiana, Ohio, Pennsylvania, New York
16. Alaska
17. Alaska
18. California, Arizona, New Mexico, Texas
19. Washington, Idaho, Montana, North Dakota, Minnesota, New York, Vermont, New Hampshire, Maine, Michigan
20. Manhattan

Page 261
wealthy
Native
cocoa
tomatoes
diseases
Smallpox
seventy-five
America
labor
tools
utensils
chickens

Page 262
1. ice skating
2. pewter
3. spoon
4. stocks
5. dugout
6. bayberry
7. samplers
8. peddlers
9. linen
10. trencher
11. dame school
12. indigo
13. linseed
14. lye
15. quoits
16. hornbook

17. doublet
18. johnnycake
19. saltbox
20. Sabbath

Page 263
1. Paris: 49°N 2°E
2. Yorktown: 37°N, 76°W
3. Quebec: 47°N, 71°W
4. Savannah: 32°N, 81°W
5. Saratoga: 43°N, 74°W
6. Guilford Courthouse: 36°N, 80°W
7. London: 51°N, 0° (Prime Meridian)
8. Boston: 42°N, 71°W
9. West Point: 41°N, 74°W
10. Cowpens: 35°N, 82°W

Page 264
1. soddy
2. corn dodgers
3. forty-niners
4. chips
5. emigrants
6. ague
7. rustlers
8. schooner

Page 265
1. Ohio River: 39°N, 83°W
2. Fort Sumter: 33°N, 80°W
3. Richmond: 37°N, 77°W
4. Harper's Ferry: 39°N, 78°W
5. Vicksburg: 32°N, 91°W
6. Andersonville: 32°N, 84°W
7. Chattanooga: 35°N, 85°W
8. Gettysburg: 40°N, 77°W
9. Kansas: 38°N, 100°W
10. Savannah: 32°N, 81°W

Page 267
1. E
2. N
3. D
4. A
5. C

6. U
7. I
8. L
9. N
10. R
11. D
12. H
13. N
14. N
Riddle: lunch and dinner

Page 268
A. George M. Cohan
B. Archduke Francis Ferdinand
C. Kaiser Wilhelm
D. Woodrow Wilson
E. General John Pershing
F. General Henri Petain
G. General Ferdinand Foch
H. General Sir Hubert Gough
I. Hans Otto Bischoff
J. Lt. Colonel Wise
K. Eddie Rickenbacker

Page 269
August 3, 1914—Belgium was invaded by Germany.

April 22, 1915—Germans first used chlorine gas.

September 15, 1916—British first used army tanks.

April 6, 1917—United States declared war on Germany.

January 8, 1918—Wilson revealed his "Fourteen Points."

November 11, 1918—First Armistice Day.

Page 270
1. J
2. G
3. B
4. D
5. F
6. C
7. I
8. H
9. E
10. A

Answer Key (cont.)

Page 272

1. Continental Congress
2. Revolutionary War
3. Ben Franklin
4. New Hampshire
5. Articles of Confederation
6. Shay's Rebellion
7. Federalists
8. Louisiana Purchase
9. Virginia Plan
10. Capitol in Philadelphia
11. Constitution
12. New York
13. Virginia Plan
14. U.S. gains freedom from England
15. the Federalist Papers
16. Declaration of Independence
17. "Yankee Doodle"
18. Sedition Act

Page 273

1. They represent the 13 colonies.
2. England
3. Legislative, Executive, and Judiciary
4. Speaker of the House of Representatives
5. freed many slaves
6. The Congress
7. a democratic form of government (or a Republic)
8. The Bill of Rights
9. freedom of speech, press, religion; peaceable assembly
10. George Washington
11. nine
12. Native Americans
13. Germany, Italy, and Japan
14. William Rehnquist
15. 26
16. 50
17. Red stands for courage, white stands for truth, and blue stands for justice.
18. to make laws

Page 274

1. Teddy
2. Washington
3. Delano
4. Madison
5. February
6. Adams
7. Honolulu
8. Carter
9. Lincoln
10. Nixon
11. Virginia
12. Mount Vernon
13. Alaska
14. Roosevelt (Theodore)
15. Congress

Page 275

1. "out of many, one"
2. six years
3. Abraham Lincoln
4. San Antonio, Texas
5. 1861-1865
6. Francis Bellamy
7. executive branch
8. Ronald Reagan
9. courage
10. John F. Kennedy
11. Eli Whitney
12. Hawaii
13. her right
14. Sir Francis Drake
15. "Hail to the Chief"

Page 276

1. I
2. C
3. B
4. L
5. K
6. E
7. H
8. M
9. G
10. O
11. A
12. F
13. D
14. N
15. J

Page 277

1. John
2. Dwight
3. Ronald
4. Thomas
5. Richard
6. Abraham
7. Jimmy
8. Herbert
9. Theodore or Franklin
10. George
11. Calvin
12. Grover
13. Ulysses
14. Zachary
15. William or Benjamin
16. Harry
17. James
18. James
19. James
20. Lyndon or Andrew

Page 278

1. Abraham Lincoln
2. James Madison
3. John Adams
4. Thomas Jefferson
5. Grover Cleveland
6. Zachary Taylor
7. Abraham Lincoln
8. John Kennedy and William Taft
9. Franklin D. Roosevelt
10. James Madison
11. Benjamin Harrison
12. James Buchanan
13. James Buchanan
14. Richard Nixon
15. John Garfield, Herbert Hoover, Harry Truman, Gerald Ford, Ronald Reagan, George Bush, and Bill Clinton